Hiking
OREGON'S GEOLOGY

SECOND EDITION

ELLEN MORRIS BISHOP

THE MOUNTAINEERS BOOKS

P9-DTR-805

Dedication

To Bob and Spirits Little Wolf,
and all those who love wild places.

THE MOUNTAINEERS BOOKS
is the nonprofit publishing arm of The Mountaineers Club,
an organization founded in 1906 and dedicated to the exploration,
preservation, and enjoyment of outdoor and wilderness areas.

1001 SW Klickitat Way, Suite 201, Seattle, WA 98134

Second edition, 2004

Published simultaneously in Great Britain by Cordee, 3a DeMontfort Street, Leicester,
England, LE1 7HD

Manufactured in the United States of America

Project Editor: Margaret Sullivan
Copy Editor: Paula Thurman
Cover and Book Design: The Mountaineers Books
Layout: Ani Rucki
Cartographer: Warren Huskey

All photographs by the author unless otherwise noted.

Cover photographs: *Closeup of clay surface, The Painted Hills, John Day Fossil Beds National
Monument.* Inset photo: *Fold in obsidian at Big Obsidian Flow, Newberry Volcanic National
Monument*

Library of Congress Cataloging-in-Publication Data
Bishop, Ellen Morris.
  Hiking Oregon's geology / Ellen Morris Bishop and John Eliot Allen.—
2nd ed.
     p. cm.
Includes bibliographical references and index.
  ISBN 0-89886-847-5 (pbk.)
  1. Hiking—Oregon—Guidebooks. 2. Geology—Oregon—Guidebooks. 3.
Oregon—Guidebooks. I. Allen, John Eliot, 1908- II. Title.
  GV199.42.O7B57 2004
  917.95—dc22
                          2003026888

Contents

Acknowledgments   7
Preface   8

INTRODUCTION   9
   Oregon's Diverse Geology   10
   Oregon's Geologic History   13
   Oregon's Active Landscapes   19
   Oregon's Geologic Provinces   21
   Gearing Up for Field Geology   24

**CHAPTER 1. THE KLAMATH MOUNTAINS AND
SOUTHERNMOST COAST**   29
   1. *Jack London Trail*   33
   2. *Upper Table Rock*   34
   3. *Mount Ashland and the Pacific Crest Trail to Wrangle Gap*   37
   4. *Pilot Rock*   39
   5. *Gin Lin Mine Trail*   41
   6. *Summit Lake*   43
   7. *Echo Lake, Red Buttes Wilderness*   45
   8. *Wild Rogue River: Graves Creek to Russian Creek*   48
   9. *Oregon Caves National Monument*   50
   10. *Vulcan Lake*   53
   11. *Chetco Lake and Chetco Peak*   55
   12. *Wild Rogue River: Illahe to Marial*   57
   13. *Humbug Mountain*   59
   14. *Cape Blanco*   62

**CHAPTER 2. THE COAST RANGE AND
CENTRAL-NORTHERN OREGON COAST**   65
   15. *Banks-Vernonia Trail at Tophill*   68
   16. *Saddle Mountain*   70
   17. *Cape Lookout: The North Trail*   72
   18. *Cape Lookout: The Main Trail*   74
   19. *Cape Kiwanda*   75
   20. *Hug Point*   77
   21. *Devils Punchbowl and Otter Crest*   78
   22. *Marys Peak*   80
   23. *Tahkenitch Dunes*   82
   24. *Coast Trail: Shore Acres and Sunset Bay to Cape Arago*   83

CHAPTER 3. THE WILLAMETTE VALLEY 87

25. *Mount Tabor* 90
26. *Powell Butte* 92
27. *Sauvie Island: Warrior Rock* 93
28. *Spencers Butte* 96
29. *Silver Creek Canyon and Rim Trail* 98
30. *Erratic Rock State Natural Site* 100

CHAPTER 4. THE COLUMBIA RIVER GORGE 102

31. *Latourell Falls* 105
32. *Angels Rest* 106
33. *Multnomah Falls to Larch Mountain* 108
34. *Eagle Creek* 110
35. *Rowena Crest and Tom McCall Preserve* 112

CHAPTER 5. THE CASCADES 115

36. *Ramona Falls and Sandy Glacier Volcano* 125
37. *Timberline Trail: Cloud Cap to Timberline Lodge* 127
38. *Lost Creek Nature Trail* 129
39. *Table Rock, Molalla* 131
40. *Rooster Rock, Menagerie Wilderness (via the Trout Creek Trail)* 132
41. *Jefferson Park via South Breitenbush Trail* 133
42. *Sand Mountain Cinder Cones* 136
43. *Metolius River Headwaters* 137
44. *South Sister Summit* 139

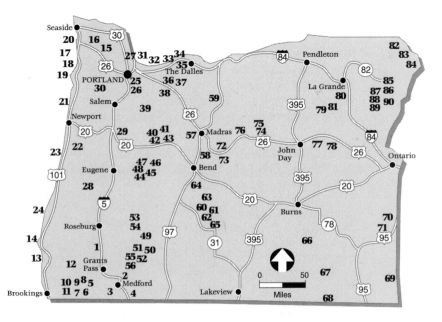

45. Broken Top: Todd Lake to Crater Creek   142
46. Yapoah and Collier Cones, Three Sisters   145
47. Lava River Trail and Little Belknap Crater   148
48. Tidbits Mountain   150
49. Mount Thielsen   151
50. Crater Lake: Mount Scott   153
51. Crater Lake: The Watchman   154
52. Crater Lake: The Pinnacles   155
53. Toketee Falls   157
54. Watson Falls   159
55. Upper Rogue River: Natural Bridge to Big Bend   160
56. Upper Rogue River: Takelma Gorge   162

CHAPTER 6. THE DESCHUTES BASIN   167
57. Cove Palisades   169
58. Smith Rock   171
59. White River Falls   175

CHAPTER 7. THE HIGH LAVA PLAINS   177
60. Paulina Peak Trail   180
61. Big Obsidian Flow   182
62. The Dome   183
63. Lava Cast Forest Trail   184
64. Trail of the Molten Land: Lava Butte and Lava Lands Visitor Center   185
65. Fort Rock State Natural Area   187
66. Diamond Craters Natural Area   189

CHAPTER 8. THE BASIN AND RANGE   192
67. Steens Mountain Rim Walk   194
68. Pueblo Mountains   197

CHAPTER 9. THE OWYHEES   201
69. Owyhee River, Three Forks   202
70. Leslie Gulch and Juniper Creek Trail   204
71. Jordan Craters   205

CHAPTER 10. THE BLUE MOUNTAINS AND THE COLUMBIA PLATEAU   208
72. Twin Pillars, Mill Creek Wilderness   211
73. Lookout Mountain: Summit and Independent Mine Loop   213
74. John Day Fossil Beds: Blue Basin Loop   216
75. Foree Picnic Area, Flood of Fire   218
76. Painted Hills   219
77. Canyon Mountain Trail: Pine Creek Trail, Strawberry Wilderness   221

78. *Strawberry Lake and Little Strawberry Lake* **224**
79. *North Fork John Day River: Granite Creek to Big Creek* **226**
80. *Hoffer Lakes and Anthony Lake* **229**
81. *Elkhorn Crest Trail, Anthony Lake to Marble Canyon* **230**
82. *Coon Hollow, with a Side Trip to Buckhorn Overlook* **233**
83. *Imnaha River Trail to Eureka Mine and Eureka Bar* **235**
84. *Nee Me Poo National Historic Trail, Hells Canyon* **237**
85. *Maxwell Lake* **239**
86. *Hurricane Creek Trail to Lakes Basin* **240**
87. *Burger Pass to Tombstone Lake* **243**
88. *Summit Point to Cornucopia and Crater Lake* **246**
89. *Pine Lakes and Pine Creek* **248**
90. *Sugarloaf Butte* **249**

Geologic Time Chart   252
Glossary   253
Recommended Reading   256
Appendix A: Mineral and Rock Identification   257
Appendix B: Geologic Maps List   263
Appendix C: Addresses   267
Index   269

Acknowledgments

Many friends contributed more than they know to this book, and without them this volume would still be in the netherworld of unborn books. John Eliot Allen's guidance gave the book direction. Joe and Marge Bernard provided long-time logistic and moral support. Ted Brown provided expertise from the hiker's perspective. Many geologists, especially Bev Vogt, Tracy Vallier, Ted Fremd, Mark Ferns, Terry Geisler, and Mike Cummings, contributed expertise. My energetic canine companions—Alaskan malamutes Wolf, Huffi, and Bear, and more recently Dundee, an Australian shepherd, and Meesha, a gentle border collie mixed breed—insisted that I get the hikes done. Most important, my husband David's patience, encouragement, understanding, advice, support, and proofreading prowess brought this book from the shadows of an idea into the sunlight of reality. However, I take all responsibility for any errors or omissions of geologic facts, dates, or other information.

—*Ellen Morris Bishop*

Preface

Few subjects transcend our modern, harried world as fully as geology. We are surrounded by stones that gauge time and tragedy in millions of years. When we consider the enduring history of the landscapes around us, many daily frustrations, from discourteous drivers to garden bugs, retreat into triviality. A hike that explores Oregon's geologic history provides not only fresh air and stress-relieving exercise but also some comforting insight into what is truly significant and what might be laughably transient in the scope of geologic time.

This book is written for the geologic layperson. It allows me to share some places that I know and love, as well as a knowledge of Oregon's long and distinguished past. Today, with a little imagination and geologic savvy we can visit tropical islands sequestered in the Wallowa Mountains, ancient volcanoes in the depths of Hells Canyon, the soils where dog-sized horses lolled in the oak-laden forests of the Painted Hills, muddy, clam-crowded sea bottom in the Coast Range, and glacially grooved Cascade valleys where ice once towered far above our heads.

But Oregon's geologic history also provides us with valuable and urgent lessons that we should heed today, including the inevitability of global warming as methane and carbon dioxide levels rise and the finality of extinction. The doe-eyed ichthyosaurs entombed in Wallowa Mountain limestone and Cretaceous sediments near Mitchell were exterminated by a catastrophic meteorite impact 65 million years ago. Though they might have been well adapted to modern seas, they are simply gone. In the earth's most severe extinction, 248 million years ago, at the end of the Permian period, methane and carbon-dioxide-driven global warming and changing sea levels coupled with meteorite impact eradicated 95 percent of life on the planet, including the Permian sea life now preserved as fossils in Hells Canyon. It behooves us all to consider the stories told by mute and stolid stones.

The best place to find Oregon's geology and the stories that it tells is in the backcountry, among wild rocks. Few of these tales are finished. Many have yet to be found and told. Newcomers to the landscape and the science often bring new insight and ask unconventional questions, revealing a history that geologists with long acquaintance and too-practiced eyes may have overlooked. There is no such thing as a dumb question, especially when looking at landscapes and considering their history. And, as you'll see, there is a lot of history to consider.

Introduction

Geology seems remote from our everyday concerns. What could ancient, inanimate rocks possibly have to do with modern ecosystems, with the lives and travails of salmon, or old growth, or highway congestion? Everything, as it turns out. For in geology there is an undeniable record of the finality of extinction, the devastating effects of climate change, and the displacement and chaos of ecosystems beset by invading exotic plants and animals—all threats to us today. Sea levels drop and 90 percent of marine species go extinct. The Permian extinction, 248 million years ago, provides an example. Increase atmospheric carbon dioxide sufficiently, and then warm the seas so formerly frozen methane hydrates are released as methane gas, and global temperatures rise, with normal daytime highs of 130 to 140 degrees Fahrenheit. As paleontologist Michael Benton of Oxford University has noted in *The Book of Life* (W. W. Norton & Co.; 1996), the planet experienced "slow suffocation, while the land fell silent and the sea stagnated." It is all there in the geologic record of the Permian extinction and other geologic events—as solidly written in stone as the Ten Commandments may have been.

And then there is this: although the dimensions and timescale of geology often seem far-removed from human experience, in fact we satisfy our every need from the earth. The air we breathe came first as gases from a cooling planet and is renewed each day by plants that depend on soils crafted from rocks. All our metals, concrete, plastics, fuels, and even wood and food supply come directly or indirectly from stone. Geology controls our water supplies. Groundwater follows some rock formations and is absent from others, is trapped in *faults,* and is funneled by *joints.* Rivers, creeks, and streams—and the ecosystems that depend upon them—all follow the dictates of tectonics and rocks. To live well and wisely, we need geology.

Landscapes and the geology that supports them nourish our aesthetic and spiritual needs as well as providing our physical requirements. Artists of all traditions have found inspiration in landscapes. In truth, the earth moves and breathes, although generally at timescales—both very fast and very slow—at the bounds of human understanding. Knowing how the scenery formed—whether you are photographing a volcano or a fault-bounded peak—provides new options for artistic expression. That cloud above Mount Hood may lend ominous meaning in one photograph, while in another at Steens Mountain,

Columbia River basalt flows mingle with sedimentary rocks at Hug Point and throughout much of the northern Oregon coast.

such a cloud may be just another suspended collection of condensed water vapor. The faulted linearity of Steens's steep east face gains new meaning, though, if you visualize a vast rent through the earth's tender crust. So whether we are prospecting for a gold deposit, fishing for steelhead trout, or simply out for fresh air and sunshine, there is some aspect of geology that is important to each of us—whether we know it or not.

OREGON'S DIVERSE GEOLOGY

Oregon's diverse geology incorporates nearly every variety of rock known, from soft, *sedimentary shales* and *limestones* to hard, dense *igneous rocks* of the earth's *mantle*. Oregon's oldest rocks are limestones east of Prineville dated at almost 400 million years in age. The youngest rocks—solid, brittle igneous rocks as opposed to newly deposited soft sediments—include the 1200-year-old *obsidian* flow at Newberry National Volcanic Monument (Hike 61) and the Devils Chain and Rock Mesa on the south flank of South Sister (Hike 44). The debris flow deposits and small *dacite dome* created by Mount Hood's most recent major eruption in 1781–82 rank as the state's youngest true rocks. However, each day water and wind deposit a new generation of Oregon's geology.

Much of Oregon's landscape has been built by multiple generations of volcanoes, including 45- to 55-million-year-old Clarno vents near Prineville and

Mitchell (Hikes 73–76) and an ancient, 35–25-million-year-old range that pre-dates the modern Cascades, and today comprises the Cascade foothills near Sweet Home and Detroit (Hikes 44 and 48). Rocks initially deposited as sands and muddy seafloors are less abundant. Today they comprise much of the Coast Range and the deep underpinnings of the Willamette Valley (Hikes 15, 20, 22, 24). *Metamorphic rocks*—ancient formations that have been changed and greatly deformed by heat and pressure—are confined to parts of Oregon's old-est *terranes*—the Klamath Mountains (Hikes 6–14) and the Blue Mountains (Hikes 77, 79, 82, 88), including the Wallowa, Elkhorn, and Strawberry Ranges.

Faults have uplifted several major mountain ranges, including Steens Moun-tain (Hike 67), the Wallowa Mountains (Hikes 85–90), Elkhorn Ridge (Hikes 80, 81), and the Strawberry Range (Hikes 77, 78). Active faults today generate earthquakes in the Portland area as the Portland Basin and Willamette Valley expand, near Klamath Falls and other parts of the Basin and Range, and in the Blue Mountains, especially near La Grande and Baker City, as part of the Olympic-Wallowa Lineament. The gentler process of *folding* has upwarped the Ochocos and the Blue Mountains south of Pendleton. In Oregon, the Cascades are the only mountain range built and maintained by volcanoes.

By far the most abundant rock in Oregon is *basalt*—a dark, iron- and magnesium-rich *volcanic rock*, erupted as a hot, fluid *lava* and cooled into a dark rock that often displays holes (or *vesicles*) that betray the presence of gases in the original lava. In Oregon, basalts are found from almost every geologic time, beginning more than 200 million years ago to some of the most recent eruptions at Dia-mond Craters only 6000 years ago. Basalt rock forms the dark, layered cliffs of the Columbia River Gorge, the layer-cake landscape of the Wenaha and Imnaha River Gorges, and the dark faces of Steens Mountain, Abert Rim, Winter Rim, and much of the High Desert landscape be-tween Bend and Burns. North Sister and the rocks of McKenzie Pass are basalt. The stacks and sea cliffs of Cape Lookout, Cannon Beach, Otter Rock, and Cascade Head, as well as the northern coastal peaks—Onion Mountain and Saddle Mountain—are composed of basalt. The

Pahoehoe basalts at Diamond Craters still look as fresh and fluid as the day they erupted some 6000 years ago.

young lava flows at Jordan Craters and Diamond Craters are also basalt.

This profusion of basalt is a consequence of Oregon's position at the western brink of the continent. A mantle plume—a jet of rising basalt *magma*—erupted basalt across much of eastern Oregon about 17 to 15 million years ago. As North America has moved west across the plume, it has produced the lavas of the Snake River Plain and today functions as the source of geothermal heat—and potentially huge eruptions—at Yellowstone. The basalts of the Cascades are related to *subduction*—the consumption of the Pacific Plate beneath the western edge of North America. And those of southeastern Oregon's Basin and Range seem to have erupted as part of the upper mantle bleeding through a stretched and paper-thin crust.

While basalt is so common that it is almost everywhere, another familiar

Alpine meadows, like those near Anthony Lake and Hoffer Lakes, are the legacy of Pleistocene glaciers that virtually disappeared about 10,000 years ago.

igneous (cooled from a molten fluid) rock—*granite*—is among Oregon's most rare. True granite is a rock that is abundant closer to the middle of the continent—in the Rocky Mountains of Wyoming, Montana, Utah, and eastern Idaho—as well as in the Appalachian Mountains of New England. It contains an abundance of potassium—an element that is a hallmark of the ancient continental core. Potassium—and true granite—are rare here. The coarse-grained white rocks of the Wallowas and Blue Mountains and the *plutons* of the Klamaths are not true granite but instead close cousins known as *granodiorite, diorite,* or *tonalite.*

Most of Oregon's sedimentary rocks—layered rocks deposited by wind or water—are *sandstones, shales,* or *mudstones.* Sandstone, a rock composed of sand-size particles pressed together and then cemented by silica or calcium carbonate (calcite) marks the site of ancient beaches or offshore deltas and deep sea fans. Today, sandstones are found in the Coast Range as part of a 40-million-year-old coastline and fan system, and in central Oregon near Mitchell and southern Oregon near Ashland as 100-million-year-old beaches and off-shore sandbars. Finer-grained shales and mudstones are also associated with these deposits. Finer-grained sandstones found along the Oregon coast today are much younger deposits, ranging from about 20 to 5 million years old. They record the rise and fall of sea levels, as well as the tectonic emergence of the Oregon coast. *Limestone,* a product of tropical or subtropical warm seas and marine life, is among the rarest of sedimentary rocks in Oregon. A few scattered exposures of limestone occur near Dallas—just west of Salem. Ancient limestones, more than 200 million years old, appear in Hells Canyon, the Wallowa Mountains, and the Ochocos. Similar rocks host Oregon Caves (Oregon's Caves National Monument) in the Klamath Mountains.

OREGON'S GEOLOGIC HISTORY

Oregon's landscapes began to take shape about 400 million years ago off the Idaho shore. At that time, known as the Devonian period, Boise would likely have been a coastal town. The dominant animals were heavy-jawed armored fish. The first land animals—a few awkward amphibians—had ventured out of the water. Land plants were largely a ferny assemblage, including a variety of mosses and horsetail rush, *Equisetum,* that grows on roadsides and in bogs today, a plant virtually unchanged in 400 million years.

The rocks that would become Oregon began as coral reefs and limy shallow-water banks in a subtropical sea. Today there are only a few tattered remnants of these stones scattered across the Blue Mountains. The most accessible is a small outcrop on the crest of the Greenhorn Mountains, a hundred yards or so below the iconic "green horn." Others are on private lands.

This collection of reefs would grow into a long-lived chain of volcanic islands,

13

known as the Blue Mountain *island arc,* that erupted generally north of the equator from about 400 to 170 million years ago. The rocks that occupy the Klamath Mountains of southwestern Oregon and northern California developed in a similar setting and may have been part of the same island chain. At least three generations of volcanoes erupted and died as the island chains evolved.

In the Blue Mountains, the oldest of these rocks include the 309-million-year-old rocks at Cougar Creek in the bowels of Hells Canyon, the 270-million-year-old altered volcanic rocks near Oxbow Dam on the Snake River, and the 278-million-year-old rocks of Canyon Mountain. Oregon's oldest known outcrop is a Devonian limestone on the GI Ranch, nearly 400 million years old, that rises above the surrounding grassland like a great stone whale breaching in a bunchgrass sea. The ecosystems entombed in these stones include clamlike mollusks and anemonelike crinoids. These animals were virtually erased in the Permian extinction event, 248 million years ago, that paved the way for the age of dinosaurs by wiping out almost 95 percent of existing species with high atmospheric CO_2 and methane levels, sizzling terrestrial and ocean temperatures, and meteorite impact.

Island arc volcanoes again erupted 235 to 225 million years ago. These younger Triassic rocks, including remnants of the coral reefs on the volcanoes' flanks, can be seen at Summit Point (Hike 88) and throughout the northern part of Hells Canyon (Hike 82).

The final eruptive episode in building the ancient basement of the Blue Mountains was a series of late Triassic and early Jurassic eruptions about 180 million years ago. The rocks are exposed along the Snake River near Huntington. Sedimentary rocks of similar age occur in Coon Hollow of Hells Canyon (Hike 82), in the Wallowa Mountains, and across much of the Aldrich Mountains south of John Day.

Many rock formations of Oregon's Klamath Mountains also date to the late Triassic and Jurassic. They include

Collisions between different terranes as well as with North America heated and deformed rocks in the exotic terranes of the Klamaths and Blue Mountains.

remnants of Jurassic seafloor and upper mantle exposed in the Kalmiopsis Wilderness, including Vulcan and Chetco Peaks (Hikes 10, 11), and the Red Buttes Wilderness on the Oregon-California border (Hike 7).

About 160 million years ago, North America began to move westward as the North Atlantic Ocean opened. By 140 million years ago, the continent had begun a long process of colliding with the volcanic islands. The collision generated *granitic* intrusions now exposed in the Klamaths (Hikes 3, 9) and in the Wallowas and Elkhorn Mountains (Hikes 80, 81, 85, 86, 87, 89). These intrusions generated and emplaced the gold deposits that brought mining—and eventually grazing and farming—to the Klamaths and the Blue Mountains (Hikes 5, 88).

By the early Cretaceous, about 120 million years ago, the process of accretion was virtually complete. The volcanic islands, along with their coral reefs, beaches, and bays, had become part of North America. And the shoreline was now near Mitchell. The collision likely forced up a range of high coastal mountains that kept the dinosaurs of Montana at bay—no dinosaurs have been found in Oregon yet, save for one hadrosaur that was moved north from California by faulting long, long after its death. Oregon does boast the remnants of ichthyosaurs—swimming, porpoiselike reptiles that gave birth to live young—and of pterosaurs—toothy bat-winged reptiles that could soar over mountains and oceans.

The Cretaceous sedimentary rocks near Mitchell and Ashland suggest that Oregon's first coastline was rugged, fed by fast-flowing rivers that ran into a shallow, rocky bay. In the uplands, giant tree ferns known as *Tempskya* grew, along with stubby palms. It seems to have been a barebones landscape. And most of its plants and animals, like those of the planet, were extinguished by the multiple impacts of meteorites 65 million years ago, including the devastating collision that created Mexico's Chixulxub Crater.

In the ensuing Paleocene period, life recovered, haltingly at first. Mammals grew in size; deciduous trees began to dominate. In Oregon, the Paleocene record is scarce, but can be found along Birch Creek east of Pilot Rock, about 30 miles south of Pendleton. Here, the leaves of a 60-million-year-old forest that included early versions of alder, oak, and gingko are preserved.

About 55 million years ago, Oregon's first native volcanoes began to erupt. Known as the Clarno Formation, these vents sprouted near Fossil, Mitchell, east to near Baker City, and west almost to Prineville (Hikes 73, 76). They erupted in a warm climate and may have grown to the size of the modern Cascades. Today, all that is left are eroded volcanic necks and a thick accumulation of debris flows and mudflows—now part of the John Day Fossil Beds. These rocks have provided an exquisite record of life in this period, known as the Eocene, when dog-sized, three-toed horses browsed on shrubs and vines

Cretaceous rocks near Mitchell are the remnants of the Pacific shoreline in central and eastern Oregon about 100 million years ago.

and saber-toothed, catlike nimravids waited to pounce for a meal.

Near the end of the Eocene about 38 million years ago, the *subduction zone* off the Oregon coast shifted, cutting off the supply of magma to the Clarno volcanoes and beginning a new generation of volcanoes—the Western Cascades. Today, Pilot Rock, a monolith south of Ashland, marks one of these early Western Cascade volcanoes (Hike 4). This range grew with time until, about 30 to 25 million years ago, it may, like the Clarno volcanoes before it, have rivaled the modern High Cascades in scale. Still, Oregon would have looked very different. The coastline ran along the eastern side of today's Willamette Valley. Silver Falls State Park marked the Oligocene coastline (Hike 29). The Willamette Valley was a huge sound, perhaps similar to modern Puget Sound in size. In the Oligocene, the Oregon coast acquired its most recent exotic terrane—a line of *seamounts* and oceanic basalts that now are sequestered in the Coast Range (Hike 22).

The enormous basalt flows that now characterize much of Oregon's landscape occurred in the Miocene, about 17 to 15 million years ago. They began as almost simultaneous fissure eruptions in southeast Oregon, where Steens Mountain is today (Hike 67), and in northeast Oregon, near the town of Imnaha (Hike 84). These eruptions were fundamentally different from what we consider a volcano. Instead of erupting from a single point (central vent), long fractures several miles to tens of miles opened in the earth's crust. Basalt lava flowed from this opening like blood rushing from an elongate wound. Ultimately, these basalts—more than 100 flows during a million years—covered more than 70,000 square miles beneath as much as 15,000 feet of basalt. Some of the most voluminous flows extended from eastern Oregon to

16

Columnar joints on the south side of Pilot Rock are part of a 38-million-year-old volcano near Ashland.

the Pacific. Today they form Cape Lookout, Haystack Rock at Cannon Beach, Saddle Mountain, and other coastal landmarks (Hikes 16–21), as well as the cliffs of the Columbia River Gorge and Steens Mountain. Known as Columbia

17

Three Fingered Jack is a Pleistocene volcano that was severely eroded by glaciation in the last 100,000 years.

River basalts and Steens basalts, these rocks are world-renowned examples of flood basalts.

At nearly the same time that vast basaltic eruptions spread across northern and central Oregon, powerful eruptions of hot, gassy ash emanated from huge circular vents called *calderas* in southeast Oregon's Owyhees. Today the products of these eruptions form the pockmarked cliffs of Leslie Gulch and the Honeycombs (Hikes 69, 70).

Near the end of the Miocene, 7 to 5 million years ago, faulting began to open Basin and Range landscapes and uplift the mountains of eastern Oregon. In the past 5 million years, the Wallowa, Elkhorn, Strawberry, Steens, and Pueblo Mountains, along with Basin and Range rimrocks like Abert Rim and Poker Jim Ridge, have risen above the adjacent landscape.

The period from 5 to about 1.8 million years ago, know as the Pliocene, was marked by a huge lake in what is today a desert region of southeast Oregon as well as southern Idaho. Known as Lake Idaho, this huge body of water supported 8-foot-long salmon. At the same time, small volcanoes began to erupt across what is today the Portland Basin. Known as the Boring volcanics (for their abundance near the town of Boring), these volcanoes continued to erupt through the late Pleistocene, with some vents dated as less than 100,000 years ago. The eruptions may not be finished yet (Hikes 25, 26).

Oregon's Ice Age, or Pleistocene, began 1.8 million years ago, as global cooling that began in the Miocene accelerated. The Pleistocene brought alpine glaciers to the Cascades, Wallowas, Elkhorns, Greenhorns, and Strawberry Range. Steens Mountain sported a thick ice cap. Near the close of the Pleistocene, between 13,500 and about 12,000 years ago, a series of huge floods unleashed from a glacially dammed lake in Montana scoured the Columbia River Gorge and repeatedly converted the Willamette Valley into a lake (Hike 30). Today, Willamette Valley farmers grow their crops in Idaho and Washington soils washed into the valley by floodwaters. Throughout the Pleistocene,

Cascade volcanoes tried to erupt as glaciers sought to wear them down. Mount Washington and Three Fingered Jack are examples of volcanoes that grew dormant and lost the battle with the ice; Mount Hood and Mount Jefferson are examples of volcanoes that persisted in building their cones while the ice tried to wear them down.

Since the end of the Pleistocene, the High Cascades and other Oregon volcanoes have continued to erupt and the subduction zone beneath our feet has continued to shift. The last major subduction zone earthquake on Oregon's coast occurred in 1700. Two well-exposed and young basalt lava fields can be found at Jordan Craters and Diamond Craters in southeast Oregon. Mount Mazama erupted catastrophically about 7700 years ago, about the same time as Mount Hood's Parkdale flow and the eruptions at Diamond Craters. About 1200 years ago, less bombastic eruptions emanated from Newberry Crater (Big Obsidian Flow) and South Sister (Devils Chain; Rock Mesa). Mount Hood last erupted significantly in 1781–82 (Hikes 37, 38). And South Sister presently is showing signs of preparing for another volcanic episode.

OREGON'S ACTIVE LANDSCAPES

Oregon's landscapes have been crafted by geologic processes for the past 400 million years. These processes continue every day. Most of this modern geologic activity falls into the categories of either tectonics (otherwise known as faulting and folding) or volcanism (otherwise known as erupting volcanoes). But landslides and floods also mold the earth's face.

Two active fault zones slice across the state, and several areas, including the Portland Basin and Willamette Valley, are in the process of being tectonically shaken and stretched. One of the major fault zones is known as the Olympic-Wallowa Lineament, or OWL. This complex system of faults extends from the Snake River near Brownlee Dam and Halfway northwest along both the northern and southern flanks of the Wallowa Mountains through the Grand Ronde valley and Milton Freewater, ultimately leading through Hanford Nuclear Reservation and diffusing into the faulted basins of Seattle. In 1936 an earthquake of about magnitude 4 shook the area around Milton Freewater and Umapine. Small earthquakes of magnitude 3 or less are common along these faults. Some geologists have calculated that the system is capable of a magnitude 7 quake.

Farther to the south, the Brothers fault zone accommodates the expansion of the Basin and Range. The small faults extend from south and east of Burns through Brothers and then west almost to the southern flank of South Sister. Recorded earthquakes along the Brothers fault zone have been mild. However, earthquakes in the Basin and Range, generated by the shifting and expanding crust, can be severe. In 1996 two quakes of magnitude 6 occurred on the westernmost Basin and Range faults near Klamath Falls. They resulted in one

Talus, at the base of Yokum ridge was spalled from a thick andesite.

death and millions of dollars in structural damage.

Other fault systems, including the Mount Angel system that cuts across the landscape north of Salem and the West Hills Fault in Portland and Forest Park, accommodate crustal stretching and rotation in the Willamette Valley and near Portland. These faults have produced magnitude 4 and 5 quakes as well as a noteworthy magnitude 6 "spring-break" quake that damaged the state capital building, also in 1996.

By far the most ominous tectonic threat comes from a future great, magnitude 9 subduction zone earthquake. Studies of past quakes along Oregon's coast indicate that such devastating temblors occur every 300 to 400 years. The last one happened in 1700.

Oregon sits above a tectonic time bomb. Just off our coast, the Juan de Fuca Ridge produces fresh ocean floor along a line of undersea volcanoes. This new seafloor moves at the rate of about an inch per year. When it reaches the coastline and the continent, the ocean floor bends downward and slides beneath North America. At a depth of about 30 miles (or 30 miles beneath the summit of Mount Hood), this down-going seafloor eventually melts and engenders melting in the surrounding mantle. The resulting hot, molten rock rises and may erupt, helping to maintain the Cascade volcanoes. But sometimes the down-going slab of seafloor gets stuck. Pressure builds up, and when (or if) it begins to move again, it does so with a jerk. To those of us who live on Oregon's coast or in the Willamette Valley, this "jerk" is a magnitude 9 earthquake—the equivalent of the 1964 Alaska earthquake.

Given the active nature of geology here, Oregon's volcanoes are also unlikely to be quiescent in the future. Mount Hood's most recent noteworthy eruption in 1781–82 sent voluminous mud, rocks, ash, and sand down the Sandy River. At the Sandy's mouth, the flow of the Columbia was shoved into a narrow, half-mile-wide channel—or so Lewis and Clark noted when they passed by the Sandy River's (or, as they called it, the Quicksand River) mouth in 1805, two decades after Hood's eruption. Mount Hood has experienced a number of small earthquake swarms in recent years that may portend the slow

The stump of a whitebark pine, toppled by Mount Hood's eruption in 1781-82, attests to volcanic violence.

start of more molten material toward the surface. South Sister has an undeniable bulge on its southwestern flank that suggests a gathering volcanic storm.

Although we cannot yet predict exactly when an earthquake or volcanic eruption may occur, we can be sure that Oregon's changing landscape will experience them in the future.

OREGON'S GEOLOGIC PROVINCES

The diverse landscapes of Oregon can be categorized into geologic "provinces" based upon the processes that formed them and the type and ages of the rocks found.

This is a relatively intuitive process, for Oregon's geology parallels its geography. Each set of rocks defines a different landscape, a unique climate, and different challenges for the hiker. From oldest to youngest, Oregon's major geologic subdivisions are as follows:

The Blue Mountains: Though similar to the Klamath Mountains, the Blue Mountains generally represent a single, long-lived system of volcanic islands that may have been similar to the modern Marianas, 400 to 170 million years in age, which was added to North America about 120 million years ago. These highly deformed and altered rocks are covered by younger volcanic rocks, including the Columbia River basalts.

The Klamath Mountains: Mostly rocks of the seafloor and tropical

21

volcanic archipelagos, 300 to 100 million years in age, the Klamaths were added to North America about 100 million years ago. Many consider their metamorphosed and igneous rocks to have been initially formed in a setting similar to the Blue Mountains. Older rocks occur in the California Klamaths.

The Cascades: The Cascades are two mountain ranges in one. Both are volcanic. The Western Cascades, 40 to about 10 million years in age, occupy the Cascade foothills; the High Cascades, whose reigning volcanoes are less than 1 million years old, parade as scenic peaks.

The Coast Range: These low mountains are composed of seafloor sediments and seamounts. Their rocks are 60 to 25 million years old, but most were added to North America about 30 million years ago.

The Willamette Valley: North of the Klamath Mountains, between the Coast Range and the Cascades, lies the Willamette Valley. Geologists used to think this valley simply lay passively between two mountain ranges. But we are discovering that the Willamette Valley is a dynamic place. During the last 10 million years earthquakes and volcanic eruptions have sculpted this landscape. The Portland Basin, which lies at the northern end of the Willamette Valley, is among the most seismically active areas in Oregon.

The Columbia River Gorge: Most closely allied with the Cascades, the Gorge is lined with basalts of the Columbia River group from 16 to 6 million years in age. These basalts erupted from vents in eastern Oregon and Washington. Some followed the ancestral channel of the Columbia all the way to the sea.

The Basin and Range: This vast region of southeast Oregon is seismically active. Here, the earth's crust is stretching, and has been for the last 15 million years. Volcanic rocks predominate; a few layered sedimentary rocks represent accumulations of ash in shallow lakes. The basalt rimrocks of Abert Rim, Poker Jim Rim, and Steens Mountain are about 16 million years in age.

The Owyhees: Lying unobtrusively east of the Basin and Range, the Owyhees are a dissected upland of giant volcanic calderas and fine-grained gold deposits. The huge volcanoes erupted 15 to 10 million years ago. A few young basalts, less than 1 million years in age, have flooded local basins and created rubbly rims.

The Deschutes Basin: Between Bend and Warm Springs, and near The Dalles, ash, stream sediments, and lavas from the Cascades accumulated between 7 and 4 million years ago. Today they form a volcanic layer-cake of ash-rich sediments and volcanic flows that comprises the Deschutes Basin.

The High Lava Plains: A chain of volcanoes, mostly *rhyolite* and basalt eruptions, the High Lava Plains vents and volcanic rocks become progressively younger to the west. The most recent eruptions built Newberry Volcano. Here

Columbia River basalt dikes cut through Cornucopia stock in the southeast Wallowa Mountains.

the Big Obsidian Flow, a glassy rhyolite flow, is only 1200 years in age and ranks among Oregon's youngest volcanic rocks.

GEARING UP FOR FIELD GEOLOGY

Field geologists are pretty much hikers with some extra knowledge of the earth sciences and a specific problem to solve. By using this book and learning a few basics, you can become a field geologist too.

WHAT TO BRING

Begin with the basics for hiking, including comfortable and appropriate clothes, sturdy boots, a day pack or backpack, a hat, a whistle, a space blanket, et cetera. Be sure to always carry items from the Ten Essentials: A Systems Approach:

1. Navigation (map and compass)
2. Sun protection (sunglasses and sunscreen)
3. Insulation (extra clothing)
4. Illumination (headlamp or flashlight)
5. First-aid supplies
6. Fire (firestarter and matches/lighter)
7. Repair kit and tools (including knife)
8. Nutrition (extra food)
9. Hydration (extra water)
10. Emergency shelter

A GPS unit is helpful, especially if you want to find a route to a specific feature that is off the trail. If you have a GPS, learn to use it before embarking on a long off-trail sojourn. GPS units with built-in altimeters and compasses are especially helpful for geologists. Be careful to avoid private property when navigating cross country. Use topographic maps, preferably 7.5' USGS maps, and if a published geologic map of the area is available, you might find it helpful. For more information on maps, see the next section, Books and Maps.

To explore and understand geologic features, a few other items to include are a hand lens, preferably 10X, to examine the small-scale features of rocks; a hammer, to break open rocks so you can examine a fresh surface (weathered surfaces often do not even remotely resemble the real rock); and safety glasses. It is critical to wear eye protection, and to keep others at a safe distance when breaking rock with a hammer (or with anything else), because rock chips and steel slivers from the hammer frequently fly in all directions and can seriously injure eyes or cut you or bystanders. Bring safety glasses and use them. And also, if you have brought along a geologist's rock hammer—the kind with the pointy end—avoid the temptation to bash at rocks with the pointed part of the instrument. This point is used properly for prying, not pounding, and you'll immediately alert the world to your amateur status if you whack away at an outcrop with the wrong end of the hammer. Steel slivers have been known to fly off such misused hammers and present a danger to people nearby. When breaking rocks with a hammer, choose your target with care, and never use the pointy end for forceful blows.

A notebook is handy to record observations. Commercially available field notebooks are more durable than spiral-bound books from stationery stores, but any notebook is better than none. If you want to collect samples, consider taking something to wrap them in so that they are protected and your gear is protected from your samples. Newspaper is light, cheap, and effective. A felt-tip, waterproof pen can be useful to mark sample numbers on each rock and key it to notes about where it was collected or other thoughts.

Using a hand lens for a geologist's eye view of a rock

The two most essential things to take are focused curiosity and keen observation. These are inexpensive, lightweight, durable, and indispensable. And everyone has free access to them.

BOOKS AND MAPS

Because this book is not meant as a comprehensive field guide to solving all geologic problems, you might want to invest in a book or two specifically about field geology. See Recommended Reading at the end of this book for some suggestions. Many technical papers that explain geology in great detail are also available in larger libraries.

Topographic maps provide information about elevation and topography as well as trail location. The standard, and most easily readable, is the US Geological Survey's 7.5' quadrangle map format. Other USGS maps, including USGS 1:100,000 scale, are available as well.

Topographic maps of most wilderness areas are published by or in cooperation with the US Forest Service and Bureau of Land Management and may be obtained at most ranger districts or in outdoor stores.

Geologic maps show the type of rock formations present. Most have a topographic base, so they provide both geologic and topographic information. However, the topographic information may be difficult to read, so a separate topographic map is recommended. A list of geologic maps for the hikes in this book is found in Appendix B, Geologic Maps List.

Geologic maps and USGS topographic maps, as well as many other books and some geologic and topographic maps, are available from The Nature of Oregon, a sales office of the Oregon Department of Geology and Mineral Industries and US Forest Service, located in the State Office Building in northeast Portland. For addresses of these agencies and other resources, see Appendix C, Addresses.

HOW TO USE THIS BOOK

Each chapter is devoted to one of Oregon's ten geologic provinces; the chapters follow a geographic progression from west to east. Each chapter begins with an overview of the geologic province, then lists one or more hikes in the area.

Each hike is numbered, and its title, subtitle, and summary provide information on location and special features to help you quickly select hikes that interest you. An information block further summarizes the hike's profile:

Distance: The hike's length is given in miles, round trip unless stated otherwise.

Elevation: The change in elevation is given by listing the hike's low and high points in feet.

Difficulty: Ratings are *easy, moderate,* or *strenuous.* Easy hikes are on level terrain, are usually less than 2 miles long, and follow well-marked, broad, unobstructed trails. Strenuous hikes traverse more than 2000 feet in elevation change, follow rugged trails, and/or require either long day hikes of more than 8 miles or an overnight pack trip. Moderate hikes fall in between these two extremes.

Topographic Maps: The USGS 7.5' quadrangle map or maps for the hike are listed.

Geologic Maps: Geologic maps in Appendix B, Geologic Maps List, have been given a unique number; here, the map or maps for the hike are indicated by that number. Refer to the appendix for the map's name and facts of publication.

Fees/Regulations: Many hikes in this book require a parking or use fee. Oregon State Parks and some Natural Areas require an annual or day pass; Forest Service trails require a Northwest Forest Pass for parking and, where appropriate, a no-fee wilderness permit.

Overlook, Painted Hills, John Day Fossil Beds National Monument

Precautions: Crucial information regarding access, trail conditions, and safety concerns are listed here.

Information: The agency that manages the land in which the hike is located is given here; addresses are found in Appendix C, Addresses.

Following the information block are the **Directions,** which describe how to get to the trailhead. Next comes the section **About the Landscape,** which highlights the geologic features of interest on the hike. Last is the **Trail Guide,** which gives details about the hike's route.

At the back of the book are a Geologic Time Chart, a Glossary of geologic terms, a list of Recommended Reading, and a Mineral and Rock Identification aide.

THE CHANGING LANDSCAPE

When we enter the backcountry we step away from processes that humans control and into the changing landscape. Here, what seem like catastrophes to us—floods, forest fires, earthquakes, windstorms, and volcanic eruptions—are merely planetary housecleaning. No place on earth is immune to catastrophic change, and the trails discussed in this book are no exception. For example, in 1995, high winds felled trees and closed trails on Marys Peak while floods and landslides damaged trails in the Columbia River Gorge. In 1996 and again

27

in 2002, major forest fires swept through Hells Canyon, the Elkhorn Mountains, and the Strawberry Mountains. Most of the Kalmiopsis Wilderness was closed to entry during the summer of 2002 due to the extensive Biscuit forest fires. Old fires may present new hazards. Areas that have been burned in previous years may eventually produce trails clogged by fallen trees.

Hikers especially need to be aware that conditions along a trail may change abruptly. Check trail conditions with the pertinent agency before embarking on a lengthy trip. Remember, too, that the US Forest Service's policy of returning fire to the ecosystem means that lightning-caused forest fires, especially in wilderness areas, are often allowed to burn. Be aware of forest conditions and storm activity when hiking in late summer. And as you hike, consider how past disturbances, including earthquakes, landslides, volcanic eruptions, and fires, have created the landscape that you, for the moment, are a part of.

A NOTE ABOUT SAFETY

Safety is an important concern in all outdoor activities. No guidebook can alert you to every hazard or anticipate the limitations of every reader. Therefore, the information presented and the techniques described in this book are not representations that a particular activity will be safe for you or your party. When you engage in any of the activities described in this book, you assume responsibility for your own safety. Under normal conditions, such excursions require the usual attention to traffic, road and trail conditions, weather, terrain, the capabilities of your party, and other factors. Keeping informed on current conditions and exercising common sense are the keys to a safe, enjoyable outing.

—The Mountaineers Books

Chapter 1

THE KLAMATH MOUNTAINS AND SOUTHERNMOST COAST

The Klamath Mountains are one of the most eclectic ranges in Oregon. They spill over into California and encompass the welter of peaks called the Siskiyous. Their rocks include slivers of the earth's mantle, seafloor, and old volcanoes; scraps of the continent; and gold-bearing granites. Their exotic geology is similar to that of the Blue Mountains: they once were islands far from the Oregon coast, and were added to North America more than 100 million years ago. The oldest rocks of the Klamath Mountains reside in northern

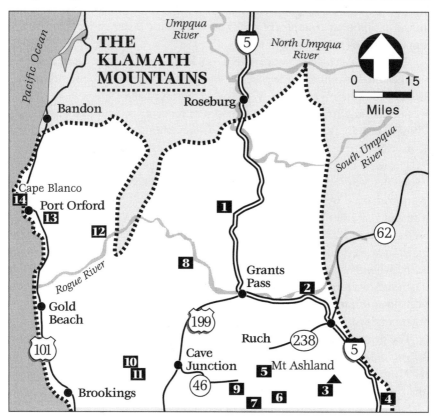

Layered peridotite outcrops near Little Vulcan Lake

California, where scraps of seafloor that may be older than 500 million years huddle in the shadows of Mount Shasta.

Oregon's Klamaths are hard-pressed to reveal ages older than about 200 million years. But despite their relative youth, Oregon's Klamath terranes reveal exceptional examples of *peridotite*—rare, dark, dense rocks of the earth's upper mantle (Hikes 7, 10, 11).

There are also high-pressure *schists*—rocks that have been squeezed, folded, and heated deep beneath the surface. These rocks, known as schist, occur near Condry Mountain—and also on Hike 6 to Summit Lake.

Rocks of the Ashland pluton, exposed in roadcuts as well as along the Pacific Crest Trail, illustrate the slow but often violent process of granitic intrusions (Hike 3).

The rocks and "terranes" of the Klamaths have been shorn from a multitude of arcs that were amalgamated, or joined together, just before their collision with North America. By hiking from one part of the Klamath Mountains to another, you can visit islands that may have formed millions of years and hundreds of miles apart—and also traipse across the accordioned seafloor that once separated them in space and time. Each relatively coherent sliver of rock—forming identifiable geologic settings, such as seafloor (Hikes 9, 12, 13) or a volcano (Hike 1)—is called a terrane—a sort of geologic pun on the more normal word *terrain*. A geologic terrane is a long-vanished landscape, one that can only be envisioned if you understand how and where the rocks of the terrane formed.

The principal terranes of Oregon's Klamath Mountains that are recognized by geologists include the following:

The Sixes River terrane: The scraps of Cretaceous seamounts and ocean floor that make up this terrane are found near Cape Blanco.

Snow Camp terrane: Magma chambers beneath Cretaceous island arc volcanoes are exposed on the lower Rogue River (Hike 12).

Gold Beach terrane: This zone of Jurassic sedimentary and igneous rocks is found today along the Oregon coast between Gold Beach and Cape Blanco.

Yolla Bolly terrane: The sandstones and shales of a Jurassic beach extend from Brookings northward.

Western Klamath terrane: This extensive, Jurassic island arc complex has five recognized subterranes, or subdivisions of the main terrane, representing parts of the island arc. They include the Rogue River subterrane—arc volcanoes—and the Dry Butte subterrane—the roots of those volcanoes. Hikes 10, 11 and 12 traverse these rocks.

Applegate or Western Paleozoic and Triassic terrane: This terrane represents the oldest rocks of Oregon's Klamath Mountains and includes fragments of ancient ocean crust. The *marbles* of Oregon Caves (Hike 9) and the rocks of Red Butte on Hike 7 are part of this terrane.

Many of these terranes collided with one another to form a collage of terranes before they encountered North America. By the time the continent arrived, many had amalgamated into a mini-continent. The Klamath terranes became part of North America by about 130 million years ago. Beaches offshore collected sands and nourished huge, spiral-shelled ammonites. Beginning about 50 million years ago, sedimentary rocks of the Coast Range buried the old rocks on the north, and lava flows from the Cascades covered the Klamath terranes' connection with the continent.

Gneiss and deformed rocks along the Applegate River attest to the heat, pressure, and force of collision between the continent and terranes of the Klamaths.

KLAMATH MOUNTAINS: ISLAND ARCS, SUBDUCTION ZONES, AND EXOTIC TERRANES

Many of Oregon's oldest rock formations—found in the Klamath Mountains and Blue Mountains—are not natives to the state. They originated as volcanoes, coral reefs, and other parts of Pacific island systems, known as island arcs.

These island systems, as well as similar, modern island chains, including the Aleutians, Kuriles, and Marianas, mark places where the seafloor plunges more than 400 miles into the earth's mantle, creating a deep oceanic trench as it goes. The path of the down-going crust is known as a subduction zone.

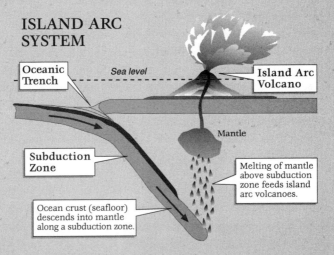

ISLAND ARC SYSTEM

Oceanic Trench

Sea level

Island Arc Volcano

Mantle

Subduction Zone

Melting of mantle above subduction zone feeds island arc volcanoes.

Ocean crust (seafloor) descends into mantle along a subduction zone.

The descending crust adds volatile new material to the mantle, stirring the plastic rocks there and causing part of the mantle to melt and thus creating a magma that rises to the surface and erupts as a volcano. On a map, the chains of volcanoes above the oceanic trench curve slightly. Hence they are known as volcanic arcs. When the volcanoes erupt in the ocean, forming islands, they are called an island arc.

Island arcs are often swept up and added to the prow of moving continents. In this collision, the island arc is added, or accreted, to the continent. This newly acquired landscape is called an exotic terrane. Western North America has grown westward more than 400 miles in the last 600 million years by this process of accretion.

Hike 1

JACK LONDON TRAIL

Follow the path of a famous writer to find volcanic greenstones atop this peak.

DISTANCE ■ 5 miles round trip

ELEVATION ■ 1230–2850 feet

DIFFICULTY ■ Moderate

TOPOGRAPHIC MAP ■ Glendale

GEOLOGIC MAP ■ 1

PRECAUTIONS ■ Some poison oak is present along the way.

INFORMATION ■ Jackson County Parks and Recreation: (541) 774-8183 or *parksinfo@jacksoncounty.org;* Wolf Creek Tavern: (541) 866-2474 or *www.thewolfcreekinn.com*

Directions: Follow Interstate 5 to exit 76, Wolf Creek, about 20 miles north of Grants Pass. Continue 0.5 mile to the now-restored historic tavern. (They serve excellent meals here.) From the tavern, continue west, following signs for Wolf Creek Park. The trailhead is at the south side of the park, along Wolf Creek.

About the Landscape: This hike allegedly follows the same path the writer Jack London did one afternoon when he stopped overnight at the Wolf Creek Tavern. Local residents secretly believe that he wrote *Call of the Wild* on the summit, but in reality, he only wrote part of an unpublished story.

Still, London's trek did take him farther into the wild than he might have imagined—on a hike across a 170-million-year-old volcanic landscape—or what remains of it. London Peak is composed of altered basalts and andesites—now pistachio-colored rocks called volcanic *greenstones.* These are part of the Rogue Formation and

Greenstones form the upper part of London Peak.

33

represent the carapace of a Jurassic volcano that once raised its head far from the Oregon coast and was accreted to the continent about 130 million years ago, along with the rest of the Klamaths.

Trail Guide: From the trailhead, the path crosses Wolf Creek, then begins a very, very long, 1.8-mile switch-backing ascent. The path climbs through second-growth Douglas fir and madrone. With increasing elevation, the trees are larger. Watch for poison oak along the way.

At 1.8 miles the trail turns a bit to follow the flat line of a side-ridge toward the peak. Expect to see some wildlife here, including deer. This respite is only temporary. After 0.2 mile that path steepens considerably and gets serious about summiting. As you near the top, a nice park bench provides a view of the freeway below—a bit different than the scene that greeted London.

The bench marks the official summit, but to find the best exposures of Rogue River greenstones, continue another 0.5 mile. This part of the path is a handicapped-accessible trail that leads to a mountain-top road and parking area. Along the way, major greenstone outcrops greet the hiker. At the road, turn right to find a nice quarry, where the angular, green volcanic rocks are exposed and easy to examine. Return as you came.

Hike
2
UPPER TABLE ROCK

An easy walk up to an ancient riverbed provides an exceptional view of the modern Rogue River and the valley.

DISTANCE ■ **4 miles round trip**
ELEVATION ■ **1300–2050 feet**
DIFFICULTY ■ **Easy**
TOPOGRAPHIC MAP ■ **Sams Valley**
GEOLOGIC MAP ■ **2**
PRECAUTIONS ■ Avoid contact with and transporting flowers or seeds of yellowstar thistle, an exotic pest plant that prospers on Table Rocks. Take adequate water; there is no potable water on Table Rocks. Dogs are prohibited.
INFORMATION ■ Medford Bureau of Land Management: (541) 770-2200; The Nature Conservancy of Oregon (503) 230-1221

Directions: To reach Upper Table Rock trailhead from Medford, take Table Rock Road north 5 miles. At a Y intersection, turn right on Modoc Road and follow the road about 1.5 miles to the trailhead.

About the Landscape: The large, flat-topped mesas north of Medford (called, rather unimaginatively, Upper Table Rock and Lower Table Rock) overlie the

Lower and Upper Table Rock are remnants of lava flows that filled the ancestral Rogue River gorge about 7.1 million years ago.

Klamath terranes. They look large and square, but a map view or a hiker's exploration prove them to be horseshoe-shaped. Table Rocks preserve the form of the ancestral Rogue River's meanders. They are a classic example of inverted topography: the lowest feature—the Rogue River's ancestral channel—has now become the highest.

Near today's town of Prospect, along the modern Upper Rogue's channel, lava from the Cascades erupted about 7 million years ago and filled the ancient river canyon with hard, resistant *andesite*. As time passed, the rock on either side of the lava-filled canyon eroded away, preserving the lava cast of the ancestral Rogue's course. Today, Upper and Lower Table Rocks' horseshoe-shaped forms are the remnants of the thick, canyon-filling lava flow—meanders of the ancient Rogue frozen in stone.

The proximity of the modern Rogue River to this old canyon suggests that the river course and drainage patterns have changed little during the past 7 million years. The climate, vegetation, and ecosystems are different though. Seven million years ago Oregon's climate was temperate, a bit warmer overall than today, and relatively dry, with strong seasonal fluctuations. Grass had become a dominant plant. Trees may have included oaks and gingkoes, and a few lingering metasequoia (dawn redwood), alder, and river birch in wetter locations. The animals that lived along the Rogue probably included the small, early horses *Merychippus* and *Plesippus,* both of which were adapted to grazing grasses rather than browsing shrubs. A few gomphotheres—large browsing ancestral elephants, may have passed through the landscape on their way to extinction as the forests they needed for habitat shrank in the face of the drying climate.

The dark volcanic rocks that cap both Upper and Lower Table Rock look like basalt. They have columns like basalt. And most references discuss the "basalt" of Table Rocks. But, technically, this rock, like many other rocks of the Cascades, is andesite. Sandstone, shale, and conglomerates lie buried beneath the 200-foot-thick volcanic flow. These sedimentary rocks, poorly exposed along the oak-shaded lower portion of the Table Rocks trails, are relicts of an even older river system, about 38 million years in age (late Eocene).

Trail Guide: This hike threads through moss-festooned, gall-infested scrub oak to the base of the high andesite caprock of Upper Table Rock. This area was logged in the 1950s, and pine has not regenerated well on the dry, hot slopes.

The trail departs the parking area and clambers up the gradual slopes of old slumps, landslides, and talus. There is little geology to see at Upper Table Rock until you reach the base of the cliffs about 1 mile into the walk. Here, blocks from the adjacent cliffs form a jumbled, coarse talus. The base of the flow is buried in crumbled rocks. Once you reach the flat summit of Upper Table Rock in about 1.5 miles, the subtle geology unveils itself slowly.

Elongate furrows and narrow rock crevasses define extensive vertical cracks in the lava flow. These cracks form as erosion strips away the support for the cliffs.

From where the trail emerges onto the top of Upper Table Rock, a cross-country walk 0.5 mile west reveals the opposite side's cliffs, with not only cracks but a mounded topography. Similar mounds of soils perch atop basalt bedrock worldwide. Known generally as biscuit scabland, they form by a variety of mechanisms. These include freezing and thawing, the activity of gophers, collection of fine material into regularly spaced mounds by violent shaking during earthquakes, and the capacity of grass and other vegetation to catch and hold windblown silts and clays. On Upper Table Rock, the mounds' north-south orientation parallels the prevailing winds and suggests that here wind was a factor in their formation.

Explore the top of Upper Table Rock, watching for the deep vertical tension cracks that cross this plateau. The overall horseshoe shape of Upper Table Rock is evident from the vantage point of its western cliffs. Return along the same route down the cliffs and along the trail to the trailhead.

MOUNT ASHLAND AND THE PACIFIC CREST TRAIL TO WRANGLE GAP

Hike

3

Visit an example of how a pluton intrudes, digests, and assimilates the surrounding country rock.

DISTANCE ▪ 12 miles round trip

ELEVATION ▪ 5800–6200 feet

DIFFICULTY ▪ Easy

TOPOGRAPHIC MAPS ▪ Mount Ashland, Siskiyou Peak, Dutchman Peak

GEOLOGIC MAPS ▪ 5, 6

FEES/REGULATIONS ▪ Northwest Forest Pass required for trailhead parking.

PRECAUTIONS ▪ Because of this hike's length, it is recommended as an overnight backpack.

INFORMATION ▪ Ashland Ranger District, Rogue River-Siskiyou National Forest: (541) 552-2900

Directions: From Interstate 5 south of Ashland, take exit 6, Mount Ashland, and take Mount Ashland Road toward Mount Ashland Ski Area. This road becomes USFS Road 20 at the Siskiyou National Forest boundary. High roadcuts from mile 2 to mile 4 along this paved and well-maintained roadway show, in progression, (1) sedimentary rocks cross-cut and intruded by small granitic *dikes;* (2) sedimentary rocks enmeshed in a network of granite; (3) dark, angular globs of recrystallized sedimentary rock *(xenoliths)* floating in a granitic matrix; (4)

Granite outcrops along the Pacific Crest Trail

irregular, small blobs of recrystallized sedimentary rock entombed in granitic rock; and (5) granitic rocks with a few small, dark, rounded xenoliths.

At Grouse Gap, 1.5 miles west of the Mount Ashland Ski Area, at the intersection of USFS Road 20 and the Pacific Crest Trail (PCT), also called USFS Trail 2000, find the trailhead. Parking is available at the Grouse Gap shelter if you plan to be on the trail overnight.

About the Landscape: The Ashland pluton is one of eight major granitic intrusions in the Klamath Mountains. This large body of granitic rocks is mostly granodiorite, 160 to 147 million years old. It has deformed, baked, and digested the rocks of the Applegate terrane, the oldest rocks of the Oregon Klamath Mountains.

This relatively level hike explores Mount Ashland and the Ashland pluton. One of the best parts of the journey is the exceptional lesson of how the Mount Ashland granitic pluton intruded the surrounding shale. This process is exposed in roadcuts on the way to the hike's beginning. Plan to stop and check out several of these roadcuts and perhaps arrange an auto-hiker relay if you drive up the mountain with a companion.

Trail Guide: The first 5 miles meander through the Ashland pluton. Large outcrops are rare along the hike, but many boulders and small exposures along the trail show off the Ashland pluton's textures and rock types. Notable things to look for include the large square pink to white orthoclase (potassium-rich) *feldspar* crystals that are a hallmark of many Ashland pluton rocks, and dark, strung-out xenoliths, or relics of the old sedimentary rocks intruded, partly

Light-colored granitic rock intrudes dark shale along Mount Ashland Road.

melted, and captured by the pluton. These features are prominent near Grouse Gap. The closer you approach the edge of the Ashland pluton, the finer-grained the granitic rocks become. Within 200 yards of this contact, the granitic rocks develop a noticeable layering or, in geological terms, foliation.

At about 5 miles, the rocks change abruptly from the monotonous gray of the Ashland pluton's granodiorite to finer-grained metamorphic rocks. The trail makes a wide swing to the north around the aptly, if unimaginatively, named Big Red Mountain. It is composed of metamorphosed peridotite. Metamorphism has enhanced the reddish brown color of the weathered stone by oxidizing the iron in the peridotite. Long, bladed crystals of the magnesium-rich mineral anthophyllite form interesting textures in these rocks.

The trail eases around the barren slopes of Big Red Mountain and 1 mile farther, at Wrangle Gap, a small but shaded and well-developed campground with water and toilets waits on USFS Road 20, just beyond its intersection with the trail. Return to the trailhead at Grouse Gap via the PCT, or walk along the USFS road for slightly different scenery.

Hike
4

PILOT ROCK

Take a short stroll along the Pacific Crest Trail to the throat of one of the Cascades' first volcanoes.

DISTANCE ■ 1 mile round trip

ELEVATION ■ 5100–5500 feet (trail); summit is 5908 feet

DIFFICULTY ■ Moderate (trail), very difficult summit

TOPOGRAPHIC MAP ■ Siskiyou Pass, Oregon-California

GEOLOGIC MAP ■ 1

FEES/REGULATIONS ■ Northwest Forest Pass required for trailhead parking.

PRECAUTIONS ■ The climb to the summit on slippery rocks is difficult and dangerous, especially when the rocks are wet. This climb is *not* part of the hike and is nonessential to explore and understand the geology of Pilot Rock.

INFORMATION ■ Ashland Ranger District, Rogue River-Siskiyou National Forest: (541) 552-2900

Directions: From Ashland, drive south on Interstate 5 to exit 6, Mount Ashland. Take this exit and continue on old Highway 99 past the turnoff for Mount Ashland Ski Area. In 0.7 mile from the exit, follow the road under the freeway and continue to Siskiyou Pass. Just beyond the pass, turn left on Pilot Rock Road. Follow this road 2.9 miles to a parking area on the left. Pilot Rock is visible on the right.

Pilot Rock is the 38-million-year-old remnant of an early Western Cascades volcano just southeast of Ashland.

About the Landscape: Until about 40 million years ago, there were no Cascade volcanoes in Oregon, Washington, or California. Instead, volcanoes of the Clarno Formation erupted near Mitchell, Prineville, Fossil, Condon, and Baker City—all in what we consider today as eastern Oregon. But at about 38 million years ago, a shift in the subduction zone off the Oregon coastline brought a halt to Clarno eruptions—and initiated the Cascades.

This humble beginning can be seen today at Pilot Rock, just southeast of Ashland. Here, gray, columned cliffs rise abruptly—this is the last relict of an andesite vent and lava flow. The rock is gray in color and proudly displays dark *hornblendes* on a freshly broken surface—a telltale sign that this is andesite rather than the darker, more iron-rich basalt.

Trail Guide: This trail leads from the parking lot quite directly to Pilot Rock's bare countenance a little less than 0.5 mile away. Once at the base, you may choose whether to turn left or right. A trip to the left leads to a scrambling climb and a view of eroded columns. The way to the top is difficult (some would merely consider it challenging) and provides little extra insight to Pilot Rock's origins.

If you turn to the right as you first approach the base, a rude, informal trail leads to the south flank. Here, the columnar joints are exquisitely exposed and loom somewhat ominously above hikers' heads. Black hornblende crystals can be found in the rocks of the talus slope at Pilots Rock's base.

Either way, the hiking distance is limited. Return as you came.

Hike 5

GIN LIN MINE TRAIL

Explore the vestiges of Chinese placer mines on a short but scenic interpretive trail.

DISTANCE ■ 0.8-mile loop

ELEVATION ■ 1690–1730 feet

DIFFICULTY ■ Easy

TOPOGRAPHIC MAP ■ Squaw Lakes, Oregon-California

GEOLOGIC MAP ■ 1

FEES/REGULATIONS ■ Northwest Forest Pass required for trailhead parking.

PRECAUTIONS ■ Poison oak is present near much of the trail.

INFORMATION ■ Applegate Ranger District, Rogue River-Siskiyou National Forest: (541) 899-3800

Directions: From Interstate 5 just north of Medford take exit 30, Jacksonville, and stay on Highway 238 through Jacksonville to Ruch. Turn left (south) on Upper Applegate Road and drive 12 miles south. Turn right on USFS Road 1095 (about 1 mile past the Applegate Ranger Station) marked for Gin Lin Trail and Flummet Flat Campground. The entrance to the trailhead parking lot is about 0.4 mile on the right, just past the campground.

About the Landscape: In the 1850s, miners began to move north from the California goldfields into Oregon. Placer gold was discovered along Jackson Creek near Jacksonville, in December 1851, by two pack-string owners, James Cluggage and James R. Poole. By the summer of 1852 the area around Jacksonville swarmed with miners. Placer miners constructed vast systems of ditches to bring water to unlikely hill slopes where "hydraulick mining" could be practiced—and whole hillsides were washed through sluice boxes by high-pressure hoses. The Gin Lin Trail traverses one of these sites, a place known as Palmer Diggings when it was first mined by hydraulic methods in the 1860s.

By 1880, this area was considered unprofitable. A Chinese miner named Gin Lin purchased the site in 1881, brought in more Chinese to work the claim, and turned it into a profitable mine by working the ground more methodically and carefully—still using hydraulic methods.

Trail Guide: From the trailhead, the interpreted path heads uphill, navigating a narrow, clay-sided ravine carved out by hydraulic hoses. Sluice boxes—wooden boxes in which the flow of water was slowed by a series of baffles that caught gold nuggets and flakes—once operated in this ravine, after it was mined out by hoses. The clays, sands, and gravels throughout this trail are all the ancient deposits of the Applegate River.

At the top of the ravine, piles of river cobbles make up the tailings that attest to the Chinese miners' painstaking hand work here. This spot also offers a nice view of the Applegate River below. From here, the path meanders through a sugar and ponderosa pine/madrone-rich forest, finding several more cuts made by hydraulic miners and climbing past some robust poison oak before joining the original Palmer Ditch at about 0.5 mile into the walk. Beyond the ditch, the path—and a handy bench—overlook an area now filled with manzanita and madrone that was extensively eroded by hydraulic hoses. Another short ravine that held sluice boxes leads the path to its final discovery—a long and straight tailings pile of water-worn cobbles that complete the loop hike at the original trailhead.

The Gin Lin Trail

SUMMIT LAKE

Hike 6

Find some true schist—one of Oregon's rarest rock-types.

DISTANCE ■ 4 miles round trip
ELEVATION ■ 3080–4730 feet
DIFFICULTY ■ Difficult
TOPOGRAPHIC MAP ■ Squaw Lakes, Oregon-California
GEOLOGIC MAP ■ 25
FEES/REGULATIONS ■ Northwest Forest Pass required for trailhead parking.
PRECAUTIONS ■ Watch for bears on this trail.
INFORMATION ■ Applegate Ranger District, Rogue River-Siskiyou National Forest: (541) 899-3800

Directions: From Interstate 5 take exit 30, Jacksonville, and stay on Highway 238 through Jacksonville to Ruch. Turn left (south) on Upper Applegate Road and drive 14.5 miles to Applegate Dam. Turn left, cross the dam, and continue on this road (USFS Road 1075) for 8.5 miles to Squaw Lakes. The trailhead is on the right, in the upper parking lot; keep to your right as you navigate the many cars at the popular entry to Squaw Lakes. The last 5 miles of USFS Road 1075 is a single-track narrow gravel road. Watch for traffic, including occasional log trucks.

About the Landscape: In addition to slivers of ancient volcanic islands, seafloor basalts, and chunks of the upper mantle, the Klamath Mountains also harbor metamorphosed sedimentary rocks that collected in ocean basins between and around islands. The limestones (now metamorphosed into marble) of Oregon Caves are one such sediment—part of the Applegate terrane. The Condrey Mountain schist is another—though more mysterious in its heritage. This high-pressure rock is related to the Josephine ophiolite—a chunk of the mantle that lies in the eastern Kalmiopsis Wilderness. The Condrey Mountain schist represents seafloor that was squeezed during the lengthy process of placing the upper mantle peridotites onto the crust where they can be found today. Its rare minerals—blue-green-colored amphiboles—indicate that the original shales were metamorphosed at high pressures and low temperatures in the process of deep-seated faulting.

Trail Guide: Summit "Lake" is a grassy, wetland depression rimmed by beautiful old-growth pine that is somewhat boggy in the spring as snow melts, but a nice soft place to rest after a hard 2-mile climb in the summer. In early July the lake's surface shimmers with a long-forgotten blue color of delicate violet blooms.

Condrey Mountain schist is a rare, high-pressure metamorphic rock exposed along the trail to Summit Lake.

From the trailhead, the Summit Lake Trail climbs evenly at an easy grade for the first 0.5 mile, crossing a wooden bridge and switch-backing as though it knew what switchbacks were for. There's no water here—at least not in late summer—and no water along the trail. Look for an osprey nest in a tall pine snag just a few hundred yards up the trail. After the second bend, the trail begins to climb in earnest, gradually steepening its slope like a drag racer accelerating for the finish line.

At about 1 mile, the trail ducks behind a slope, tempers its rise, and lets you explore a natural outcropping. These rocks are Condrey Mountain schist, a blue-green rock that once was a shalelike seafloor sediment, but was heated and recrystallized as the diverse terranes of the Klamath block were amalgamated into one large microcontinent about 160 million years ago. These rocks are an orphaned and misplaced part of the Klamath's Western Jurassic Belt— the same general group of rocks as the peridotites at Vulcan Lake and Chetco Peak (Hikes 10, 11) in the southern Kalmiopsis Wilderness.

Here, at the first large outcrop of Condrey Mountain schist, you enter bear country—look for signs, including droppings, dead trees that have been ripped open in search of ants and grubs, and large rocks rolled over in similar hunts for food. The diverse forest along the way includes madrone, Douglas fir, ponderosa pine, sugar pine, and cedar.

At 1.7 miles the trail skirts a huge clearing—vestige of a 1980 forest fire that was subsequently logged so as not to "waste" wood. Only one or two lonely snags remain standing. (Now we know that the number of birds actually increase in a burned area as species such as flickers, nuthatches, and pileated woodpeckers harvest the insects that come to feed on damaged or dead trees.) At the upper end of the clearing, the trail zigzags and then joins USFS spur road 700. There are several more outcrops of Condrey Mountain schist, along with Jurassic volcanic greenstone—once part of a Jurassic seafloor—here. Just before the junction, an unmarked trail leads gently downslope 100 yards to the grassy meadow of Summit Lake.

Once here, you can stretch your legs in this clearing. There are nice views of the Siskiyous from the logged-over fire area, and an opportunity to explore the old-growth pine grove that encloses Summit Lake. Return as you came.

ECHO LAKE, RED BUTTES WILDERNESS

Examine part of the earth's deep crust and upper mantle in the Red Buttes Wilderness.

DISTANCE ▪ **8 miles round trip**

ELEVATION ▪ **2200–5860 feet**

DIFFICULTY ▪ **Difficult**

TOPOGRAPHIC MAP ▪ **Kangaroo Mountain, Oregon-California**

GEOLOGIC MAP ▪ **5**

FEES/REGULATIONS ▪ **Northwest Forest Pass required for trailhead parking.**

PRECAUTIONS ▪ **The upper part—approximately the last 2 miles—of this trail is not maintained. Expect to encounter downed trees (some quite large) and other obstacles, especially above Butte Fork Creek.**

INFORMATION ▪ **Applegate Ranger District, Rogue River-Siskiyou National Forest: (541) 899-3800**

Directions: From Interstate 5 just north of Medford take exit 30, Jacksonville, and follow Highway 238 14 miles through Jacksonville to Ruch. Turn south on Upper Applegate Road. Continue 19 miles to a T intersection at the upper end of Applegate Reservoir. Turn left and follow this road 1.3 miles to a large gravel open area where USFS Road 1040 turns sharply right, downhill. Follow Road 1040 (narrow, gravel, single lane, but a good road) along the Middle Fork of the Applegate River 5.8 miles, cross a bridge across Cook and Green Creeks, and turn into a parking loop.

About the Landscape: The earth's upper mantle is normally buried tens of miles beneath our feet. But when islands and continents collide, the slow-motion tectonic violence often heaves up chunks of mantle and the oceanic crust just above it onto the continent's edge like a beached whale. One of the few places on the planet where we can stroll across rocks typical of the earth's upper mantle is in the Klamath Mountains. The landscape, from the Applegate River to the summit of No-Name Butte and Red Butte, 4 miles to the south, provides an abbreviated cross section of lower crust and upper mantle—and a graphic example of the titanic forces involved in dredging mantle rocks to the surface.

If you pause along the Applegate River before you take to the trail, you'll notice dark and wildly banded rocks in the river's gorge. These are *amphibolites*. Once, 230 million years or so ago, they were *gabbro*—a rock that looks like granite but is darker and contains much more iron. But faulting, shearing, and thrusting at high temperatures transformed these gabbros into the harlequin rocks along the Applegate—and in the first few miles of the trail. They served as a sort of hot, plastic lubricant or cushion on which the peridotites of Red Buttes slid into place.

These rocks, and the peridotites in the Red Buttes Wilderness, are part of the Klamath Mountain's Western Paleozoic and Triassic belt, among the oldest rocks in the Oregon Klamaths.

Trail Guide: This trail leads to an alpine lake in the Red Buttes Wilderness, and to the ridge above it with outstanding views and access to some side hikes over the tawny outcrops of Red Butte and No-Name Butte. There are two major creek crossings, and also Echo Lake itself—a smallish tree-cloistered pond. The trail in the last half is not well maintained, so expect a real workout, including detours around fallen trees, on the hike upward. The geology and view at the summit is worth the effort.

From the trailhead, the path follows a small stream for the first 0.25 mile, shouldering by several dark and heat-radiating outcrops of banded amphibolite. The trail begins to switchback upslope, and at 0.5 mile splits, with Butte Fork Trail 957 sauntering right and Trail 958—the trail that you are following—sprinting ominously uphill straight ahead.

The trail's steep pitch moderates soon. It passes through a forest of ponderosa pine, sugar pine, madrone, and Douglas fir, where hermit thrush provide fluty music. After a 0.5-mile straight uphill stretch the path switch-backs across more black-and-white-striped amphibolite outcrops to several nice views of the Butte Fork landslide. Red Butte—a red-colored peridotite peak at the head of the trail's destination—peers over the top of the slide.

You may have to clamber over several fallen trees along the next segment of the trail—a more evenly paced path that rises to 4000 feet in elevation amid giant sugar pine and ponderosa pine in a flat area known as Horse Camp before dropping about 100 feet in elevation to meet Butte Fork Creek at mile 1.8—nearly the hike's midpoint. This is a welcome wet place. The cool, shallow water is ideal for cooling off.

Beyond the creek, the trail is less traveled, less well maintained, and rises more steeply. More fallen trees require detours. After another uncivilized mile the trail enters the meadows below Echo Lake. These meadows were once

Red Butte, a monolith composed of peridotite (a rock of the upper mantle) looms above Applegate Lake.

lakes. But in the 10,000 years since the retreat of glaciers, they have filled in to become marshes. Small streams flow through them. These wetlands are important reservoirs of upland water, holding cool water in soils through the long dry summer when a real, open lake might have evaporated. The trail is challenging to follow through these meadows. A few rock cairns mark it in the rare locations where rocks were handy to pile.

To find Echo Lake, a tiny wet refuge below the eastern buttress of Red Butte, continue on the trail as it leads east seemingly away from the valley. After winding about 0.25 mile thorough a thinly forested slope, a spur trail leads to the left. Marked "Echo Lake," this trail leads slightly downward to the lakeshore of the 300- by 200-foot shallow lake. Half-submerged logs line the shore and accessing the water can be difficult. The main trail continues left for another 0.5 mile to the ridge top. From here, elevation 5860 feet, you can see the landscape of northern California and southwest Oregon at your feet, including Mount Shasta, the Trinity Alps, and Grayback Mountain. Red Butte and No-Name Peak rise just to the west of you. The trail connects with the Pacific Crest Trail (PCT) here, though you will have to hunt for it amid the bushes.

You can follow the PCT about 0.25 mile west toward Red Butte. The red rock here is peridotite. Most of it has been somewhat altered to *serpentinite*—a less-dense and often shiny greenish rock that retains the same external red color as peridotite. Much of the original layering and textures of the upper mantle are preserved. In these rocks, as in the peridotites of Vulcan Lake and Chetco Peak (Hikes 10, 11), the layering is an artifact of flow in the upper mantle, where these solid rocks once had the viscosity of silly putty, and flowed, as a highly plastic solid, at the rate of several millimeters per year.

Return as you came.

WILD ROGUE RIVER: GRAVES CREEK TO RUSSIAN CREEK

Hike

8

Hike part of the Rogue's most rugged canyon, lined with the wreckage of Jurassic seafloor.

DISTANCE ■ **11 miles round trip**

ELEVATION ■ **550–645 feet**

DIFFICULTY ■ **Moderate**

TOPOGRAPHIC MAPS ■ **Mount Ruben, Bunker Creek**

GEOLOGIC MAP ■ **5**

PRECAUTIONS ■ **Poison oak is present on some parts of the trail. The trail is hot, with sparse shade in the summer—it's a good winter or late fall hike. Carry water.**

INFORMATION ■ **Medford Bureau of Land Management: (541) 770-2200**

Directions: From Interstate 5 about 5 miles north of Grants Pass, take exit 61, Merlin. Drive 2 miles west to Merlin, then continue 11.2 miles west along the Rogue River on County Road 2400 (Galice-Hellgate Byway). At a junction with Galice Road, continue straight on County Road 2400, which turns into a broad, well-graded gravel road past the BLM's Rand Visitor Center as it continues to follow the river. The Graves Creek Bridge appears 18.6 miles past Merlin. The main trailhead is on the far (north) side of the bridge.

About the Landscape: Much of the lower Rogue River, from Graves Creek to Gold Beach, slices through the Jurassic remnants of volcanic islands and the adjacent sea bottom. Along the road that leads to the Graves Creek Trailhead, as well as along the first 3 miles of the river hike, slanting, shiny, flat rock surfaces catch the eye. They are the remnants of *bedding*—and other surfaces known as cleavage planes—in the slightly metamorphosed and highly polished shales of the Galice Formation. Part of the Klamath Mountain's Western Klamath terrane, these rocks are part of the same subgroup as the Vulcan Lake and Chetco

Peak (Hikes 10, 11). Their deformation into tough, thinly layered slates occurred when the rocks of the Josephine ophiolite (Vulcan Lake and Chetco Peak areas) were thrust over the top of them. Faulting, folding, and erosion during the ensuing 155 million years have since removed the overlying peridotite here, but the evidence of pressure and shearing remains in the Galice's highly compressed rocks.

Trail Guide: The trail along the Rogue strikes out from a large and busy parking area. This is a popular take-out and put-in for rafters. The trail skirts dark and stark-looking outcrops of the Galice Formation's *slate*—this rock will be your companion for most of the 5.5-mile trip to Russian Creek. It bears scratches (officially called *striations*) caused by its fellow rocks sliding over it during deformation.

The Rogue River cuts a rugged canyon through slate and greenstone downstream from Graves Creek.

The trail is carved into outcrops above the river, providing you with great views of rapids and Rainie Falls. Watch the waters for brave water ouzels. Canyon live oak provide shade in many side drainages where you can also find water—but be sure to filter it. You'll find a less welcome companion here as well—poison oak, which is prolific in some sections of this trail.

At 3.5 miles, the trail reaches a junction with a side road. This trail leads away from the river for 0.2 mile, finding Whiskey Creek Cabin—an old gold-miner's camp and now a preserved historic site.

You can continue past Whiskey to Russian Creek, 5.5 miles from the trailhead, for a nice day hike. Russian Creek is also the site of an old mining camp. It also marks the boundary between the Jurassic rocks of the Galice Formation and slightly younger and less orderly rocks of the Dothan Formation—a major boundary marked by the Valen Lake thrust fault. You can't see the fault along the river, but downstream from Russian Creek and its big, luxurious bar, you'll find the Rogue's canyon is increasingly rugged. The Dothan Formation includes sedimentary rocks and slightly metamorphosed volcanic rocks, in a somewhat jumbled order. Russian Bar is a popular

Grooves and slickensides on Jurassic slates attest to severe folding and deformation.

and very suitable place for an overnight camp, should you want to explore farther down the river.

Hike 9 OREGON CAVES NATIONAL MONUMENT

Tour a cave to get inside a tropical reef.

DISTANCE ▪ About 1 mile round trip

ELEVATION ▪ 1200–2000 feet

DIFFICULTY ▪ Moderate

TOPOGRAPHIC MAP ▪ Oregon Caves (Underground passages are not shown.)

GEOLOGIC MAPS ▪ 1, 5, 6

FEES/REGULATIONS ▪ The National Park Service–sponsored 90-minute commercial tour has an admission fee of $7.50 (in 2003).

PRECAUTIONS ▪ A portion of the hike requires climbing 210 vertical feet on skinny, slippery metal staircases. In peak summer season, there may be long waits for spaces on the cave tours. Try to arrive early in the day.

INFORMATION ▪ Oregon Caves National Monument: (541) 592-3400; tour information: (541) 592-3400, ext. 260

Directions: From Cave Junction, drive east on Oregon Highway 46 for 19.3 miles to Oregon Caves National Monument.

About the Landscape: The marble of Oregon Caves National Monument is part of the Applegate terrane, a coral reef that flourished about 220 million years ago in tropical seas somewhere west of its location today. Some of the original, folded bedding can be seen in outcrops along the walk from the park-

50

ing area to the cave entrance, and on the road from Cave Junction. As sediments piled up on the seafloor, the limestones were buried slowly beneath a thick pile of shales. Deep burial, plus the force of collision with North America, recrystallized the limestone and transformed it into a low grade of marble. These rocks are similar in age and origin to the Martin Bridge limestone of the Wallowa Mountains, leading some geologists to hypothesize a connection between the two.

Granitic plutons intruded the marble of Oregon Caves and the Applegate terrane 160 million years ago, about the time these Klamath Mountain rocks collided with North America. They became part of North America more than

Stalactites and stalagmites in Oregon Caves (Photo courtesy Oregon Dept. of Transportation)

120 million years ago. These granitic rocks are evident east of Oregon Caves if you hike the trails that lead from the monument up the ridges to the "Big Tree" and Mount Elijah. Since that time, the rocks that form Oregon Caves have been folded, tilted, and faulted. All this activity created faults and cracks in the rock.

Oregon Caves were formed as these imperfections were gradually enlarged through the dissolving and eroding action mostly of groundwaters, rather than of surface streams. However, significant erosion and deposition of silt and gravels into Oregon Caves was accomplished by rivers or streams that flowed into sink-holes and then deposited their gravels in the passageways below.

Trail Guide: The tour begins at the cave entrance.

At the first lights-out stop, the guide spins the tale of the cave's discovery. Other stops discuss the effects of faults and earthquakes on the cave, the growth of stalactites and stalagmites and other cave-related rock formations, and the biology and life cycles of the cave's bats.

Several stops, mostly early in the walk, examine the fanciful dripstone and flowstone formations that often attract people to caves. About midway through the tour, in a straight and rather narrow passageway, you can see the actual pencil signature of pioneering geologist Thomas Condon, who, with his entire University of Oregon geology class, visited the cave in 1883 shortly after its discovery. The signature has been covered and protected naturally by transparent calcite in the ensuing century, but it is still visible. It seems a fitting way to preserve Condon's autograph.

The observant hiker will find much on the tour that is not mentioned by the Oregon Caves guide, including diorite dikes, small faults, and a variety of shale and sandstone interbedded with the cave's marble. When the lights come on in large open chambers, look for small diorite dikes and interbedded shales that cut through the marble, as well as the relict bedding, now somewhat contorted, that hints at the marble's original sedimentary heritage. Narrow passageways provide excellent close-up views of stalactites and other dripstone formations. The cool dampness of the cave is a good reminder that most limestone caves are created and maintained by water.

After your tour through the cave, try the Big Tree Trail to see what the marbles look like in natural outcroppings. This loop begins near the Visitor's Center and shop, and returns in 1.2 miles after introducing you to the "Big Tree"—a 13-foot-diameter Douglas fir. For a longer and more diverse geological hike, turn onto the Mount Elijah Trail at 0.5 mile into the Big Tree loop. In 1.2 miles this path leads to the nearby summit of Mount Elijah—a high outcropping of granite, part of the Grayback pluton, about 155 million years in age. This intrusive body is responsible for the transformation of the cave's limestones into granular marble (long before the cave was created), and for the narrow igneous dikes dimly visible in the cave's artificial light.

VULCAN LAKE

Cross two major terranes of the Klamath Mountains and see unusual carnivorous plants.

DISTANCE ▪ 8 miles round trip

ELEVATION ▪ 3200–4000 feet

DIFFICULTY ▪ Moderate

TOPOGRAPHIC MAP ▪ Vulcan Peak

GEOLOGIC MAPS ▪ 3, 4

FEES/REGULATIONS ▪ Northwest Forest Pass required for trailhead parking.

PRECAUTIONS ▪ Although the drive to the trailhead is only about 36 miles, most of this is on remote gravel and dirt roads; a full gas tank is a good idea when you start. The mine shaft at the Gardiner Mine is inviting but unsafe; do not enter this mine.

INFORMATION ▪ Chetco Ranger District, Rogue River-Siskiyou National Forest: (541) 412-6000

Directions: The long drive to the trailhead begins from Brookings by taking the North Bank Road up the Chetco River. At Little Redwood Campground, 10 miles from Brookings, the single-lane paved road with turnouts becomes USFS Road 1376. Pavement ends 1 mile past the campground, where the road becomes a first-rate wide gravel highway. The road crosses the Chetco River and at about 16 miles from Brookings arrives at a T intersection where a sign says "Kalmiopsis Wilderness, 24 Miles" and points to the left. Either way will get you there, but you would do better to turn right onto USFS Road 1909 (improved greatly since the weathered sign was posted) and follow it the remaining 20 or so miles to the trailhead. At a road junction 1 mile before the Vulcan Peak trailhead, continue left to Vulcan Lakes/Peak.

About the Landscape: The Vulcan Peak and Chetco Peak areas once formed the base of an island arc. The red rocks of Vulcan Peak are peridotite, a rare rock that comes only from the earth's mantle. Two varieties of peridotite occur around Vulcan Peak. One has a knobby surface and is called harzburgite, named for similar rocks in the Harz Mountains of Germany. The other is a smooth-surfaced, tawny or red-brown rock called dunite, named for its dun color and for Dun Mountain, New Zealand, which is composed of similar rock.

If you examine the smooth-surfaced dunite carefully, you can find small, shiny specks about the size of coarsely ground pepper. This black mineral is chromite. In sufficient concentration it becomes an economically valuable deposit, and the rock is mined as chrome ore. Before the Kalmiopsis was a designated wilderness, a major chrome mine (the Gardiner Mine) operated here. Whereas granite is usually associated with gold, peridotite bears chrome and platinum as well as other rare metals.

North of Vulcan Lake, a major fault forms the boundary between two subterranes: the Smith River subterrane (peridotite) and the Dry Butte subterrane (gabbro). Both are part of the Western Klamath terrane—a fragment of Jurassic mantle, seafloor, and island arc volcanoes. This fault is marked by layered igneous rocks and amphibolite metamorphic rocks.

Between Dry Butte and Johnson Butte, Valen Lake occupies a glacially carved *cirque,* nestled into the northwest side of Dry Butte. The Dry Butte–Johnson Butte Trail crosses the Valen Lake fault in the area above Valen Lake; this is the hike's final destination. The Valen Lake fault is the boundary between two major terranes of the Klamaths: the Western Klamath terrane and the Yolla Bolly terrane.

Trail Guide: This is a loop hike with spurs of varying lengths to visit Vulcan Lake, Little Vulcan Lake, and the view of Valen Lake from the Dry Butte–Johnson Butte Trail. Both Vulcan Lake and Little Vulcan Lake rest in cirques carved during the Pleistocene. Both make fine and very popular camping sites.

Trail 110A, to Vulcan Lakes, leaves the trailhead parking area along an old road. From this broad, level entry road, the trail branches to the right and climbs over the ridge ahead toward Vulcan Lake. This path rises through red-brown peridotite—once part of the earth's mantle. A short spur trail about 0.75 mile into the walk coaxes the hiker to Vulcan Lake, less than 0.5 mile away, and its dark shoreline lined with red-brown peridotite.

From Vulcan Lake, retrace your steps to Trail 110A, which continues on toward Little Vulcan Lake. This trail is sometimes difficult to follow but is well marked by hikers' cairns. To the north and 0.5 mile downslope of Vulcan Lake, another short spur leads to Little Vulcan Lake, which harbors a botanical reserve where pitcher plants prosper.

On the rise just north of Little Vulcan Lake, excellent exposures of glacially polished peridotite can be found. An exploration of the 200-yard-wide area between the lake and the abrupt drop into the valley below reveals beautiful examples of layered peridotite, as well as the rectangular pattern of joints that dictate much of the regional landscape.

From Little Vulcan Lake, retrace the spur path to Trail 112A, which leads north to the Gardiner Mine and on to Dry Butte. Trail 112A is well marked by cairns. The footpath merges with an old road after about 0.5 mile, and the road continues 0.25 mile to the abandoned Gardiner Mine. You can find chunks of shiny black chrome ore in the nearby piles of mine tailings.

From the mine, the road leads another 0.25 mile to the ridge top. The layered rocks and amphibolites of the Madstone Cabin thrust fault appear along this ridge top. They have been squeezed into banded black and white rocks called amphibolite. The Madstone Cabin thrust fault has not been active for perhaps 100 million years, but it is a major fault that divides two terranes. As you proceed along the trail, you cross gradually from the Smith River subterrane (mantle peridotite) to the Dry Butte subterrane (gabbro of the ocean floor).

At the ridge top, turn right (north) along an old logging/mining road (Road 1110). The walk to the end of this road is an easy one; in 1 mile merge with the more traditional 3-mile-long trail that continues toward Dry Butte, Johnson Butte, and Valen Lake. This trail leads into the younger gabbro on the north side of the Madstone Cabin thrust fault. Halfway between Dry Butte and Johnson Butte, just above Valen Lake, the bedrock changes abruptly from tough gabbros to soft shales.

Valen Lake is significant for a second geological reason: the Valen Lake thrust fault that cuts through the slope just above the lake. Like the Madstone Cabin fault that you crossed earlier, the Valen Lake fault has not been active since the Klamaths became part of North America. Long ago this major fault lifted the old igneous rocks of the Western Klamath terrane (which includes the peridotite and gabbro you have just hiked across) up and over the younger sedimentary shales of the Yolla Bolly terrane.

As you near Johnson Butte, you will find the intersection of Trails 1110 and 1112. This means you have crossed the Valen Thrust—the mission of this hike—and can return the same way you came along Trail 1110 and along the old mine access road to Trails 112A and 110A to the Vulcan Peak/Vulcan Lakes trailhead.

Hike
11

CHETCO LAKE AND CHETCO PEAK

Explore the earth's upper mantle.

DISTANCE ▪ **10 miles round trip**
ELEVATION ▪ **3800–3980 feet**
DIFFICULTY ▪ **Moderate**
TOPOGRAPHIC MAPS ▪ **Quail Mountain, Chetco Peak**
GEOLOGIC MAPS ▪ **3, 4**
FEES/REGULATIONS ▪ **Northwest Forest Pass required for trailhead parking; wilderness permit for hike.**
PRECAUTIONS ▪ **Little shade and a rough, rocky trail.**
INFORMATION ▪ **Chetco Ranger District, Rogue River-Siskiyou National Forest: (541) 412-6000**

Directions: From Brookings, drive east on the North Bank Road up the Chetco River. In 10 miles, at Little Redwood Campground, the paved country road morphs into gravel, USFS Road 1376. At 16 miles, the road crosses the Chetco River on a high bridge. Turn right at a T intersection just across the bridge, and follow USFS Road 1909 21 miles to an intersection marked for Chetco Lake Trail, to the right, and Vulcan Lake Trail to the left. Bear right. The trailhead is 0.8 mile from the intersection.

About the Landscape: This hike takes you even deeper into the mantle than the Vulcan Lake hike (Hike 10). Look for well-developed layering in much of the peridotite near Chetco Peak and Lake, as well as clumps of pepper-sized shiny black chromite—the stuff of which chrome bumpers used to be made. These rocks are Jurassic in age and outliers of the Josephine ophiolite—essentially the floor of a Jurassic sea that opened between a number of Klamath "islands" off the North American shore, and then rapidly closed. Some 180 million years ago, ichthyosaurs—large-eyed, dolphinlike marine reptiles—likely swam in the warm sea waves above the present summit of Chetco Peak.

Just to the south of the hike, a major thrust fault, the Madstone Cabin Thrust, is the plane along which the Josephine ophiolite (including the rocks of Chetco Peak and Vulcan Peak) was moved over the top of adjacent sediments (now the Galice Formation). The fault is delineated by dark, banded rocks known as amphibolites that appear just south of the trail. The movement on the thrust fault occurred about 155 million years ago.

Trail Guide: This hike tours the south side of Vulcan Peak, following a two-track, long-abandoned mining road into the ridges east of the peak, then drops into the small Chetco Lake basin. The hike provides breathtaking views of the Kalmiopsis Wilderness to the north, and Red Buttes Wilderness and Mount Shasta to the south and east. There is shade periodically and two springs along the way.

From the roadside trailhead, the broad and very rocky path leads upward along the south side of Vulcan Peak. The trail here is very, very rocky.

The odd-looking, orange-colored rocks are peridotite—a rock that is characteristic of the earth's mantle. Like the rocks at Vulcan Lake, these were uplifted many miles by folding and faulting when North America collided with the Klamath microcontinent about 130 million years ago. Break open the orange rocks and you'll see that the true color of peridotite is a very dark green. Generally, the denser (or "heavier") the rock, the less altered and the truer it is to its original mantle composition.

The trail tours upward through largely open slopes—the magnesium-rich peridotite-laden soils here discourage most plant growth. Jeffery pines and brushy junipers provide sporadic shade. Oregon grape and stunted manzanitas form an understory, and a few azaleas show off spring flowers. At 1.3 miles, a trail leads downslope about 2 miles to the site of a 1944 plane crash and a monument to its U.S. Navy crew. The main trail plods into the wilderness and toward the ridge. Once at the ridge crest, 2 miles into the hike, amazing vistas open to the north, south, and east.

At 2.7 miles, a side trail leads about 0.25 mile downhill to Van Pelt Spring. You can fill water bottles here. Bountiful iris and other wildflowers make the side trip doubly worthwhile. At 3.5 miles, the trail reaches the ridge top and levels out. The surrounding landscape is rugged, with Chetco Lake in view, beckoning and still a mile ahead. At 4.5 miles into the hike, there is a junction. The path to the right drops gently into the lake's small, pine- and juniper-lined basin. There are campsites and shady spots for a well-deserved rest among the trees. The open landscape invites plenty of exploration here. Try a scramble to the top of Chetco Peak, where there are many outstanding examples of layered peridotite. Return as you came.

Hike

WILD ROGUE RIVER: ILLAHE TO MARIAL

Explore the volcanic rocks and conduit system of an exotic island arc, plus spectacular scenery of the wild Rogue River.

DISTANCE ▪ 15 miles one way

ELEVATION ▪ 207–320 feet

DIFFICULTY ▪ Moderate

TOPOGRAPHIC MAPS ▪ Agness, Marial

GEOLOGIC MAPS ▪ 7, 8

FEES/REGULATIONS ▪ Northwest Forest Pass required for trailhead parking.

PRECAUTIONS ▪ The hike begins at Illahe trailhead, where access does not require a 4WD vehicle, and ends at Marial, where trailhead access is on steep, narrow, and sometimes deeply muddy roads. This hike requires either a shuttle vehicle at the Marial trailhead or an overnight at Marial before retracing the route back to the Illahe trailhead. If you plan to stay overnight at Marial Lodge, make reservations well in advance.

INFORMATION ▪ Gold Beach Ranger District, Rogue River-Siskiyou National Forest: (541) 247-3600; Marial Lodge: (541) 474-2057

Directions: To reach the Illahe trailhead from Gold Beach, at the south end of the US Highway 101 Rogue River bridge, turn east onto Jerrys Flat Road and USFS Road 33. Drive 30 miles to Curry County Road 375 (marked "To Illahe/Rogue River Trail"). Illahe is 1 mile past this junction; here, cliffs and roadcuts provide an intimate view of sedimentary rocks. These are the Flournoy Formation—marine sediments about 45 million years old. Continue about 3 miles

Conglomerate outcrop along the Rogue River

to the trailhead—an abrupt right turn into a broad field.

About the Landscape: This hike tours the Snow Camp terrane, a remnant of a Jurassic island arc tossed casually into the Klamath Mountains like an anchovy onto a pizza. To the east, upstream from Marial, the older Rogue River subterrane provides gold deposits. The Snow Camp terrane displays island arc crust. The rocky cliffs along the Rogue expose dikes and gabbro, but the light-colored, silica-rich volcanic rocks upstream are the upper parts of island arc volcanoes. The Snow Camp terrane's rocks are an errant scrap of island arc that once looked as inviting as Bora-Bora, but they have been changed by stress and time to the aged, wrinkled rocks that today confine the Rogue.

Trail Guide: The first mile of the hike skirts the field and provides a good view of river terraces and the lower Rogue River. As the trail joins the river, it threads through second-growth forest. The lodge at Clay Hill, 6 miles into the hike, appears just before the Riddle Formation's brittle, thinly bedded metamorphosed shales.

One mile farther, at Tate Creek, the trail begins its journey through the magma chambers of ancient volcanoes that once erupted far from Oregon's coastline. These rocks are Jurassic, dated at about 160 million years. They represent the Snow Camp terrane. At Solitude Bar, 8 miles into the hike, darker, fine-grained rocks are the metamorphosed remnants of Jurassic basalt flows. Blossom Bar Rapids at 13 miles flows over ancient andesites—rocks 150 million years old that once formed a volcano like Mount Hood.

Some of the most interesting rocks of this old volcanic complex are the sheeted dikes at 14 miles that form Inspiration Point, create Stair Creek Falls, and support the last mile of trail from Inspiration Point to Marial. These sheeted dikes served as the conduits for multiple intrusions, perhaps serving as the path upward for the lavas of tens of eruptions over hundreds or thousands of years. The bands in these rocks are the chilled margins of each upward pulse of lava. The coarse-grained rocks (gabbro) enclosed by these dark, fine-grained volcanic greenstones are remnants of the solid rock these dikes cut through on their way to the surface and eruption.

At Marial, either stay overnight—camping is available, as are accommodations at Marial Lodge—and the next day return the way you came or drive your shuttle vehicle back to the Illahe trailhead.

Hike 13

HUMBUG MOUNTAIN

Climb a coastal landmark built from ancient cobble-rich beaches.

DISTANCE ■ **5.5 miles round trip**

ELEVATION ■ **40–1730 feet**

DIFFICULTY ■ **Moderate**

TOPOGRAPHIC MAP ■ **Port Orford**

GEOLOGIC MAP ■ **1**

FEES/REGULATIONS ■ **Oregon State Parks annual pass or day fee.**

PRECAUTIONS ■ **Outcrops are sparse on Humbug Mountain. For a better view of the Humbug Mountain conglomerate, take the trail from campground to the beach, and explore the stark cliffs along the beach at low tide.**

INFORMATION ■ **Oregon State Parks: (800) 551-6949**

Directions: Take US Highway 101 5.5 miles south of Port Orford to Humbug Mountain State Park. The parking lot is on the west side of the highway just past where the road swings away from the beach.

About the Landscape: In the early Cretaceous, the scattered islands of the Klamath arcs were welded into a single block. This series of multiple collisions and faulting uplifted the terranes and provided new opportunities for erosion. Rivers rushed down steepened slopes of the Klamath microcontinent, carrying coarse sands and cobbles to the sea. These sediments piled up offshore and along ancient Klamath beaches, creating deposits of conglomerate and sandstones. These rocks were strongly folded and uplifted as the Klamath microcontinent collided with North America about 130 million years ago. Today these early Cretaceous rocks, known as the Humbug Mountain Formation, form most of Humbug Mountain. The steep slopes and crashing surf make much of the mountain's best outcrops difficult to access except at very low tide. But a hike to the mountain's summit will provide a few glimpses of these ancient island beaches.

Trail Guide: The 2-mile walk to the top of Humbug Mountain is more a pilgrimage than a hike. One of the most-climbed summits on Oregon's coast, Humbug Mountain is a memorable trek through a vigorous coastal forest, with a certain feeling of accomplishment when you reach the summit. But don't expect great views. Except for a tunneled glimpse of the coast to the south, and a few rare, tree-obscured views to the north in the first mile of hiking, about all you will see from anyplace on this hike are the trees, the forest, and a few other hikers.

The Humbug Mountain Trail begins either from a tunnel in the campground between the A and B Loops or from a roadside parking lot along US Highway 101, 10 miles south of Port Orford in Humbug Mountain State Park. There are virtually no exposures of rock until you near the summit, and then there are only shy glimpses of the Humbug Mountain conglomerate. Still, it's nice to know that you are accomplishing the hike on an uplifted and very ancient (about 140 million years) cobbled island beach.

The trail leads into a forest of big leaf maple, Douglas fir, and myrtle trees, rising at a brisk-but-hikable rate, switch-backing past a stream and a number of old-growth Douglas fir that still show scars from a fire that burned much of this coastal area almost a century ago. The steepest part of the trail is the first 0.5 mile—a climb of 420 feet. The trail crosses the stream twice, first at 0.5 mile (about 550 feet elevation), and later, on a higher switchback, at 0.75 mile. Wildflowers, including Columbia lily, adorn the trailside along with maidenhair ferns.

Just before the 1-mile marker, the trail splits. Here, it also offers a bench for planning the next phase of your ascent. The path to the east tracks through the drier side of Humbug Mountain, and is slightly less steep, reaching the summit in 2 miles. To make your uphill trudge a bit easier, take this path. It leads through tanoak groves of many small-diameter trees. Wild rhododendrons share the forest with an understory of salal and sword ferns. The summit area is a small meadow with several rock outcroppings. Here, you are

Humbug Mountain is composed of massive conglomerates, Cretaceous in age.

finally rewarded with the cobbled visage of the Humbug Mountain conglomerate and a limited view of Cape Sebastian and Gold Beach to the south.

To return to the trailhead, try the steeper, west trail. This path is somewhat
rockier that the up-bound route. It switchbacks downward, exploring a more
dense forest on the wetter, western slopes of Humbug Mountain where Douglas fir and Port Orford cedar—some including large second-growth trees and
a few old-growth giants—far outnumber tanoak. Rock outcrops are noticeable
along the upper 0.5 mile of the trail These are classic examples of the Cretaceous Humbug Mountain conglomerate—full of rounded granitic cobbles and
pebbles of greenstone, all eroded from the older rocks of the Klamaths.

After a quick, steep switch-backed drop, the western trail hits a saddle and
sashays through a brighter forest where salal and vanilla leaf form the understory. The forest here is relatively open for good reason. In 1968, Oregon's
infamous Columbus Day storm uprooted and blew down so many trees here
that this portion of the trail was closed and did not reopen for more than 20
years. The western loop joins the main trail 0.9 mile from the summit. Return
as you came.

Hike 14

CAPE BLANCO

Discover the ancient rocks of Oregon's westernmost, fastest-rising headland.

DISTANCE ■ 2 miles round trip
ELEVATION ■ sea level–200 feet
DIFFICULTY ■ Moderate
TOPOGRAPHIC MAP ■ Cape Blanco
GEOLOGIC MAP ■ 1
FEES/REGULATIONS ■ Oregon State Parks annual pass or day fee.
PRECAUTIONS ■ Time your beach hike to coincide with low tide. Be prepared for wind!
INFORMATION ■ Oregon State Parks: (800) 551-6949

Directions: From Port Orford, drive north on US Highway 101 about 4 miles and turn left (west) on Cape Blanco Road—also marked for Cape Blanco State Park. Follow this road 6 miles to its end at the parking lot just east of the lighthouse. Informal trails lead to the beach on the south side of the cape for the best view of its geology. The Oregon Coast Trail and other short trails also explore the landscape in the state park atop the cape.

About the Landscape: Cape Blanco is an amalgamation of several rock types and sources. The oldest, darkest rocks that form the base of the cape and the sea stacks to the south are part of the Otter Point Formation—a jumbled Jurassic conglomerate. These 180-million-year-old rocks are part of the Gold Beach terrane and comprise some of the younger rocks of the Klamath Mountains. They are also highly faulted, with displacement along strike-slip faults that measure in tens of miles. Rocks of this terrane contain the tattered remnants of the only real dinosaur found in Oregon—a Jurassic hadrosaur. However, this dinosaur is really a Californian—one of the first California residents to immigrate to Oregon—carried north by a fault long after its death.

Above the dark rocks of the Otter Point Formation there is a whole new generation of geology. Gray sediments just above the dark Jurassic rocks are part of the Eocene Tyee group. They are about 45 million years in age. These sands and clays eroded from newly uplifted Klamath Mountains deposited after the Klamath microcontinent became part of North America. Above these somber sediments are the white rocks that gave Cape Blanco its name—fine-grained white sands and silts of the Empire Formation, about 10 to 7 million years in age. Studded with the fossil shells of clams, these rocks represent a time when Oregon's climate began to change gradually from a warm, mild, temperate regime to a cooler and more extreme climate. The lavas that filled the old Rogue River's channel to form Table Rocks near Medford were erupted at about the same time as these rocks were deposited.

Finally, Cape Blanco is an excellent place to witness the rapid rise of the coast since the Pleistocene. To the east of the cape, a series of stair-stepping flat meadows and forested terraces represent uplifted beaches. Cape Blanco is being uplifted by coastal deformation above the subduction zone at a rate of about 1 inch per 30 years—the fastest rate of crustal deformation in Oregon—if not globally.

Trail Guide: From the parking lot, the two trails lead to the beach. The best views of Cape Blanco's geology come from the south side, and it requires a bit of a scramble down the grassy slope and its anastamosing (branching) informal trails to get there. Easier beach access to the south side can be attained by driving into the Cape Blanco Campground and taking a short spur road that leads almost to the beach. From there it's a 200-yard hike to the shore—and a 0.5-mile walk along the beach to see Cape Blanco's diverse geology up close.

Headlands and beached logs at Cape Blanco

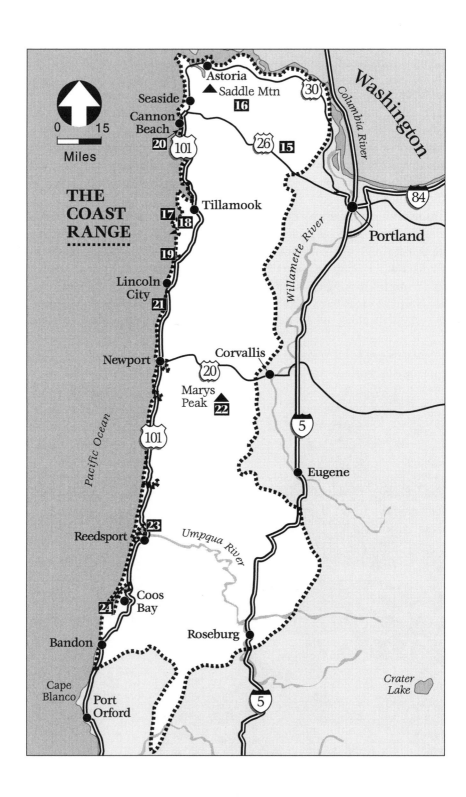

THE
COAST
RANGE
··············

Washington

Astoria
▲ Saddle Mtn
16
Seaside
Cannon
Beach
20 (101)
26 **15**

Columbia River

(30)

(84)

Portland

Willamette River

17
18
Tillamook

19

Lincoln
City
21

Newport
(20)
Corvallis

Marys
Peak ▲
22

(101)

(5)

Eugene

Pacific Ocean

23
Reedsport
Umpqua River

Coos
24 Bay

Roseburg

Bandon

Cape
Blanco
Port
Orford

(5)

Crater
Lake

0   15
Miles

Chapter 2
THE COAST RANGE AND CENTRAL-NORTHERN OREGON COAST

Oregon's Coast Range perches on the northern rim of the Klamath Mountains. Like most everything else in Oregon, the Coast Range is largely an added attraction. Many of its major peaks, including Mount Hebo and Marys Peak (Hike 22), first formed as ocean floor sediments and seamounts from about 60 to 45 million years ago, in the Paleocene and Eocene. At the time, the major land-based volcanoes in Oregon erupted near Mitchell and Prineville, as part of the Clarno Formation. The climate on land was semitropical and similar to modern Veracruz, Mexico. Palms and magnolias were common trees, along with wetland cypress, walnuts, and moonseeds.

Oregon collided with the seamounts about 25–35 million years ago, adding them as its last exotic terrane. Today, this exotic terrane is known as Siletzia, named for the Siletz River volcanics—one of the major groups of seafloor basalts that are now found on Marys Peak and along the Siletz River. The Siletz River volcanics are the foundation of the Coast Range. The rocks include lumpy pillow basalts—tell-tale signs that much of the Siletz River volcanics erupted beneath the sea.

Even after their collision with North America, these rocks remained submerged for millions of years, creating a relatively shallow ocean basin north of the Klamath Mountains that filled with sediment. For the most part, Oregon's coast and Coast Range are composed of somewhat younger sedimentary rocks draped over a skeletal structure of the old, accreted Eocene seamounts' basalt. These younger sedimentary rocks include the gas-bearing Oligocene and Miocene rocks near Mist, fossil-rich mudstones between Banks and Veneta (Hike 15), and the Miocene Astoria Formation, a repository of many fossil mollusks that is exposed along much of Oregon's northern beaches (Hikes 19, 20).

The Oregon modern coastline began to take shape about 25 million years ago as the accreted seamount chain emerged from the sea. By Miocene time, 18 million years ago, the coast's configuration resembled what we see today.

One of the most astounding episodes in Oregon's coastal geology occurred about 16 million years ago. At that time, there were no lofty High Cascades. An ancestral Columbia River ran just south of where Mount Hood towers today.

And down this ancient channel ran basalt lavas. At least twelve large flows of Columbia River basalt streamed more than 300 miles from vents in eastern Oregon and Washington all the way to Oregon's coast. The basalt headlands at Seal Rocks, Otter Rocks, Depoe Bay, Yaquina Head, Cape Lookout, Cape Meares, Cape Falcon, and Tillamook Head are all Columbia River basalt (Hikes 16, 17, 18, 21).

Oregon's coast is still forming. As the Pacific Ocean floor slides beneath the shoreline, beaches on the north and south are rising. Cape Blanco is being lifted several millimeters per year—an astounding rate, geologically speaking. Broad, wave-cut terraces stair-step away from the southern Oregon shore. While the north and south ends are lifting, the central Oregon coast seems to be folding down. Hence the coastal topography around Newport and Florence is subdued and sand dunes are the landscape of tectonic choice.

About every 300 to 400 years, a major earthquake (magnitude 9) shakes the Oregon and Washington coast. The last major earthquake, likely a magnitude 9, occurred on January 26, 1700. The precise date was determined by narrowing the range of dates to between 1658 and 1720 by carbon-14 dates of drowned trees along the Oregon coastline. This research was carried out by Curt Peterson and Brian Atwater. Then four Japanese researchers, led by Kenji Satake, found records of a major *tsunami* (tidal wave) that damaged several Japanese fishing villages on January 27, 1700—but the tsunami was not associated with any known Japanese quake. Allowing for travel of this wave across the Pacific, the timing of the last great subduction zone quake in the Pacific Northwest was calculated to be late in the day on January 26, 1700. In many areas along Oregon's north and south coast, a record of many other periodic great earthquakes is preserved in drowned marshes and in the coarse sands of tsunami deposits.

Eocene pillow basalts and lava tubes in a roadcut near Marys Peak

FOLDS AND FAULTS

Rocks respond to stress in one of two ways: by bending or breaking. Bending, if you are a rock, is also known as folding. Breaking, or snapping suddenly, is also known as faulting.

Most commonly, folds occur as an up-fold, known as an anticline, or a down-fold, known as a syncline. Generally, stress that produces folding is of geologically long duration, and regional in scope.

When rocks are stressed more quickly, they (like us) tend to snap. In rocks (and in people) this is called a fault. The snapping process is called an earthquake. When rocks are squeezed together relatively quickly, the resulting faults are known as reverse faults, or sometimes thrust faults, where one part of the formation slides over extensive areas of the other. The John Day fault is a reverse fault that has uplifted the Strawberry and Aldrich Ranges about 4000 feet above the John Day valley. In the Klamath Mountains, thrust faults that include the Madstone Cabin and Valen faults have shuffled many terranes, including placing part of a Jurassic seafloor and upper mantle over the top of adjacent, older rocks (Hike 10).

Where the earth's crust is being stretched apart like cold taffy, normal faults accommodate the action. The Alvord fault is a normal fault that allowed Steens Mountain to rise a mile above the adjacent Alvord Desert (Hike 67).

Some fault systems allow mostly lateral motion. In Oregon, the faults of the Brothers fault zone and Olympic-Wallowa Lineament (OWL) act as "zippers," letting the Basin and Range of Nevada and southeast Oregon expand.

Faults and folds are most easily recognized where they offset beds of sedimentary rock or other horizontal strata. Because motion along a fault breaks the stone, a fault is often marked by the presence of *breccia*—broken, angular rocks in a clay matrix. The bedrock surface may be polished along a fault by the pressure of one stone on another. This polish, and the grooves on the polished surface, are called slickensides.

Rock folds

BANKS-VERNONIA TRAIL AT TOPHILL

Explore the muddy bottom and sea-life of an ancient bay.

DISTANCE ■ 12 miles one way

ELEVATION ■ 360–1040 feet

DIFFICULTY ■ Moderate

TOPOGRAPHIC MAPS ■ Vernonia, Buxton

GEOLOGIC MAP ■ 1

FEES/REGULATIONS ■ Oregon State Parks annual pass or day fee.

PRECAUTIONS ■ This trail is extremely popular with mountain bikers. Horses and hikers with dogs use it as well.

INFORMATION ■ Oregon State Parks: (800) 551-6949

Directions: From Portland, drive about 30 miles west on US Highway 26. Turn right (north) on Oregon Highway 47, toward Vernonia. Drive 12 miles west on the highway. You'll pass under a very high curved wooden trestle, just before reaching the Tophill trailhead parking lot on the left.

About the Landscape: Much of the Coast Range and northern Oregon coast is mantled in relatively soft mudstones and fine-grained sandstones, reflecting a placid and organic-rich sedimentary basin. In the Oligocene, what is today the Willamette Valley was a large shallow marine bay, perhaps similar to, but much warmer than, today's Puget Sound, with lower and less rugged topography surrounding it. (Think modern Willapa Bay, perhaps.) Clams, anemonelike crinoids, and a variety of mollusks thrived. In the area near Vernonia, rocks that record this marine embayment include the Keasey, Pittsburg Bluff, and Scappose Formations. Most fossils are found in the fragile olive-colored mudstones of the Oligocene Pittsburg Bluff Formation.

Trail Guide: This ambitious hiking trail is part of the first Rails-to-Trails park in Oregon. It follows a narrow-gauge rail line built in the 1920s that carried lumber and logs from a mill in Vernonia and passengers from Keasey to Portland. When the mill closed in 1957, the line was converted to a steam-excursion train use. The last train ran in 1965, and the line was abandoned in 1973. The right-of-way has been an Oregon State Park since 1990.

Before you begin the main hike, you might want to explore the outcrops, including an old quarry, less than a mile along the path in the opposite direction. (Remember that it is illegal to hammer on outcrops or collect fossils—or anything—at an Oregon State Park. Please leave your finds for others to enjoy.) To reach the old quarry, cross Highway 47 and follow the trail across the

Fossils of Oligocene clams and gastropods (snails) are present in sedimentary rocks along the trail near Veneta. (But please just look!)

creek, up a slope, and about 0.25 mile north. Where the vegetation opens into a small clearing, look for an informal trail to the right that leads past a small dam and to a high, light-colored cliff. Signs remind you not to disturb anything.

From the Tophill trailhead the old grade turns west toward Beaver Creek, seemingly taking the wrong direction and heading back toward the Beaver Creek start. But just when you think all is lost, the path swings south, climbing steadily to the summit about 1.6 miles from the trailhead. This first, 2-mile-long segment of the trail, from trailhead to the summit, contains some of the best outcrops. The crumbly, soft mudstone weathers very quickly. Fossils exposed here have only a short time to witness daylight again, for the first time in 20 million years, before they dissolve in the weather.

The trail drops to cross Nowakoski Road. It turns again, continuing its descent through oak- and maple-cluttered woods, reaching Highway 47 in 0.3 mile. The path crosses the road on a railroad bridge and crosses the West Fork of Dairy Creek on a footbridge, passing through the wetland headwaters of a tributary and then climbing very gradually once again.

The next 3 miles are the most remote and rugged on the trail, crossing Brook Creeks in another mile, before rising slightly and dropping into the valley of Williams Creek. These woods offer a variety of big-leaf maple, white oak, and vine maple, with an understory of ferns. Expect to see deer on spring and summer hikes.

Four miles from the Tophill trailhead, the trail finds the valley of Mendenhall Creek, winding downhill until it reaches and crosses Bacona Road and then Mendenhall Creek. Here, the Buxton Trestle towers above the trailhead 5 miles from the beginning.

You may arrange for a pickup here, on Bacona Road, or choose to continue as the trail crosses the road and continues along a hillslope for another 1.5 miles to the Banks-Vernonia State Park headquarters just off Highway 47.

Hike

16 SADDLE MOUNTAIN

This hike tours basalt that flowed more than 250 miles from eastern Washington to the Oregon coast.

DISTANCE ▪ **6.5 miles round trip**

ELEVATION ▪ **1650–3280 feet**

DIFFICULTY ▪ **Strenuous**

TOPOGRAPHIC MAP ▪ Saddle Mountain

GEOLOGIC MAP ▪ 1

FEES/REGULATIONS ▪ Oregon State Parks annual pass or day fee.

PRECAUTIONS ▪ Carry water. Upper portions of the trail are slick paths on narrow ledges. Avoid the summits in wet conditions.

INFORMATION ▪ Oregon State Parks: (800) 551-6949

Directions: From Portland, take US Highway 26 west toward Astoria. About 4.8 miles west of the David Douglas Wayside, turn north onto Saddle Mountain Road. A sign to Saddle Mountain State Park marks this road. The park is 7 miles north at the road's end.

About the Landscape: Saddle Mountain's dark peaks are composed of a single thick flow of Columbia River basalt. It is mind-boggling that the source of this lava flow is a basalt dike in eastern Washington, about 250 miles away. The flow at the top of Saddle Mountain is part of the Frenchman Springs flows in the Wanapum group of Columbia River basalts. These erupted about 14.5 million years ago, as the major Columbia River basalt eruptions began to dwindle.

The peaks of Saddle Mountain are corrugated. The basalt breaks away from the cliffs in little, irregular chunks. Instead of columns, the cliffs bear a latticework of cracks and thin bands, occasionally punctuated by a thick, solid dike shooting its way to the top. The type of cracks, or joints, that developed in many of the later Columbia River basalt flows—like the Frenchman Springs flow here or the Pomona flow that forms Crown Point in the Columbia River Gorge—is decidedly different from the stately columns of the Columbia River Gorge.

Saddle Mountain, like many highlands and headlands on Oregon's north coast, is composed of a Columbia River basalt flow that originated almost 300 miles to the east.

The Frenchman Springs flow, nearing the Miocene coast as it ran through a river valley, cooled rapidly and explosively as it encountered the sea, which, at the time, must have been here. The result was breccia—broken, fragmented basalt. The vertical dikes that cut through Saddle Mountain's basalt cliffs are not standard intrusive dikes that carried lava from a deep magma chamber to the surface. Instead, they were generated by still-fluid portions of the same basalt flow forcing its way down through the broken, brecciated basalt. The process was rather like squeezing caulking into cracks or pressure-sealing concrete. Other Columbia River basalt flows that reached the coast also produced such invasive dikes. They include the semicircular basalt dikes exposed at low tide north of Otter Rocks and the basalts near Depoe Bay.

The steadily rising trail to the summit of Saddle Mountain remains in second-growth forest for most of its length. Riotous vegetation covers the sedimentary rocks—primarily marine sandstones and siltstones, about 20 to 15 million years old—at the base of Saddle Mountain.

Trail Guide: The trail begins at the east side of the parking area. About 1 mile along the steadily climbing trail, trees thin and the bare double basaltic peaks of Saddle Mountain loom ahead. The remaining 1.3 miles is a winding climb to the north and highest summit.

Along this part of the trail, you get an up-close view of these unusual rocks. Instead of the stately black columnar basalt familiar to us in the Columbia River Gorge, these rocks are reddish and fragmented. Their broken (or, geologically, brecciated) appearance is the result of quick cooling and interactions with water as they chilled. There was no time to form columns here. This was a place of steamy and violent explosions as the basalt met seawater and chilled.

A 0.25-mile portion of the trail threads a narrow ridge with only a cable as a handhold.

At the summit, the broken nature of Saddle Mountain's venturesome Columbia River basalt is even more evident. Fresh black basalt is rare; most rock is glued-together basaltic rubble. The view of the sea and the Coast Range is a great reward for the climb. Return as you came.

Hike
17

CAPE LOOKOUT: THE NORTH TRAIL

Hike through old-growth forest to a beach of broken basalt.

DISTANCE ▪ **5.2 miles round trip**
ELEVATION ▪ **sea level–890 feet**
DIFFICULTY ▪ **Moderate**
TOPOGRAPHIC MAP ▪ **Sand Lake**
GEOLOGIC MAP ▪ **1**
FEES/REGULATIONS ▪ **Oregon State Parks annual pass or day fee.**
PRECAUTIONS ▪ **Try to time your hike along the beach at the lower end of the trail for low tide.**
INFORMATION ▪ **Oregon State Parks: (800) 551-6949**

Directions: From Tillamook, drive south 11 miles on US Highway 101. Turn right (west) on County Road 871. Continue 4.2 miles and turn right (north) on USFS Road 11, marked for Cape Lookout. The large parking area is 3 miles on your left (west) at the crest of a long hill.

About the Landscape: Cape Lookout is one of many Oregon coastal headlands that, like Saddle Mountain, are composed of errant Columbia River basalt. Its long protrusion into the Pacific suggests that here the basalt flows may have followed a canyon or valley that extended west.

Trail Guide: From the parking area, the trail down the north side of Cape Lookout leads to the beach and Cape Lookout State Park in 2.6 miles. Along the way there are views of Netarts Spit to the north, as well as a nice stream.

The path leaves the parking area on the northwest side. This trailhead is separate from the trailhead for the main path to the end of Cape Lookout. It ambles through a forest sprinkled with mammoth Sitka spruce, reaching Cape Creek in 0.9 mile. From the creek, the path climbs across a long and ingenious

The North Trail on Cape Lookout leads to the state park campground, and Netarts Spit.

set of steps, then flattens and crosses a ridge where it offers a tantalizing view of the ocean.

From this spot, 1.5 miles into the hike, the trail begins dropping. It edges briefly along the top of cliffs—the drop-offs are screened and cushioned by salal and shore pine. Occasional gaps in the salal fringe permit glimpses of the beach below.

At 2.2 miles, the trail begins an earnest, switch-backing descent to the campground area. Before it enters the Cape Lookout Campground, the path crosses an inviting creek. Once on the beach, you may follow the beach south for close-up views of the fragmented, brecciated Columbia River basalt flow that comprises most of Cape Lookout. There are also places where the sands that this flow invaded and displaced are surrounded and baked by basalt. This beach is a great place to poke around and explore the varied textures created by basalt-sediment interactions. Return as you came.

Hike 18

CAPE LOOKOUT: THE MAIN TRAIL

Follow a basalt flow's seaward path.

DISTANCE ■ 5 miles round trip

ELEVATION ■ 440–890 feet

DIFFICULTY ■ Moderate

TOPOGRAPHIC MAP ■ Sand Lake

GEOLOGIC MAP ■ 1

FEES/REGULATIONS ■ Oregon State Parks annual pass or day fee.

PRECAUTIONS ■ Portions of the trail lead along the edges of abrupt 700-foot cliffs with little protection from falling.

INFORMATION ■ Oregon State Parks: (800) 551-6949

Directions: From Tillamook, drive south 11 miles on US Highway 101. Turn right (west) on County Road 871. Continue 4.2 miles and turn right (north) on USFS Road 11, marked for Cape Lookout. The large parking area is 3 miles on your left (west) at the crest of a long hill.

About the Landscape: Cape Lookout is, simply, the elongate cast of a coastal valley and channel system that was filled by a Columbia River basalt flow about 15.5 million years ago. Like the basalt flows that form Saddle Mountain and Onion Peak, this flow followed stream valleys through what was then a very low Coast Range, a landscape that likely was a grassy savannah that included oaks, maples, gingkoes, and a few pine and spruce, with hemlocks on low hilltops.

Trail Guide: The trail to the west end of Cape Lookout leaves from

The Cape Lookout Trail follows the top of a 15.5-million-year old Columbia River basalt lava flow.

the west side of the parking lot. In about 25 yards, another trail darts sharply to the left, downhill. This path leads to the beach on the south side of the cape. It is worth hiking if you have extra energy to burn, as it provides a nice view of the well-defined columnar jointing on the south side of this long, thick basalt flow—a feature that is very rare among the coastal Columbia River basalts.

The principal path to the end of Cape Lookout is hard to stray from. It leads through a spruce-rich forest, offering occasional heart-stopping views of the coast to the south at 0.6 mile into the hike, and a view to the north at 1.3 miles into the walk, as well as a history lesson—the site of a World War II bomber's crash—remembered with a brass plaque on a cliff at about shoulder height at 0.7 mile into the hike.

There is actually more topography to navigate than might seem possible. The trail dips into a small valley at 1.3 miles and again at about 1.8 miles. The surf seems very, very far below as the path edges along cliffs near the trail's end at 2.5 miles.

The views from the north side reveal Netarts Spit extending northward. To the south, Cape Kiwanda, a compilation of Astoria Formation sandstone, appears on the coastline. Return as you came.

Hike 19 CAPE KIWANDA

Sculpted sandstones reveal a 15-million-year-old beach.

DISTANCE ▪ 0.5 mile round trip
ELEVATION ▪ Flat, sea level
DIFFICULTY ▪ Very, very easy
TOPOGRAPHIC MAP ▪ Sand Lake
GEOLOGIC MAP ▪ 1
PRECAUTIONS ▪ Visit at low tide to maximize geologic value.
INFORMATION ▪ Oregon State Park: (800) 551-6949

Directions: From Lincoln City, drive north on US Highway 101 approximately 12 miles. Turn left (west) on Brooten Road, marked for Pacific City. Follow this road 1.5 miles and turn left (west) onto Cape Drive. Follow Cape Drive approximately 0.5 mile to Cape Kiwanda State Park.

About the Landscape: Cape Kiwanda is carved from the soft, yellow sandstones of the Miocene Astoria Formation. They represent offshore sands and submarine fans, and the whole complex was built before the arrival of the Miocene Columbia River basalts. At the time these sediments were deposited on Oregon's new western shoreline, sea levels—and the position of the coast—were nearly the same as today's. (However, sea levels would drop considerably, compared to present levels, in the late Pliocene and would fluctuate greatly during the Pleistocene, or Ice Age.) Cape Kiwanda is one of the few places where the coastal invasion of the Columbia River basalts is minimal. You are left with nice views of the bedding and a few fossil clams and gastropods (marine snails) to find in the sea-washed outcrops. A hike up the beach provides nice views of sea cliffs.

Miocene sedimentary rocks at Cape Kiwanda are a great place to look for ancient—or modern—sea life.

Trail Guide: There is no real trail at Cape Kiwanda, but there is quite a lot to see. Here, the Miocene sandstones of the Astoria Formation are beautifully exposed. These cliffs are not especially full of fossils, but an occasional gastropod or clam appears if the outcrops are properly scrutinized.

From the parking lot, hike along the beach to the cape, about 0.2 mile away. At low tide, you can easily access an informal trail that crosses the neck of Cape Kiwanda. Here the sandstones are easy to examine. Look for bedding and layers of muds among the sands.

The Astoria Formation has yielded many invertebrate fossils—but sometimes larger vertebrates, including sea lions, sharks, turtles, and an occasional whale have been found, though none of these has yet been recovered from Cape Kiwanda.

The path also leads toward a large parabolic dune. This is one of the few places along the northern Oregon coast that supports this type of isolated dune. The sand is transported from beaches to the north near Sand Lake.

Hike 20

HUG POINT

Explore sea caves and a waterfall where basalts met the beach.

DISTANCE ■ **2 miles round trip**

ELEVATION ■ **Flat, sea level**

DIFFICULTY ■ **Easy**

TOPOGRAPHIC MAP ■ **Arch Cape**

GEOLOGIC MAP ■ **1**

PRECAUTIONS ■ **Visit at low tide to access old roadway and caves. Beware of becoming stranded as the tide rises.**

INFORMATION ■ **Oregon State Parks: (800) 551-6949**

Directions: From Cannon Beach, drive 3.5 miles south on US Highway 101. Turn right into a large parking area for Hug Point State Park. Steps lead down to the beach at the western end of the parking lot.

About the Landscape: Here, just south of Cannon Beach and its Columbia River basalts, a long expanse of elegantly exposed rocks reveal the process of basalt "invasion." The coastal cliffs expose narrow basalt dikes that, unlike most dikes, do not thicken downward. Instead, they fade out, thicker at the top, and disappear into the soft yellow sedimentary rocks (Astoria Formation) below. The more solid exposures of basalt that occur at the south end of the Hug Point beach are highly fractured, like the basalts of Cape Lookout and Saddle Mountain and other examples of the coastal Columbia River basalts.

Trail Guide: The beach is really your trail here, and the delightful thing about Hug Point is its unusual and varied beach-cliff landscapes.

If you turn south from the stairway onto the sands, you'll find sea stacks and sea cliffs hewn from basalts by wave action. A closer look reveals fascinating textures, including broken or brecciated basalts (no stately columns here) and places where the basalts mixed with, flowed around, and even incorporated sediments. There are layers of umber-red basalts—the result of oxidation as seawater boiled at the touch of hot basalt lava. If you round the small point at the south end of the beach, you'll be back in the territory of sedimentary rocks again.

If you turn north from the stairway, you'll begin a 0.5-mile stroll past a sandstone cliff with a sea cave and basalt dikes knifing down into the sandstone. You can continue north along the beach at low tide. Here you'll find a waterfall where Fall Creek plunges over a small cliff onto the beach, and there are more small caves and sediment contorted by the invasive basalts. A bit farther north,

Stringers and dikes of invasive basalt converge at a sea cave near Hug Point.

there is a wagon road that has been carved into the Astoria sandstone. It leads around the point, revealing tide pools at low tide. Return as you came.

Hike 21 — DEVILS PUNCHBOWL AND OTTER CREST

Find invasive breccias and "ring dikes" on a cloistered beach.

DISTANCE ■ 1 mile round trip

ELEVATION ■ Sea level–400 feet

DIFFICULTY ■ Moderate to strenuous (stairway)

TOPOGRAPHIC MAPS ■ Newport, North and Depot Bay

GEOLOGIC MAP ■ 1

PRECAUTIONS ■ Plan your visit to coincide with low tide to optimize your access to geology and your view of "ring dikes." This hike involves descending and climbing wooden stairs that can be slippery when wet and provide a workout on your return from the beach. Requires Oregon State Parks day use pass or annual pass.

INFORMATION ■ Oregon State Parks: (800) 551-6949

Directions: From Newport, drive north on U.S. Highway 101 approximately 7 miles to Otter Crest Loop Road (signed for Devils Punchbowl). Continue about 0.25 mile on Otter Crest Loop, then turn left (west) on First Avenue and drive 0.5 mile to the parking area. En route, you may wish to explore the beach at Beverly Beach State Park, where Miocene sandstones of the Astoria

Formation occasionally reveal fossils along the beach. To view the arcuate "ring dikes" of Otter Crest, continue on Otter Crest Loop 1.3 miles past First Avenue to a viewpoint atop the seacliffs.

About the Landscape: Most geologists now accept the invasive nature of the Columbia River basalt "intrusions" found along Oregon's coast. These lavas were driven down into soft sediments by their weight, rather than following the normal igneous process of intruding upward from magma chambers deep below. But when the coastal basalts were first mapped and described, they were assumed to have intruded and erupted in place more normally—from vents on the coast. The curving exposures of basalt "dikes" exposed at Otter Crest, and easily visible at low tide from the Otter Crest overlook, were often cited as classical examples of "ring dikes"—a pattern of intrusion that develops when intrusion is especially sudden and forceful. (In fact, as of this writing, the interpretive sign at the overlook still describes the invasive basalt as "ring dikes".) Only after the similarity of these rocks' age and composition to rocks in the Columbia River Gorge and eastern Oregon aroused suspicions, and new technology (gravity and magnetic surveys) proved the intrusions to be rootless, with no deep source, were geologists able to accept the curving "ring dikes" at Otter Crest as imposters. The hot heavy lavas worked their way down into soft sands and sandstones, exploiting subtle joints and folds and propagating fractures downward by their weight.

Trail Guide: From the parking area at Devils Punchbowl Natural Area, a path around the cliff–top offers a view of the basalts in Otter Crest's small bay, and also a view into sea caves and arches excavated into the soft Miocene sandstones of the Astoria Formation. Heat from the nearby basalts may have hardened some sandstone here to help it withstand the constant battering of waves. To reach the beach, look for a stairway and sign that says "Beach Trail" near the restrooms, about 50 yards east of the parking area.

The staircase deposits you at the base of soft sandstone sea cliffs. This is the Miocene Astoria Formation—the sands that basalt lavas invaded. At the time, about 15.5 million years ago, this spot was just offshore—a position close to today's environment. These sands have been uplifted several hundred feet from their original position. Look for dark "concretions" in the sandstone—small, hard, rounded clay and sometimes clay—pyrite nodules that develop around fossils or larger pebbles in the fine sands.

At low tide, you can scramble around the point here and examine small exposures of broken and unstable basalt on the north side and on the beach just below the Inn at Otter Crest (but take care that rising tides don't trap you!). The sound and fury of incoming waves is only a dim reminder of the steamy violence that prevailed here, 15.5 million years ago when hot lava invaded the cold water and damp sediments of the Pacific.

MARYS PEAK

An unusual intrusive formation caps Marys Peak and provides a grand view of the Coast Range and the Cascades.

DISTANCE ■ 9.6 miles round trip

ELEVATION ■ 2500–4097 feet

DIFFICULTY ■ Strenuous

TOPOGRAPHIC MAPS ■ Marys Peak, Alsea

GEOLOGIC MAP ■ 9

FEES/REGULATIONS ■ Northwest Forest Pass required for trailhead parking.

PRECAUTIONS ■ Poison oak is present in some places. Carry water.

INFORMATION ■ Siuslaw National Forest, Supervisor's Office, Corvallis: (541) 750-7000

Directions: To reach the trailhead, from Corvallis take US Highway 20 west for about 5 miles and turn south on Oregon Highway 34 (Alsea Highway). Drive 9 miles west on Highway 34 to USFS Road 30 (Marys Peak Road) and turn right. Follow the winding road upward for 3.5 miles until you reach a turnout on the left, which provides an overview to the west. A gated gravel road here leads 0.25 mile west to an exquisite exposure of *pillow lava* in an abandoned quarry. From this stop, continue on Marys Peak Road another 2 miles to milepost 5.5. Turn right into the parking area for the East Ridge trailhead (Trail 1324).

About the Landscape: For a quick trip to the seafloor, nothing beats the 56-million-year-old Siletz River volcanics on Marys Peak. These are perhaps the best example of pillowed basalt anywhere. Their globby forms and glassy exterior indicate that the molten lava chilled and solidified very quickly. Although they are invisible along the uphill-bound trail, these rocks are beautifully exposed in a quarry near Marys Peak Road (USFS Road 30).

A resistant, 700-foot-thick gabbro *sill* (a flat-topped and flat-bottomed intrusion) caps Marys Peak. The rock is dark gray-green and has the same overall composition as basalt. It intruded into the sedimentary rocks (Flournoy Formation) that overlie the 56-million-year-old pillow lavas, forcing its way as a molten mass in between sedimentary layers. The Marys Peak sill is about 30 million years in age. It has many relatives scattered through the Coast Range, including rocks at the summits of Roman Nose, Fanno Peak, and Elk Mountain.

Trail Guide: This loop hike rises 1000 feet in 3 miles, passing through an area of huge noble fir before reaching the summit of Marys Peak at 4097 feet. The downward route reveals the Marys Peak sill and sandstones of the Flournoy Formation. Pillow lavas are exposed in a quarry off Marys Peak Road (USFS

Road 30), and in a narrow roadcut 3.5 miles from Highway 34.

The East Ridge Trail (1324) leads straight up a gentle grade through mixed fir and then noble fir forest. About 1 mile along the walk, the East Ridge Trail meets Trail 1313. Turn left, upslope, and continue 1 mile on Trail 1324. After another switchbacking hike through forest, the trail meets the Summit Loop Trail (Trail 1350) in another mile. Take Trail 1350 upward to cross Marys Peak Road in 0.5 mile, reaching the summit in about another 0.5 mile. From the summit, you have an excellent view of the Coast Range.

Pillow lavas, the remnants of a 50-60 million-year-old chain of seamounts, now reside on Mary's Peak and much of the coast range south to Roseburg.

Several paths lead downward through Marys Peak meadow, which receives about 100 inches of rainfall annually and supports an ecological collage of plants adapted to extreme climates. The best route is Meadow Edge Trail (Trail 1325), which can be found by retracing the Summit Loop Trail (Trail 1350) back to just before its junction with Marys Peak Road.

Follow the Meadow Edge Trail 1.6 miles downhill to Marys Peak Campground. Then follow Marys Peak Road 3 miles back to the East Ridge trailhead (be wary of traffic).

Along the way (1.5 miles from the campground), you will find an excellent exposure of the Marys Peak gabbro sill at Parker Falls. The fine-grained texture of this rock indicates that it was fairly near the surface (perhaps less than 1000 feet beneath the seafloor) when it intruded the seafloor sediments and cooled. Its composition is similar to the pillow lavas exposed in the quarry, but it is a much younger formation (about 30 million years old as opposed to 56 million years).

At 2.5 miles beyond the campground, roadcuts reveal the alternating sandstones and shales of the Flournoy Formation. These Eocene rocks, which lie just above the pillow lavas, are turbidites. Such alternating sandstone and shale sequences are created when a storm or earthquake stirs up near-shore sands into a dense cloud of sediment. That cloud of sediment moves rapidly downslope, spreading coarse sands into deeper water, where the sand is deposited in a layer. The finer-grained sediment transported with it settles to the seafloor more gradually and becomes the shale atop the sandstone layers. Close scrutiny of these beds reveals sedimentary structures such as cross-bedding and the tracks of pebbles or sticks dragged along by the fast-moving sand. The remaining 0.5-mile hike back to the trailhead follows an easy, curving downhill stretch of road.

Hike 23

TAHKENITCH DUNES

This short walk through a dune field to the ocean showcases dune forms, a lake, and, usually, plenty of solitude.

DISTANCE ■ 4-mile loop

ELEVATION ■ sea level–100 feet

DIFFICULTY ■ Easy

TOPOGRAPHIC MAP ■ Tahkenitch Creek

GEOLOGIC MAP ■ 1

PRECAUTIONS ■ Protect against wind-blown sand. Avoid disturbing snowy plover habitat; keep dogs on leash.

INFORMATION ■ Oregon Dunes National Recreation Area: (541) 271-3611

Directions: From Reedsport, drive 5 miles north on US Highway 101 to the Tahkenitch Lake State Park Campground and Picnic Area. The trailhead is at the south end of this area.

About the Landscape: Most dunal forms at Oregon Dunes National Recreation Area are longitudinal dunes. These long, narrow dunes form in areas where the wind blows from different directions seasonally. Here, wind blows generally from south to north in the winter, and from north to south in the summer. The classic, crescent-shaped barchan dunes that we find in many deserts are formed by wind from a steady or constant direction, and are absent from this part of Oregon Dunes.

Trail Guide: From the trailhead, walk about 0.25 mile south on a short access trail, then turn right onto Tahkenitch Dune Trail. A 0.5-mile walk through a forest built on sand dunes brings you to the brink of dunes. This is a deflation basin, where sand is temporarily dropped, only to be picked up by the wind and moved on. Higher dunes border the area to the south and north. It is a great place to observe dune forms and the process of dune construction and destruction.

A brisk 1-mile walk across the dunes brings you to a line of pine trees and a narrow pine forest. Large wooden posts mark the trail across these dunes. At the west edge of the trees, turn south and hike about 1.5 miles to Threemile Lake, a freshwater lake perched precariously on the sand dunes. The lake's fresh water is protected from invasion of salt water by an apron of several small freshwater creeks.

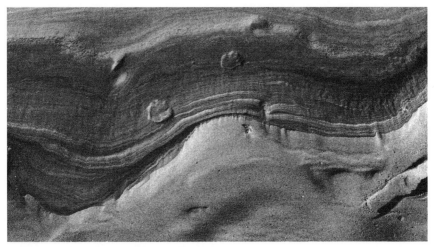

Patterns in the sand at Tahkenitch Dunes

The trail loops around the lake, crossing through snowy plover habitat and returning to the junction with the 0.25-mile access trail back to the trailhead.

COAST TRAIL: SHORE ACRES AND SUNSET BAY TO CAPE ARAGO

At low tide, rhythmically bedded sandstones and shales are exposed along the beach at Cape Arago; spectacular concretions make Shore Acres beach outcrops a macabre landscape.

DISTANCE ■ 4.3 miles one way

ELEVATION ■ sea level–120 feet

DIFFICULTY ■ Easy

TOPOGRAPHIC MAPS ■ Cape Arago, Charleston

GEOLOGIC MAP ■ 10

PRECAUTIONS ■ Be watchful for sneaker waves—high waves that appear without warning. This hike should be done at low tide. It can be done year-round. Provide a shuttle vehicle at Cape Arago State Park unless you want to double the length of the hike by retracing your route.

INFORMATION ■ Oregon State Parks: (800) 551-6949

Directions: Reach Sunset Bay State Park in about 12 miles from Coos Bay by driving west on the Empire–Coos Bay Highway to Empire, then south through

Charleston on the Cape Arago Highway. Or, from US Highway 101 5 miles north of Bandon, bear west on Seven Devils Road—a shortcut to Charleston—and turn south to Sunset Bay State Park. To reach Shore Acres, the botanical garden and outcrops on the shore, look for the Shore Acres entrance 0.5 mile south of Sunset Bay on Cape Arago Road.

About the Landscape: Sedimentary rocks and wave-cut terraces decorate the coastline at Shore Acres State Park, just south of Sunset Bay State Park. The yellow sandstones of Cape Arago and Sunset Bay are part of the Coaledo Formation and are Eocene in age, about 45 million years old. They were deposited in relatively shallow water as tidal or lagoonal sands. The name Coaledo Formation stems from the presence of coal in some layers of the formation.

Trail Guide: The Coast Trail weaves from cliff to beach to outcrop to road, providing a 4-mile walk between Sunset Bay and Cape Arago State Parks, with occasional descents to the beach. The layered sedimentary rocks of Sunset Bay Beach and Cape Arago beautifully display the patterns of Eocene ocean currents in swirling sand. Low tide permits close-up examination of the rocks and is the best time to explore here. Sea lions at Simpson Reef provide noisy accompaniment to the waves' roar.

The best views of the patterned sedimentary structures are found in the rocks at Shore Acres State Park. To find them, avoid the botanical gardens and follow paths toward the beach. The eroded patterns of the hard, iron-enriched concretions are spectacular here.

Well-exposed sandstone layers emerge from the sand south of the bay and also on its north side. A walk at low tide reveals world-class cross-bedding patterns in the stone.

After exploring the area around Sunset Bay, take the Coast Trail south from the south end of Sunset Bay Beach. South of Sunset Bay, rounded forms known as "concretions" appear in the rocks. These concretions are concentrations of clay and calcite cement that collect around a fossil or some other impurity in the rock. This process occurs after the sediment is deposited, and usually before it becomes solid stone. Several small faults cut through the rocks here and are easy to spot in the barren outcrops.

In 1 mile, the trail splits; take the Coast Trail to the right, though both trails lead to Shore Acres State Park in another 1 mile. From Shore Acres, continue on the Coast Trail to Simpson Beach and on to Simpson Reef Viewpoint in another 1.25 miles. This is the end of the Coast Trail. From here, walk about 0.5 mile south along the Cape Arago Highway to Cape Arago State Park.

An approach to the beach at Cape Arago State Park provides excellent close-up views of patterned sandstones. The Cape Arago South Cove Trail begins at the picnic area just past the south end of the Cape Arago parking lot, dropping over the edge of the cliff and winding abruptly downslope to the beach below

Concretions and contorted Eocene sandstones at Shore Acres reveal macabre patterns.

in 0.25 mile. The outcrops and tide pools are north and west of the beach. When you are finished exploring, walk back up the 0.25-mile South Cove Trail to the trailhead and your shuttle vehicle.

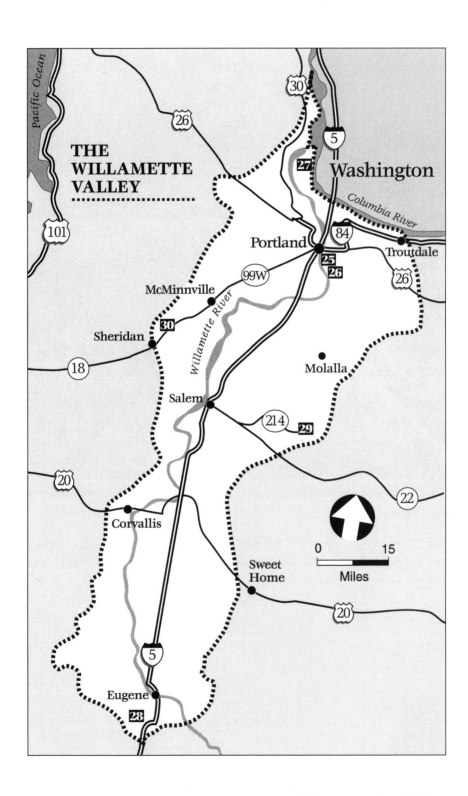

THE WILLAMETTE VALLEY

Pacific Ocean

Washington

Columbia River

Willamette River

Portland

Troutdale

McMinnville

Sheridan

Salem

Molalla

Corvallis

Sweet Home

Eugene

26

30

5

27

84

101

99W

30

18

20

214

22

20

5

28

25

26

26

29

0   15
Miles

Chapter 3
THE WILLAMETTE VALLEY

The Willamette Valley began its life about 45 million years ago as seafloor off the early Cascades. Scotts Mills, Silver Falls, and Sweet Home would have been seaports. Today, the rocks associated with the old seafloor and coastline are deeply buried beneath Ice Age and younger sediments in the valley bottom. Faults and earthquakes are sculpting the valley's modern topography.

Some of the oldest exposed rocks native to the Willamette Valley are the isolated buttes—Skinner Butte, Spencers Butte, the Coburg Hills, and Knox Butte—found in its southern half. Most geologists believe that these intrusions, lava flows, and small volcanoes, which average 30 million years in age, originated in the Western Cascades (Hike 28). In the Oligocene the Willamette Valley was covered by the sea, but by the early Miocene, about 25 million years ago, the rocks of the Coast Range had "docked" with the continent and were uplifted, creating the mountains and slowly elevating the valley above the waves. Lavas from the nearby Western Cascades flowed over the new land, which was punctuated by a few small volcanoes (Hike 28). By 16 million years ago, the valley floor was dry ground.

Columbia River basalt flows followed the river's ancestral channel into the Willamette Valley and west to the coast, reaching the sea at what is now

The small vents and cinder cones of the Boring volcanic field pepper the landscape near Portland.

Newport. Some spread out in the Willamette lowland and reached the coast near Cannon Beach and Astoria. Today, Columbia River basalts form the cliffs at Oregon City, Portland's Forest Park and West Hills, as well as the South Salem Hills, Amity Hills, and Eola Hills, and elsewhere in the northern Willamette Valley. They also line the western Cascade foothills along the Clackamas River and at Silver Falls State Park (Hike 29).

The Portland area has its share of volcanic buttes, including Mount Tabor, Rocky Butte, and Mount Sylvan. These and dozens more local buttes are part of the Boring volcanic field, named for the town of Boring. They first developed about 2 million years ago as faulting pulled the Portland Basin apart, and may have opened the Willamette Valley to the south as well. However, many of these small volcanic vents have proven to be quite young. Rocky Butte, on the east side of Portland, erupted a mere 98,000 years ago. To the north, near Vancouver, Washington, Battle Ground Lake State Park protects a volcanic vent only about 105,000 years old. Some geologists regard the Boring volcanic field as still potentially active (Hikes 25, 26).

In the Pleistocene, the Willamette Valley periodically became a huge lake. Water from an ice-dammed lake in Montana was unleashed repeatedly and swept down the ancient Columbia River channel. These so-called Missoula floods carried glacial ice and created a dam across the Columbia near what is now the town of St. Helens. Silt-laden water flooded the Willamette Valley. The water was more than 300 feet deep where Portland is today. Even today, small clusters of ice-rafted granite boulders appear in fields and backyards throughout the valley. An Oregon state park—Erratic Rock Natural Site—is dedicated to a huge boulder transported from Montana on such a raft of ice (Hike 30).

Two major fault zones are pulling the Portland Basin apart: the Portland Hills fault on the west defines Portland's West Hills, while multiple faults cut through the Gresham area. Earthquakes along these faults, and from the subduction zone beneath, have rattled Portland frequently. These quakes include magnitude 4.5 in 1953, 4.5 in 1961, and 5.6 in 1963. Geologists estimate that a magnitude 6 quake strikes the Portland area about once every 100 to 150 years, and a quake greater than 6.5 strikes every 800 to 900 years.

Another fault system, the Mount Angel fault, runs across the Willamette Valley south of Salem. In 1990 a cluster of barely noticed earthquakes (magnitude 1 and 2) tickled Woodburn. In 1992 the Scotts Mills earthquake, magnitude 5.6, on these faults cracked the state capitol dome, damaged ninety buildings and a major bridge, and caused more than $28 million in property damage. This Mount Angel fault system is part of a series of faults that are opening, extending, and rotating the Willamette Valley. Similar fault systems may await detection south of Salem.

ICE AGE FLOODS ON THE COLUMBIA

At the close of the Ice Age, some of the most catastrophic floods ever documented on earth swept down the Columbia River and inundated the Portland Basin to a depth of 350 feet. Known as the Missoula floods, they occurred between 13,500–11,000 years ago. There were at least forty separate major floods. Some geologists count 120 or more. The largest completely filled the Columbia

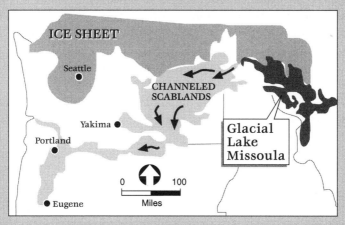

River Gorge, overtopping Crown Point and flooding the Willamette Valley as far as Eugene.

In the waning Pleistocene, a lobe of continental ice sheet in northern Idaho periodically formed an ice dam across the Clark Fork River where the stream now enters Lake Pend Oreille. Water backed up behind the dam, flooding the Missoula valley to a depth of up to 950 feet. Waves etched parallel lakeshore benches around the basin like giant bathtub rings.

Periodically, the ice dam broke and water flooded across the Washington palouse, ripping away soil and leaving a macabre, barren landscape behind—the channeled scablands. Glacial ice bearing rocks from Montana and Canada were torn into icebergs and rafted their rocky passengers down the Columbia. Some of these icebergs came to rest on hilltop islands in the Willamette Valley. The Willamette Meteorite may have been rafted into place by ice. And west of McMinnville, a 40-ton boulder of Canadian *argillite*, a fine-grained sedimentary rock, now holds a commanding view of the Willamette Valley at Erratic Rock State Natural Site (Hike 30).

MOUNT TABOR

A walk up a small, urban volcano provides a glimpse into its past and a view of the Portland Basin and its fault zones.

DISTANCE ■ About 1.8 miles round trip
ELEVATION ■ 200–650 feet
DIFFICULTY ■ Easy
TOPOGRAPHIC MAP ■ Mount Tabor
GEOLOGIC MAPS ■ 13–20
PRECAUTIONS ■ None
INFORMATION ■ Portland Parks and Recreation Department: (503) 823-7529

Directions: The walk (or drive) to the summit begins at the park's official entrance at Northeast 60th Avenue and Salmon Street. There is also an entry road on Northeast 64th Avenue that leads directly to the basketball-court volcano.

About the Landscape: Most small buttes that pimple Portland's landscape are bantam-weight volcanoes that began to erupt basalts and andesitic lavas about 3 million years ago. The youngest vents, including the lavas at Rocky Butte, erupted less than 100,000 years ago. And some geologists think this broad volcanic field that includes at least ninety-five small volcanoes may erupt again.

The small volcanoes that dot Multnomah, Clackamas, and Washington Counties and Clark County, Washington, are known as Boring volcanics, named for the small town of Boring 20 miles southeast of Portland, where the vents are abundant and the lava flows are thick. The Boring volcanics include Portland landmarks like Mount Tabor, Powell Butte, and Rocky Butte, as well as flows atop the Portland Hills (Mount Sylvan) and exposed along Interstate 205 near Oregon City. Willamette Falls plunges over a lava flow that diverted the river's course perhaps 200,000 years ago. Larch Mountain, just north of Mount Hood, is a Boring vent. So are Battle Ground Lake and Prune Hill in Clark County, Washington. The Boring volcanics seem related to the pull-apart, extensional nature of the Portland Basin. In this thin, faulted crust, basalts rise rapidly to the surface and erupt rapidly, until faulting and crustal deformation shuts off the conduits.

Despite its youth, much of the Boring volcanic field has been erased by time and floods. Although some volcanoes still have a low cone shape, many were scoured by the Missoula floods about 13,500 to 11,000 years ago. The east face of Rocky Butte still bears scars from the flood, easily visible near the junction of Interstates 84 and 205.

90

At Mount Tabor Park, a partly excavated flank and vent of a cinder cone are displayed nicely.

Trail Guide: The two important stops on the short walk are the cinder cone exposed in the basketball court–amphitheater and the tree-shrouded summit. You can drive up the entry road or hike the wood-chipped pathways. The main entry meanders uphill, passing the Mount Tabor reservoir—a major water storage facility for the City of Portland—before continuing upward to the basketball court.

The basketball court and amphitheater at about 0.6 mile from the Northeast 60th Avenue park entry provides a revealing cross section of a Boring volcanic vent. The upper portion is *scoria,* lava, and *lava bombs* in volcanic cinders. Below this, a light-colored, layered rock is made up of ash and pebbles from the underlying Troutdale gravels. The Troutdale Formation—mostly old Columbia River gravels—is now buried several hundred feet below the volcano. Lavas are about 200 feet thick around the Mount Tabor cone.

The summit of Mount Tabor provides leaf-fringed glimpses to the north, south, and west. To the north, Rocky Butte is visible. To the south, more small volcanoes, including Mount Scott and Powell Butte, appear. Boring Lavas that erupted atop Sylvan Heights are visible to the west. On the west side of Portland, the Portland Hills escarpment frames the Portland Hills fault.

Hike

26

POWELL BUTTE

Stroll through forests and meadows that cover one of Portland's biggest Boring volcanoes.

DISTANCE ■ 4.1-mile loop

ELEVATION ■ 450–630 feet

DIFFICULTY ■ Easy

TOPOGRAPHIC MAPS ■ Gladstone, Damascas

GEOLOGIC MAPS ■ 14, 20

PRECAUTIONS ■ Access hours vary and generally correspond to seasonal daylight hours.

INFORMATION ■ Portland Bureau of Environmental Services: (503) 823-7740

Directions: From Interstate 205, east of Portland, take the Powell Boulevard exit. Drive east 3.4 miles to 162nd Avenue. Turn right (south) on 162nd Avenue and drive 0.7 mile to the parking area. The main trail begins near a visitor's information kiosk on the south side of the parking area.

About the Landscape: Like Mount Tabor, Powell Butte is a Boring volcano and also a major storage facility for Portland's water supply. But here, the water tanks are buried beneath the grassy meadows near the main parking area. At Powell Butte, rock exposures are hard to come by. However, it's interesting to view the other pimply hills in the Portland Basin from this viewpoint and envision a day in the middle Pleistocene when an occasional eruption clouded the spruce- and alder-covered basin's sunny skies, sending the mastodons and dire wolves scurrying for cover, while huge birds known as terratorns—with wingspans of about 20 feet—glided away from the eruptive plume.

Trail Guide: Many formal and informal paths wind across this huge parkland. Much of Powell Butte is open meadowland—a relic of a time when dairy cows were pastured here. Expect to meet

Rock outcrops are hard to find on Powell Butte, a cinder cone of the Boring volcanics probably less than 500,000 years in age.

mountain bikes, horses, and plenty of other people and dogs.

From the trailhead, the paved Mountain View path leads south through grassland, then turns east and climbs 0.6 mile to the top of the butte. Along the way there are benches to rest on, and at the top, a "mountaintop finder" helps identify Cascade peaks. Red-tailed hawks and kestrels like to hunt the grass slopes atop Powell Butte.

Take the trail to the butte top, continuing past the first path that splits to the right. At the top of the grade continue straight, and then turn right for a short stretch downhill, then quickly left again. The dirt trail to the left is longer and accommodates hikers and horses. The graveled path is shorter and accommodates mountain bikes and hikers. Opt for the dirt path here. In 0.6 mile it circles into a Douglas fir and cedar forest and then meets a junction of four trails at a very complex intersection.

Cross the creek here, and then bear left. This path continues through forest, turning downslope and meeting the upbound trail from Southeast Ellis Street at 1.8 miles from the hike's beginning. Continue right, along the main trail here. In 0.8 mile it meets a trail to the right. Continue straight to maximize the length of your hike. From this junction, the trail continues about 1.4 miles along the north side of Powell Butte, slipping through mixed Douglas fir and big leaf maple. Return to the trailhead in 4.1 miles from the beginning.

SAUVIE ISLAND: WARRIOR ROCK

Hike

27

Find the geologic roots of Sauvie Island at an historic lighthouse.

DISTANCE ▪ **5.8 miles round trip**

ELEVATION ▪ **Flat**

DIFFICULTY ▪ **Easy**

TOPOGRAPHIC MAP ▪ Sauvie Island

GEOLOGIC MAP ▪ **15a**

PRECAUTIONS ▪ **A day or annual parking permit is required to park at or near the trailhead—or in any ODFW trailheads on the island. Permits are available at the Cracker Barrel on Sauvie Island Road, the 7–Eleven in Linnton, and Portland GI Joe's.**

INFORMATION ▪ **Oregon Department of Fish and Wildlife: (503) 621-3488**

Directions: From Portland, take Highway 30 6 miles northwest through the town of Linnton. Four miles west of Linnton, turn right to cross the Sauvie

The western end of Sauvie Island is buttressed by low-lying outcrops of Columbia River basalt that barely appear above the river surface.

Island Bridge. Continue west (left) on Sauvie Island Road and at 3.2 miles, turn right on Reeder Road. In another 8 miles, Reeder Road changes to a wide gravel road and continues as gravel 3.4 miles to the trailhead at road's end. The trailhead lies at road's end, 14.6 miles from the Sauvie Island Bridge.

About the Landscape: This 5.8-mile-long hike weaves along the Columbia River through cottonwood groves and grassy glades to a rocky point where Multnomah tribe members set out to greet the arrival of Captain William Broughton and his ship in October 1792. Broughton commanded one of the ships with Captain George Vancouver, reputedly the first European to explore the Columbia's tidewater.

This same rock, a brave outcropping of Columbia River basalt that barely holds its head above the Columbia, is one of two factors in the creation of Sauvie Island. Its presence long ago slowed the flow of the Columbia sufficiently to make the river drop a bit of its load, starting a sandbar that ultimately grew to become Sauvie Island. The second factor is that Sauvie has developed just downstream from the mouth of the Willamette River. The Willamette carries a heavy sediment load in its lower reaches, and as its waters meet the

Columbia and slow even more, some of that sediment settles to become part of Sauvie.

The plant community on Sauvie Island is an excellent example of a forest that is well adapted to disturbance. In a few million years, many of the leaves of cottonwoods and alder will be preserved in the flood sediments of the river and in the Columbia's delta and deep sea fan. Geologists worry that this propensity for preserving the forests of flood-prone and eruption-prone areas may somewhat bias the fossil record toward preserving species that grow on disturbed sites, rather than the species of old growth of climax sites. Alder, a disturbed site specialist, may be disproportionately abundant in the fossil record, whereas trees like whitebark pine, that grow in undisturbed mountain settings, may not be preserved at all.

One other geologic factor in Sauvie Island's plant community is worth noting. A majority of the plants that grow there now, including Himalayan blackberry, reed canary grass, spotted knapweed, and cheat grass *(Bromus tectorum)*, are nonnative species that were not even present in Oregon—or in fact, North America—when Captain William Broughton arrived in the late 1700s. The human-aided proliferation of exotic species and demise of native species is an event that is geologic in scale across North America. A similar invasion occurred about 3 million years ago when North America and South America were joined by the closure of the Isthmus of Panama. That new land bridge allowed big cats and wolves to migrate to South America, introducing new predators to South American ecosystems that would never be the same. The modern displacement of native plants also displaces native animals, and helps account for the rapid rates of extinction that we are witness to—an event that is geological in scope.

Trail Guide: From the parking area, the trail follows a narrow path through a wooden gate and then minces between a cow pasture and Columbia beaches that often host angler families on a summer outing. Just beyond the cow pasture, a blue stock gate offers an easy entrance to a grassy field. The narrow path leads through this gate and to the service road. Alternatively, you may follow a path along the shoreline that later joins the service road after tackling more blackberries and stepping across a partly downed wire fence.

The path leads through cottonwoods and maintains a level grade. (It's difficult to do anything else here.) The main path to the lighthouse is a double-track road that consistently bears to the right (toward the Columbia) where it junctions with other trails. Two open areas are noteworthy: one, about 0.6 mile into the hike, offers a poorly marked trail that leads left to a marshy pond. After flirting with the open sky for about 100 yards, the main trail ducks back under cover of the trees; grass gives way to a brambly wall of vegetation along a clean, soft trail. At 2 miles into the hike, there is another grassy open area of about 200 yards length. The main trail reaches the western tip of Sauvie Island at 2.9 miles. The lighthouse is just to the right of where the trail emerges.

The Columbia's currents can be treacherous here, and it is an abrupt and deep plunge from rocks into deep water, so use caution if you decide to take a quick swim. Better swimming beaches are found to the left where beaches are sandy and the water is less turbulent.

During times when the Columbia's flow and the tides permit, you may return by walking along the beach on the Columbia side. This route offers the advantages of an open view of the river and its oversized cargo vessel traffic, as well as the Ridgefield and Batchelor Island wildlife refuges across the Columbia, and of the mouth of the Lewis River.

Hike 28 SPENCERS BUTTE

Hike to the top of a large basaltic butte in the southern Willamette Valley.

DISTANCE ■ 1.5 miles
ELEVATION ■ 1250–2054 feet
DIFFICULTY ■ Moderate
TOPOGRAPHIC MAPS ■ Creswell, Fox Hollow
GEOLOGIC MAP ■ 1
PRECAUTIONS ■ Carry water. Poison oak is prolific in open areas. The trail is eroded and steep in many places.
INFORMATION ■ Lane County Parks: (541) 682-2000

Directions: To reach Spencers Butte Park, from 6th Street in downtown Eugene drive south on Willamette Street. The park and parking lot are on the left in 5 miles.

About the Landscape: The dark, pointed buttes in the Willamette Valley, including the Coburg Hills northeast of Eugene, are composed of basalt. These rocks are 24 to 32 million years old. Most are shallow intrusions or possibly the eroded remnants of lava flows. Only one, Peterson Butte, 4 miles southwest of Lebanon, seems to have erupted. Peterson Butte has a central volcanic vent with twelve radiating dikes extending outward in all directions from the center of the butte into the sediments. Skinner Butte and Spencers Butte both seem to be remnant lava flows or shallow intrusions.

This short hike takes you to the top of Spencers Butte, at 2054 feet the highest isolated basaltic butte in the Willamette Valley.

Trail Guide: The trail begins with concrete steps and immediately bears left

Basaltic outcrops mark the summit of Spencers Butte.

uphill. For most of its 0.75-mile upward-bound grade, this trail traverses a forest. The open summit, however, reveals the basalts that support Spencers Butte. These solid, dark rocks are coarse-grained and display only coarse columnar jointing, suggesting that Spencers Butte represents a shallow intrusion rather than a lava flow. The landscape to the north is pimpled with other basaltic buttes, including the Coburg Hills to the northeast. Retrace your path down the butte to the trailhead.

SILVER CREEK CANYON AND RIM TRAIL

Hike 29

Discover long-traveled basalts above an ancient Cascade shoreline.

DISTANCE ■ 9-mile loop

ELEVATION ■ 1100–1500 feet

DIFFICULTY ■ Moderate

TOPOGRAPHIC MAPS ■ Drake Crossing, Stout Mountain, Lyons

GEOLOGIC MAPS ■ 11, 12

PRECAUTIONS ■ This is a day-use fee area. Pets are *not* allowed on the Trail of Ten Falls.

INFORMATION ■ Oregon State Parks: (800) 551-6949

Directions: From Salem, drive east on Highway 22 about 6 miles, turn north on Highway 214, and follow it about 16 miles to Silver Falls State Park.

About the Landscape: On a warm summer day when you are torn between going to the mountains or heading for the beach, do both. Go to Silver Falls State Park and pitch your beach umbrella on a 25-million-year-old shoreline where waterfalls echo long-vanished waves from an ancient bayside beach.

Long ago, Oregon's shore ran along the western base of the Cascade Mountains.

The trail ducks behind 177-foot-high South Falls.

The Coast Range was visible across a wide bay. The coastline here was rocky, a warmer version of the modern Willapa Bay or Puget Sound. Headlands composed of basalts from the Cascades jutted into the bay. The sedimentary rocks deposited on that long-ago beach are known as the Scotts Mills Formation. They extend along the west side of the Willamette Valley from Silverton north to Molalla. They make fleeting guest appearances beneath the waterfalls at Silver Falls State Park.

The rocks that support the waterfalls are Columbia River basalt. They erupted between 16 and 15 million years ago in eastern Oregon and followed the ancestral valley of the Columbia River which then ran near the present location of Mount Hood. At least eight great flows of Columbia River basalt, totaling about 600 feet in thickness, are exposed in the area's waterfalls.

During the long time interval (averaging about 50,000 years) between basalt flows, soils developed atop the lavas and forest grew in the warm Miocene climate. Trees may have included alder, dawn redwood, some varieties of pine, and hemlocks. These basalt flows and the gravels of their contemporary streams buried and preserved the forest that originally grew here. If you glance upward at the rock ceiling when you stand behind North Falls or South Falls, you'll see large round holes in the basalts. These are the casts of trees that were surrounded by hot lava. The trees burned but left behind their impression in the 16-million-year-old stones.

Today, the waterfalls that proliferate at Silver Falls are a reminder that the Columbia River basalt is resistant to erosion. The falls' broad amphitheaters owe their presence to the cold winters in the Western Cascades. The misty water that surrounds the waterfalls enters and freezes in the cracks of the basalt. Frost action then loosens and wedges chunks of rock from their place on basaltic cliffs. This action, repeated over thousands or millions of years, eventually removes so much material that a broad amphitheater, like the space at North and South Falls, is created.

Trail Guide: The best place to begin this loop hike is from South Falls Day-Use Area A; a path descends to cross beneath South Falls, at 177 feet high, the most popular falls at the park. A sloping trail and stairway lets you explore all around this falls, including walking behind the cascading water. Be sure to look up to see the casts of a 16-million-year-old forest. Behind the falls and beneath the basalts you will find the shy exposures of the 25-million-year-old beach sands.

From South Falls, the main loop trail continues counterclockwise, leading to Lower South Falls in 0.8 mile for a quick tour behind this 93-foot cascade. From here, it is a 1.3-mile hike to Lower North Falls. En route, look for cedar trees amid the largely second-growth Douglas fir forest. Oregon grape and sword fern form the understory. At Lower North Falls, a short side trail up Hult Creek leads to Double Falls. The Main Trail then continues to find 106-foot-high Middle North Falls in 0.4 mile.

From Middle North Falls, the path becomes a forest trail, ambling alongside North Silver Creek for 1.2 miles before it reaches 136-foot-high North Falls. This waterfall provides a good view of the Scotts Mills Formation sandstones below the Columbia River basalts. And if you look up at the ceiling behind the falls, you'll find a forest of holes where trees once grew—a forest that likely included pines, dawn redwood, alder, and gingko that grew in a warmer and drier climate than today's. If you look closely (you'll need a powerful flashlight and binoculars), you'll see the impression of tree bark in some casts.

From North Falls, the trail climbs to the canyon rim, offers a visit to Upper North Falls on a 0.2-mile spur trail, and returns to the beginning at South Falls in another 2.5 miles of relatively flat hiking.

Hike 30 ERRATIC ROCK STATE NATURAL SITE

An iceberg-rafted boulder lies in the heart of the Willamette Valley.

DISTANCE ■ 1 mile round trip

ELEVATION ■ 300–370 feet

DIFFICULTY ■ Easy

TOPOGRAPHIC MAP ■ Muddy Valley

GEOLOGIC MAP ■ 1

PRECAUTIONS ■ None

INFORMATION ■ Oregon State Parks: (800) 551-6949

Directions: From McMinnville, drive southwest on Highway 99W to its merger with Oregon Highway 18. Continue southwest on Highway 18 for 6.3 miles to Oldsville Road. Turn right on Oldsville Road and drive 0.5 mile to the parking area for Erratic Rock State Natural Site.

About the Landscape: Once, about 13,000 years ago, the Willamette Valley was a lake. In fact, this probably happened several times, as unimaginably monstrous floods—at least 40, perhaps as many as 120—swept down the Columbia River. The largest filled the Columbia River Gorge with water, overtopping the gorge walls at Crown Point, stripping the soils and face from Rocky Butte, and filling the Willamette Valley with iceberg-laden water. These floods, known as the Missoula floods, occurred between about 13,500 and 11,000 years ago, at the close of the last Ice Age (Pleistocene). They occurred because a

Erratic Rock is a 40-ton chunk of Montana argillite (a sedimentary rock, at least 600 million years in age) rafted into the Willamette Valley on an iceberg about 13,000 years ago.

lobe of glacial ice periodically blocked the Clark Fork River and backed water up, flooding the Missoula basin to depths of 950 feet. But an ice dam is an ephemeral thing, and waters would periodically erode the dam, sending a flood rushing across eastern Washington, down the Columbia River, and eventually to the ocean—but flooding the Willamette Valley on the way. The largest of these floods, which may have occurred about 13,000 years ago, carried huge boulders rafted on icebergs. The 40-ton rock at Erratic Rock State Natural Site is one of them.

Trail Guide: A simple, paved pathway leads upslope about 0.2 mile to the large boulder perched atop a hill. This rock is argillite, a chunk of 600-million-year-old seafloor that was quarried from its home in British Columbia by a glacier, hauled south into Montana by a glacier, and remained embedded in a large iceberg as it rode the fast, swirling floodwaters from Glacial Lake Missoula across eastern Washington, down the flood-filled Columbia River Gorge, into the flood-filled Willamette Valley—then a lake known as Lake Allison—to finally beach on this nameless hilltop where it watched first alder, then grasses, pines, and spruce populate the valley floor and mastodons and dire wolves roam the wide plains, and finally two-footed humans come to hunt and plow and plant vineyards, discover the stone, assault it with hammers, build a pathway, and enshrine it with a fence. And this remnant of stone, with its 600-million-year memory of a world of sluggish, spineless sea creatures we can hardly imagine must lie here at night watching the dimming stars and wondering what will come next. Spend a little time here, and share its meditations.

Chapter 4
THE COLUMBIA RIVER GORGE

The Columbia River Gorge was forged by a 30-million-year feud between fire and water. From the Miocene to the present, the rivalry between a powerful river and persistent volcanoes built landscapes and wore them away, carved canyons and filled them. The landscape you see from Crown Point or Larch Mountain strikes a delicate balance between the earth's motile surface and its churning interior.

The Columbia River has shepherded water across Oregon for at least the last 20 million years, flowing through the active Western Cascades (Hikes 31, 34). During that time, its channel has migrated fitfully northward. Some 25 million years ago, the Columbia ran just south of the present site of Mount Hood and continued southwesterly, reaching the sea somewhere northwest of Salem.

The Columbia River provided an easy path westward for Columbia River basalt lavas: they followed the river. And they also filled the canyon, forcing the stream farther and farther north. By 14 million years ago, the Columbia River had been edged almost to its present channel by lavas and the rising Coast Range and Cascades. Its course, known as the Bridal Veil channel, lay just south of the present canyon (Hikes 31, 33, 35).

But 4 million years ago lavas and mudflows from the High Cascades and

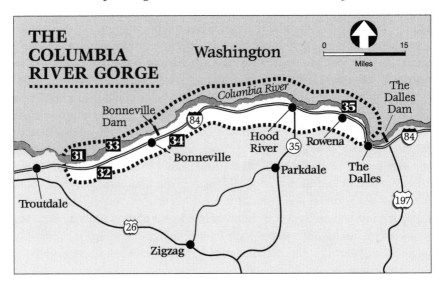

Vista House at Crown Point perches atop the Pomona Flow—a Columbia river basalt about 12 million years in age.

the Boring volcanic field (Hikes 32, 33) began to fill the Bridal Veil channel. By 2 million years ago, the Columbia had doggedly cut yet another channel through the rising Cascades, creating the deep canyon that we see today. The remnants of older channels are exposed in the sidewalls of the Gorge.

Gravels transported by the Columbia River during the last 10 million years are called the Troutdale Formation. They are found throughout the Gorge and the Portland Basin.

As the Ice Age waned 15,000 years ago, volcanoes quieted. The Columbia flexed its fluid muscles again. As a result of as many as 120 huge floods of ice-dammed lake water from Montana, the river widened its gorge, polished and steepened its sides, and spread sediment across the Willamette Valley.

Near Bonneville, humans have built a great dam 80 feet high across the Columbia. But long before the Army Corps of Engineers and bulldozers came, a landslide from the north side of the river cleaved the raw face of Table Mountain and built a dam 270 feet high across this river. It was known as Bridge of the Gods. Some geologists think this huge landslide was generated by the last big, magnitude 9 earthquake in January 1700. Others rely on carbon-14 dates of about A.D. 1550—from trees drowned by the slide. Forests as far east as The Dalles were inundated as the lake filled behind the dam. For some time before the river topped the dam, Indian tribes were able to cross the river dry-shod; once the river topped the dam it resulted in the Cascades of the Columbia. The Salish and Chinook peoples remember this natural dam and the dry-footed crossing in their stories of the Bridge of the Gods. Today, landslides and the Columbia River remain active forces in the Gorge.

COLUMBIA RIVER BASALTS AND STEENS BASALTS

The Pacific Northwest is home to world-class flood basalts. From about 17 to 12 million years ago, basaltic lavas periodically poured across Oregon and Washington. These lavas, erupted from long cracks or fissures in eastern Oregon, eastern Washington, and western Idaho, were so fluid that they did not form volcanoes. Instead, they spread across the landscape like syrup on pancakes, filling depressions and river valleys, and covering more than 63,000 square miles with basalt up to 3 miles thick. Some flows followed the ancestral Columbia River to the Pacific Ocean where today they form Cape Lookout, Otter Rocks, Saddle Mountain, and other coastal features.

The Columbia River basalts erupted in four discrete pulses. The first to erupt, beginning about 16.6 million years ago, were flows that erupted along today's Imnaha River. They are called the Imnaha basalts. The bulk of the flows, known as the Grande Ronde basalts for exposures along the lower Grande Ronde River, erupted beginning about 16 million years ago. The Grande Ronde basalts constitute about 85 percent of the Columbia River basalt's volume. As flows dwindled, two more types of basalt appeared: the Wanapum basalts, 15.5 to 14.5 million years ago, and the Saddle Mountain basalts, 14.5 to 12 million years ago.

At the same time as the Columbia River basalts began to erupt, voluminous basalt flows also began at what is today Steens Mountain. These flows, known as the Steens basalts, spread across several thousand square miles. Today the same or similar flows appear at Hart Mountain, Abert Rim, and across Oregon's Basin and Range.

The eruption of these two major flood basalts—the Columbia River basalts and Steens basalts—marked the beginning of the Yellowstone hotspot. This hotspot is a plume of fluid rock that rises from the earth's mantle. The hotspot remains relatively stationary. But the crustal plates—in this case, North America—move across it, leaving a trail of eruptive centers to track the plate's movement. Yellowstone remains a very active volcanic system, even after some 16.6 million years of eruptions that blazed the Snake River Plain across Idaho.

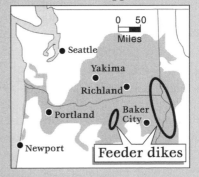

LATOURELL FALLS

Hike 31

Explore three different types of Columbia River basalts as well as the sedimentary rocks beneath them.

DISTANCE ▪ 1 mile
ELEVATION ▪ 250–650 feet
DIFFICULTY ▪ Moderate
TOPOGRAPHIC MAP ▪ Bridal Veil
GEOLOGIC MAP ▪ 1
PRECAUTIONS ▪ Short stretches of this trail edge along precipitous cliffs above the falls.
INFORMATION ▪ Columbia River Gorge National Scenic Area: (541) 386-2333

Directions: From Multnomah Falls, follow the old Columbia River Scenic Highway 6 miles west to the turnout for Latourell Falls.

About the Landscape: Three different kinds of Columbia River basalts are exposed at Latourell Falls: the Grande Ronde basalts, the Frenchman Springs flow, and the Priest Rapids flow. The Grande Ronde flow at the base of the falls is the oldest, about 15.5 million years in age. The Frenchman Springs flow above the falls originated northwest of Pendleton. These basalts were so voluminous that they clogged the Columbia's southern channel, forcing the river to move north almost to its present position about 14 million years ago. Frenchman Springs basalts are fine-grained rocks and usually display blocky or poorly developed joints. The uppermost basalt at Latourell Falls is a Priest Rapids flow. This basalt flow erupted in west-central Idaho, flowing more than 300 miles to this location about 14 million years ago. These rocks are extremely fine grained. Like the Frenchman Springs flow before it, the Priest Rapids flow filled the Columbia's canyon, forcing the river north again.

Trail Guide: This relatively easy, short loop hike leads through the lush forest of the Columbia Gorge to two major waterfalls, providing intimate views of three major types of Columbia River basalt and an example of the oldest rock in the Columbia River Gorge.

At the southwest end of the parking lot, a paved trail leads past a gray outcrop. Part of the Oligocene Skamania volcanics, this outcrop represents some of the oldest rocks (25 to 30 million years) in the Columbia River Gorge. This 0.25-mile path provides a close-up view of Latourell Creek's plunge over several flows of elegantly columned Grande Ronde Columbia River basalt, which is 16 million years old.

Return to the parking lot and take the main trail that leads upslope to an overview of Latourell Falls. Continue past the overview about 200 yards to the top of the lower falls, where the trail splits. One path leads along the east side of the creek, the other takes the west bank. Both lead to upper Latourell Falls in a level 0.5-mile walk. Visible along the way are outcrops of Frenchman Springs Columbia River basalt (about 15 million years old). At the upper falls, the creek pours over the Priest Rapids basalt, which, at about 14 million years, is the second youngest Columbia River basalt flow exposed in the Gorge.

Upper Latourell Falls

This basalt displays well-developed columnar joints. Return along the opposite side of the creek if you want to see slightly different scenery.

Hike

ANGELS REST

View the Gorge and Portland Basin from a perch on the Boring volcanics.

DISTANCE ■ **4.6 miles round trip**

ELEVATION ■ **170–1590 feet**

DIFFICULTY ■ **Moderate**

TOPOGRAPHIC MAP ■ **Bridal Veil**

GEOLOGIC MAP ■ **1**

FEES/REGULATIONS ■ **Northwest Forest Pass required for trailhead parking.**

PRECAUTIONS ■ **None**

INFORMATION ■ **Columbia River Gorge National Scenic Area: (541) 386-2333**

Directions: From Portland, drive east on Interstate 84 to exit 28, Bridal Veil. Turn right and continue 0.2 mile to a stop sign. Turn right at the stop sign and make another right immediately into the large trailhead parking lot. Overflow parking is in another 0.1 mile and provides parking with more shade. The trailhead is just across the road from the main parking lot. A spur trail connects to the overflow lot.

About the Landscape: Angels Rest is a promontory above the Columbia River Gorge that offers a stunning view of the Portland Basin and lower Columbia. The rock outcropping is different in age and lithology than most of the Gorge's 16-million-year-old Columbia River basalts. Angels Rest is composed of a stubby lava flow—the heritage of younger eruptions of the Boring volcanic field about 1 million years (or less) ago. Larch Mountain, which rises above the site, is a large Boring volcano.

Trail Guide: This relatively short hike is one of the most popular trails in the Columbia River Gorge—and in Oregon. It leads to a spectacular view. Expect to meet many hikers no matter what season or time of day. On hot days, carry plenty of water.

From the trailhead, the path heads into a forest dominated by big leaf maple and a few Douglas fir. Look for white trillium blossoms on spring hikes here. In the first 0.5 mile, the path leads uphill at a moderate pace, providing an overview of Coopey Falls and then crossing Coopey Creek.

From the wooden bridge across Coopey Creek, the trail rises through a mixed forest, with one more pause to peer into the moist canyon. Then the path climbs more steeply, touring the stark and skeletal remains of a 1991 forest fire at 1.4 miles. Most of this area is now healed into a sea of salal and ceanothis, with alder now replacing the burned Douglas fir. Shade is rare along the upper half of the hike.

At 2 miles into the hike, the path crosses rough, gray talus just below Angels

Angels Rest provides a view of the Portland Basin from atop a Boring lava flow.

Rest, and after a detour around rocky outcrops, arrives at Angels Rest in 2.3 miles from the trailhead. The views from the rocky bluffs are spectacular—to the west you can view the Portland Basin, to the east, Vista House and Beacon Rock. The blocky gray outcrop that forms the bulk of Angels Rest is andesite—probably less than 1 million years in age. Its broad columns are much larger and less distinct than most columnar joints in the Gorge.

To extend your hike past Angels Rest, continue east on the path that connects with the Wahkeena Trail. This path leads down to Wahkeena Spring in 2.5 miles and reaches Wahkeena Falls in 4.2 miles from Angels Rest.

Most hikers, however, elect to return to the trailhead directly from Angels Rest—a satisfying day hike.

MULTNOMAH FALLS TO LARCH MOUNTAIN

Hike 33

This long climb crosses eleven Columbia River basalt flows and leads to a small basalt shield volcano.

DISTANCE ■ **14 miles round trip**

ELEVATION ■ **150–4056 feet**

DIFFICULTY ■ **Strenuous**

TOPOGRAPHIC MAPS ■ **Bridal Veil, Multnomah Falls**

GEOLOGIC MAP ■ **21**

PRECAUTIONS ■ **Short stretches of the trail about 2 to 3 miles into the hike navigate steep and potentially slippery drop-offs above Multnomah Creek.**

INFORMATION ■ **Columbia River Gorge National Scenic Area: (541) 386-2333**

Directions: From Interstate 84 east of Portland, take exit 31, Multnomah Falls. (Alternatively, take the Columbia River Scenic Highway exit 28 to Multnomah Falls for a more intimate drive along the Gorge.)

About the Landscape: Eleven flows of Columbia River basalt are exposed at Multnomah Falls and along the first mile of nearly vertical, nicely switchbacked trail to Larch Mountain and Sherrad Point. Six flows are exposed from the Columbia River to the top of Multnomah Falls. Especially noteworthy is the pillow lava visible near the top of the falls. Larch Mountain (4056 feet) is a Pleistocene shield volcano—one of the most easterly vents of the Boring volcanic field—that erupted about 1.8 to 1.4 million years ago. Most of its lavas were basalts, although the rock at its summit (Sherrad Point) is iron-rich andesite. The summit provides a commanding view of the Columbia River and Portland Basin.

Pillow basalts are visible beneath Upper Multnomah Falls.

Trail Guide: The trail, USFS Trail 441, begins on the east flank of Multnomah Lodge. Note especially the pillow lavas (lumpy forms) just beneath the upper falls. Continue upward on the trail. It provides an up-close view of a moss-laden, fine-grained Grande Ronde flow. The top of the falls, at 0.9 mile, reveals a grand view of the Columbia River.

From here, the trail climbs along Multnomah Creek at a steady clip. One large falls and many cascades plunge over the Columbia River basalt Grande Ronde flows along Multnomah Creek.

At 4.5 miles into the hike, the slope steepens again as the trail encounters the young basalt of Larch Mountain's shield volcano. This rock is difficult to distinguish from Columbia River basalt. Generally, it is more brittle and lighter colored. Its small crystals are visible if you look very closely.

At almost 7 miles, the trail reaches the picnic and parking area just south of Larch Mountain summit. Another 300 yards to the viewpoint rewards the weary hiker with great views from Sherrad Point.

Hike 34

EAGLE CREEK

Visit a fossil forest of the early Miocene.

DISTANCE ▪ **11 miles round trip**
ELEVATION ▪ **225–875 feet**
DIFFICULTY ▪ **Moderate**
TOPOGRAPHIC MAP ▪ **Bonneville Dam, Oregon-Washington**
GEOLOGIC MAP ▪ **1**
FEES/REGULATIONS ▪ **Northwest Forest Pass required for trailhead parking.**
PRECAUTIONS ▪ **The trail is narrow. It edges above steep cliffs for portions of the hike. Please do not disturb fossils.**
INFORMATION ▪ **Columbia River Gorge National Scenic Area: (541) 386-2333**

Directions: From Interstate 84 east of Portland, take exit 41, Eagle Creek (also marked for Fish Hatchery). Turn right and drive 0.7 mile along a single-lane paved road to the parking lot and trailhead.

About the Landscape: The gravelly rocks along Eagle Creek are part of the Eagle Creek Formation—rocks deposited by the Early Miocene Cascade volcanoes. Little is left of the volcanoes now, but their debris flows, mudflows, ash deposits, and a few lava flows have preserved a record of their presence and of the forests that grew at their base.

If you were hiking here 25 million years ago, you would be strolling through a diverse forest of oaks, maples, gingkoes, sycamores, and sweet gum trees. Wetlands would be fringed in swamp cypress and dawn redwood. The animals might look a bit odd. They would include three types of two-toed horse about the size of a Great Dane, the camel Oxydactylus, and a plant-eating animal called a chalicothere that resembled a bear with a horse's head. The early Miocene climate was warmer and overall milder, with less seasonal variation than we experience today. And there was no Columbia River Gorge, although the ancestral Columbia likely ran somewhat south of this location.

If you scrutinize the rocks along the first 3 miles of this hike, you may find a few plant fossils. Please remember to leave them for others to enjoy.

Trail Guide: From the trailhead the path tours a variety of rocks of the Eagle Creek Formation. In the first 0.5 mile, hikers view mostly debris-flow deposits

Eagle Creek, in a calm reach, flows beside outcrops of 25-million-year-old mudflows.

from an ancient and long-vanished volcano that may have resembled Mount Hood some 25 million years ago. Large cobbles and boulders characterize the deposits from muddy avalanches that often coincided with volcanic eruptions.

In about 1 mile the trail begins to edge along a steep drop-off into Eagle Creek. Here the path clings to ash-rich deposits that resemble a concrete wall. Scrutiny here may reveal the remains of ancient leaves and stems preserved in the ashy deposits.

As the trail slowly gains elevation, the Eagle Creek Formation gives way to Columbia River basalts in about 1 mile along the path. This transition is marked by Metlako Falls, a 100-foot-high falls and the first of a series of falls along the trail. At 1.8 miles, Punchbowl Falls marks the succession of the next higher basalt flows. A mile beyond Punchbowl Falls, the trail pauses to view Loowit Falls across the canyon, then crosses a high, narrow metal bridge, and then continues, reaching Tunnel Falls at 5.5 miles from the trailhead. Here the trail creeps along the edge of a steep drop-off to cross Eagle Creek and continues behind the 100-foot-high waterfall. Beyond Tunnel Falls, the trail begins a lengthy switchbacking scramble upward to Whatum Lake (12 miles from the trailhead), and geology becomes subservient to vegetation. Return as you came.

ROWENA CREST AND TOM McCALL PRESERVE

Hike 35

Examine a macabre but lovely landscape of folds, faults, and channeled scablands.

DISTANCE ■ 4 miles round trip
ELEVATION ■ 700–1722 feet
DIFFICULTY ■ Moderate
TOPOGRAPHIC MAP ■ Lyle, Washington
GEOLOGIC MAPS ■ 1, 21
PRECAUTIONS ■ The trails cover a preserve of The Nature Conservancy; picking plants is forbidden. Hazards may include rattlesnakes, poison oak, and ticks. Dogs are not allowed on Nature Conservancy preserves.
INFORMATION ■ The Nature Conservancy of Oregon: (503) 230-1221

Directions: From Interstate 84 take exit 76, Rowena. Turn south on the Columbia River Scenic Highway and drive 3.4 miles west, up the curving old highway to Rowena Crest and the parking area.

About the Landscape: From the top of Tom McCall Point and from Interstate 84 between Hood River and The Dalles, you can see something strange on the Washington side of the river: the basalt layers are tilted. Worse yet, just where the tilt skies out, there is a crashing big collection of vertical rock spikes called the Ortley Pinnacles. They are composed of broken, angular rocks cemented together. This is a fault zone, a place where the Columbia River basalts have been violently thrust westward, one set of twelve basalt flows riding up and over the others, creating the cobbled, broken rocks of the Ortley Pinnacles. In this part of the Columbia River Gorge, the Columbia River basalts have been gently folded

as well as faulted. These folds developed in the basalts from 16 to about 10 million years ago.

On this hike you can also explore the austere landscape left by the Missoula floods, which submerged the overlook at Rowena Crest beneath as much as 200 feet of water. The initial surges of this raging, turbulent water stripped away rock, leaving a barren, knobby topography. Once the

Irregular joints are typical of the Pomona basalt near Mosier and Rowena Crest.

The lower trails of Tom McCall Preserve tour channel scabland topography sculpted by Ice Age floods 15,000 to 12,000 years ago.

high-energy, high-impact floodwaters had slowed, sand and gravel bars were left perched hundreds of feet above the present river. One lies north across the river above the town of Lyle, Washington. Another is still higher on the walls of the Klickitat River valley northwest of Lyle.

Since the floods, the active Mount St. Helens volcano repeatedly blew out clouds of volcanic ash which built up to a thickness of about 3 feet on Rowena Plateau. Subsequent erosion of this ash produced the subdued *biscuit mound* (or biscuit scabland) topography you can see all around you.

Trail Guide: The trail to the summit of Tom McCall Point departs from the end of the parking area's solid stone fence and heads across a lumpy prairie composed of Mount St. Helens ash deposited atop the basalts. In early spring (February through May) you can find an abundance of wildflowers, including grass widows, prairie stars, shooting stars, balsamroot, lupine, and Indian paintbrush here. The open grasslands are home to four plant species unique to the Columbia River Gorge: Thompson's broadleaf lupine, Columbia desert parsley, Thompson's waterleaf, and Hood River milkvetch. Hawks and larks thrive in this open landscape.

At 0.5 mile into the walk, the trail rounds a large basalt scab (a steep-sided rock outcrop) eroded by the Missoula floods and begins a more serious ascent. The trail crosses the Pomona and Priest Rapids flows of Columbia River basalt, and after a steep climb of steps literally carved into the Priest Rapids flow, emerges atop the gravels that cap Tom McCall Point, 1.5 miles from the up-bound trailhead. This vantage point provides exceptional views downstream and limited views toward The Dalles. Return as you came.

The lower trail across the relatively flat ash-mantled scabland starts at a turnout on the road near the crest; a sign just inside a wire fence marks the trailhead. This 1-mile round-trip trail provides a scenic tour of several small ponds and wetlands. These wetlands have developed in depressions scoured by the Missoula floods and later filled by ash from Mount St. Helens. You can peer over the edge of a small canyon carved into the basalts, filled by flood sediments, and now being excavated again by the tireless creek. Return as you came.

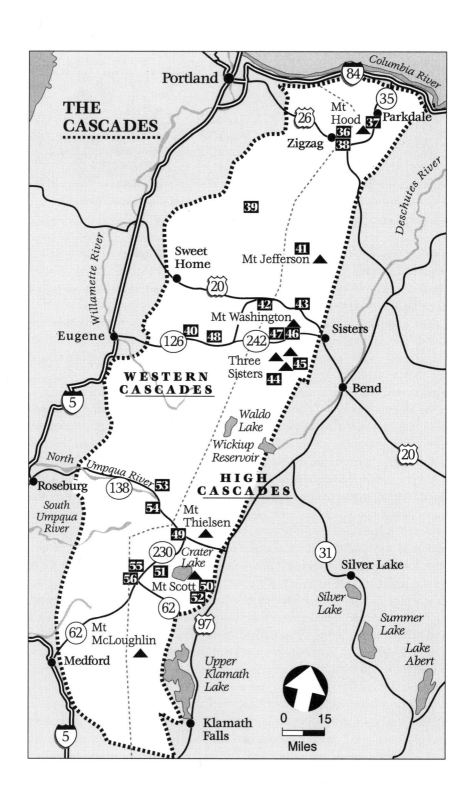

THE
CASCADES

Portland

Columbia River

84

35

Mt
Hood
36
38

37
Parkdale

26

Zigzag

Deschutes River

39

Sweet
Home

41
Mt Jefferson ▲

20

42
43

Mt Washington
47 46
Sisters

40
48
126
242 45

Three
Sisters
44

Eugene

WESTERN
CASCADES

Bend

Willamette River

Waldo
Lake

Wickiup
Reservoir

5

North Umpqua River
53
Roseburg
138

HIGH
CASCADES

20

South
Umpqua
River

54

Mt
Thielsen ▲

49

230
Crater
Lake

31

Silver Lake

Silver
Lake

55
56
51
Mt Scott 50
52

Summer
Lake

62

62 Mt
McLoughlin ▲

97

Lake
Abert

Medford

Upper
Klamath
Lake

0   15

Klamath
Falls

Miles

5

Chapter 5

THE CASCADES

The Cascade Mountains define and divide Oregon. As the state's ecologic and geologic backbone, they separate desert from rain forest and ancient rocks from young terranes. The Cascades are a community of peaks, each with a separate history, but each an integral part of the whole.

The Cascades are really two mountain ranges in one, two parallel belts of volcanic rocks of different ages. The older, steep-sloped, and heavily forested Western Cascades belt hosts the rumpled and eroded relicts of volcanoes 40 to about 7 million years in age. Today we think of this eroded, once-mighty volcanic range as merely the Cascade foothills, from Sweet Home to Detroit, or Vida to McKenzie Bridge (Hikes 40, 48).

Belknap Crater is a young volcanic feature about 2500 years old.

The younger belt of volcanoes, erupted during the last 7 million years, is called the High Cascades. The High Cascades' mountains include the familiar, photogenic volcanic peaks as well as a thick foundation of lavas beneath them. While some High Cascades volcanoes can be considered extinct, Mount Hood and South Sister are likely to erupt again.

The older Western Cascades include lavas, mudflows, and *tuffs* (consolidated ash). Their peaks once rose as high as today's volcanoes. But all we have today are their altered and eroded roots.

The Western Cascades erupted in three periods: (1) From 40 to 30 million years ago the Western Cascades built volcanoes that may have looked like today's High Cascade Range. (2) From 30 to 15 million years ago large quantities of ash erupted. Blown east by prevailing winds, this ash produced the Painted Hills. It buried rhinos and saber-toothed tigers in the John Day Fossil Beds. These silica-rich eruptions created gold deposits in the upper Santiam River basin. (3) The last volcanic activity of the Western Cascades, from 9 to about 7 million years ago, produced basalt and basaltic andesite (Hikes 39, 55, 56). At the same time, the Western Cascades began to fold gently upward, as erosion wore them down.

Oregon's High Cascades, from Crater Lake to Mount Hood, are full-fledged volcanoes, and at least two of them (Hood and South Sister) are just biding their time until they erupt again.

The High Cascades also grew in three stages: (1) From 7 to about 2 million years ago, eruptions of basalt built low-lying shield volcanoes along today's High Cascade axis (Hike 57). (2) About 2 million years ago, faulting produced a valley (called the High Cascade *graben*) along the Cascade crest. Green Ridge, east of Mount Jefferson, represents the east wall of this graben. Basalt eruptions filled this valley. (3) Beginning a little more than 1 million years ago, during the Ice Age, the modern High Cascade peaks began to erupt. Most of these volcanoes were *stratovolcanoes*.

As volcanoes grew, glaciers wore them down. The oldest High Cascade peaks are the most eroded by glaciers. Some, including Three Fingered Jack and Mount Washington, have been virtually erased by glaciation. The more vigorous volcanoes—Mount Hood (Hikes 36–38), Mount Jefferson, and South Sister (Hike 44)—maintained their youthful physique by erupting in defiance of glacial attack. Ironically, one of the oldest High Cascade peaks, the 1.4-million-year-old cinder cone of Black Butte (just west of Sisters) escaped glaciation entirely because it lies in the Cascade "rain and snow shadow" and little ice accumulated on its summit.

Cascade eruptions continued after glaciers retreated. In the past 3000 years, many cinder cones and lava vents have been active in the Cascades (Hikes 46, 47, 50–52). Most flank major peaks, although some, such as Sand

116

Mountain (Hike 42), seem isolated between major volcanic centers. Some biographical notes on major Cascade peaks follow:

MOUNT HOOD

Oregon's highest peak is also the one most likely to erupt again. Mount Hood's last major eruption occurred in 1781–82. The twisted stumps of whitebark pine executed by its force still lie in state above Mount Hood Meadows.

At least three volcanoes have occupied the area where Mount Hood rises today. The first, which produced rocks called the Rhododendron Formation, appeared about 8 million years ago. Its lavas form Zigzag and Tom, Dick, and Harry Mountains. The second, Sandy Glacier volcano, was active about 1.4 million years ago. Today it is tucked into the south flanks of Mount Hood (Hike 36). The third is Mount Hood itself.

The mountain we know as Mount Hood began its life about 700,000 years ago. Thick andesite lavas built its main cone. But by 29,000 years ago, lava eruptions dwindled. The only exception is the Parkdale flow, a 7000-year-old basalt sequestered in apple and pear orchards about 2 miles west of Parkdale.

Since the Ice Age, four periods of eruptions have shaken Mount Hood. The last eruptive episode (the Old Maid period) occurred about 1781–82.

Mount Hood, a volcano about 700,000 years in the making, has rebuilt after each glacial advance.

These eruptions vented at Crater Rock. They produced steam, ash, and a small, three-lobed dacite dome which is Crater Rock itself. The eruption melted snow and glacial ice, unleashing enormous mudflows that buried the forest on Old Maid Flat. We may still be living in the Old Maid period today (Hikes 37, 38).

In the last half century, Mount Hood's volcanic activity has killed two people. In 1934 a climber exploring the ice caves in Coalman Glacier was suffocated by the oxygen-poor, carbon-dioxide-rich gas emitted from the Crater Rock *fumaroles*. In 1980 a debris flow on Pollalie Creek spawned by rapid glacial melting killed one person and wiped out a 5-mile section of Highway 35. Even without erupting, Mount Hood remains a volcanic force to be reckoned with.

MOUNT JEFFERSON

Mount Jefferson rises to 10,495 feet, dominating the Santiam and Metolius skylines. But Oregon's second-highest peak is just a shadow of its former self. The mountain may have topped 12,000 feet before glaciers chiseled it into submission.

The lavas that formed Mount Jefferson's high cone began erupting about 680,000 years ago. These first eruptions produced basalt. Then, about 350,000 years ago, Mount Jefferson underwent a volcanic midlife crisis. Instead of

Mount Jefferson is a mostly andesite volcano that has been extensively eroded by glaciers.

Three Fingered Jack rises above the Canyon Creek trail.

basalt, it began to erupt andesite and dacite from vents such as Goat Peak on the mountain's south flank.

Although Mount Jefferson has not erupted in at least the last 15,000 years, volcanic activity near the mountain is more recent. Forked Butte, a cinder cone about 5 miles south of Jefferson's summit, produced basalt lava flows about 6500 years ago. The existence of hot springs such as Breitenbush suggests that the magma chambers below Jefferson may still be warm.

THREE FINGERED JACK

Three Fingered Jack's jaggedy, raggedy silhouette rises between Mount Jefferson and the Three Sisters. It is a mountain with racing stripes, a spectacular layered and dissected volcanic biography, a slice through time, and a full-scale cross section of a High Cascade volcano.

Three Fingered Jack began its life about 300,000 years ago as a small cinder cone. The remnants of this cone appear as the orange, red, and gray layers in the west-facing wall of the present mountain.

119

The second eruptive episode of Three Fingered Jack occurred about 250,000 years ago. The mountain built a more massive cone 0.25 mile west of the first cone. At its apex, Three Fingered Jack rose to an elevation of perhaps 9000 feet.

In its last major eruptions, perhaps 200,000 years ago, the vent of Three Fingered Jack shifted to a position near the north edge of the existing peak. This new basalt magma solidified as a broad intrusive plug that buttresses the northern flank of the mountain.

Three major glacial periods have affected Three Fingered Jack. They carved away the entire north side of the quiet, dying volcano. Three Fingered Jack, unlike Mount Hood, Jefferson, and Three Sisters, could not produce enough volume to replace what glaciers had carved away. The peak we see today is only a skeletal relict of a major volcano.

THREE SISTERS

The Three Sisters are the most popular and accessible portion of the High Cascades. They are also the most geologically complex. Although eruption of the Three Sisters area began about 5 million years ago, the peaks we see today were all built during the last third of the Pleistocene. The oldest—and most glacially eroded—volcanoes of the Three Sisters area include The Wife, The Husband, Black Crater, and Broken Top. To the north, Belknap Crater (Hike 47) and Sand Mountain (Hike 42) mark vents less than 3000 years old.

North Sister began its eruptions 300,000 years ago. It started as a small shield volcano, then built a larger cinder cone, and finally produced lava and dikes to form today's peak. Yapoah and Collier Cones, basaltic cinder cones just north of the mountain, are among the youngest (less than 5000 years old) eruptive centers in the High Cascades (Hike 46).

Middle Sister, partly submerged in glacial ice and partly carried away by it, is the least accessible and least distinctive—and the most complex—of the Three Sisters. It could never decide which of its siblings it wanted to mimic, so it erupted both basalt, like North Sister, and andesite, like South Sister.

South Sister (Hike 44) began erupting andesite and dacite more than 200,000 years ago. At the end of the Pleistocene, it constructed cinder cones on its summit. Nearby, LeConte and Cayuse Cones erupted less than 9500 years ago (Hike 45). Rock Mesa and Devils Chain are less than 2000 years old. South Sister rests uneasily. A slight but growing bulge and tiny quantities of escaping volcanic gas on its west flank suggest it may erupt in the future.

Mount Bachelor is the youngest major volcano in the Three Sisters area. It is less than 15,000 years old. Mount Bachelor began as a flat shield volcano, then shifted to erupt cinders. Egan Cone, on the west side of Mount Bachelor, is the youngest part of the mountain. It erupted between 8500 and 7000 years

Three Sisters are volcanoes with very different compositions but similar ages. South Sister is likely to erupt in the future.

ago. Lavas from Egan Cone are among the most extensive flows from Mount Bachelor. They form the youngest of the multiple lava dams of Sparks Lake.

MOUNT THIELSEN

Mount Thielsen (Hike 49) is similar to many of the basaltic andesite shields in Oregon's High Cascades. It consists of a central cone built of cindery tuff and coarse breccia. Yellow banding in the volcano's side is the result of iron-rich volcanic glass altered to a clay, called palagonite, made more spectacular by the alteration of glassy tephra to the colorful palagonite. Dikes and sills lace the cone.

Individual lava flows of Mount Thielsen are as much as 300 feet thick. Single lava flows are as thin as a few inches near their vents but thicken to more than 30 feet downslope. Fountaining from dike-fed eruptions around the edge of the cone generated coalescing spatter, which formed many of the flows.

MOUNT MAZAMA AND CRATER LAKE

The deepest lake in Oregon once ranked among the Cascades' highest peaks. Its summit reached at least 11,800 feet, which is higher than today's Mount Hood. But instead of a mountain, Mount Mazama became a hole filled with water—the third-deepest lake in the world, 1932 feet from the waterline to its mysterious bottom.

Mount Mazama first erupted 400,000 years ago in the midst of the Pleistocene (the Ice Age). At least five sizable stratovolcanoes once clustered together in one massive mountain. The oldest of these early volcanoes is called Phantom Cone. Its remnants are exposed low on Dutton Cliff along the south

121

The Phantom Ship, the oldest known remnant of Mount Mazama, dated at about 420,000 years, rises from the southeast part of Crater Lake.

shore of Crater Lake. The Phantom Ship, a ragged vessel of rock at the southeast shore of Crater Lake, is a remnant of the central vent system and feeder dikes for this oldest part of Mount Mazama.

The lavas of Mount Scott, just southeast of Crater Lake, may be the same age (Hike 50). Many other eruptions constructed a very complex mountain. By the end of the Pleistocene, 10,000 years ago, Mount Mazama formed a cluster of overlapping, eroded volcanic cones (Hike 51).

About 7800 years ago, a hundred years before Crater Lake was born, Mount Mazama erupted a viscous, silica-rich lava called *rhyodacite*. The great cliffs at Llao Rock are formed from a single flow that filled its own volcanic crater with at least a quarter cubic mile of hot, silica-rich paste. The last batch of this stuff made it to the surface just days before the climactic eruptions, and is called the Cleetwood Flow. The top of the Cleetwood Flow, on the north side of Crater Lake at Cleetwood Cove, was still soft when the rock fragments from Crater Lake's explosive eruptions hit it.

The climactic eruption of Mount Mazama developed in four stages. It began dramatically with a towering, turbulent plume of coarse ash and hot gas. The first stages of the eruption probably resembled Mount St. Helens's 1980 eruption.

In the second phase, the ongoing eruption enlarged the vent. The towering column began to collapse. Ash flows—thick, molten clouds moving at 100 mph with a temperature of 800 degrees Centigrade—blasted from the central vent. This phase of the eruption created the Wineglass *welded tuff* which to-day forms salmon-colored outcrops exposed along the trail to Grotto Cove and the boat dock.

In the third phase, the roof of the chamber began to collapse along a circular system of cracks, from which Crater Lake has inherited its rounded shape. Finally, more ash flows erupted from these cracks—at temperatures of 850 to 970 degrees Centigrade and speeds of 100 to 150 mph. As the eruption emptied the bowels of Mount Mazama, it sucked up the iron-rich basalts in the dregs of the magma chamber. The basalt from the bottom of the chamber now appears as the dark caps on the Pinnacles (Hike 52).

By the end of the eruption, almost 13 cubic miles of once-solid rock had vanished. And in its place was an awesome hole, a classic stratovolcano caldera nearly 4000 feet deep. Wizard Island and Merriam Cone, a smaller volcano on the north floor of the caldera, have erupted since the climactic caldera collapse. Hot springs and geothermal prospects also indicate that the heat of an active volcano has not been completely shut off.

Today, Crater Lake harbors the most tantalizingly inaccessible geology in the Cascades. Precipitous cliffs archive its history. Crater Lake's national park status permits hiking off road and off trail, but also discourages such use with good reason: hazards to human life as well as to the spectacular geology and a fragile alpine ecosystem.

Llao Rock, a 7800-year-old dacite, is among the last lava flows produced before Mount Mazama's cataclysmic eruption.

STRATOVOLCANOES AND SHIELD VOLCANOES

When you think of a volcano, the first image that comes to mind is probably a stratovolcano. Mount Hood. Mount St. Helens. Mount Rainier. Mount Fuji. Stratovolcanoes, sometimes called composite cones, are the classic peaks on continental margins and above subduction zones.

Eruptions of lava and ash tend to alternate in stratovolcanoes. They may erupt any kind of lava. Most produce basalt early in their history, then andesite for the bulk of their lives, and finally, like Mount St. Helens, produce explosive eruptions of silica-rich dacites and rhyodacite late in their lives. Stratovolcanoes thrive on variety: a lava here, a mudflow there, an eruption of cinders, and an eruption of ash. Most eruptions build only a small portion of the cone, although some, especially ash, may blanket the whole volcano—and the surrounding landscape.

Shield volcanoes are far more single-minded. They erupt mostly basalt. Their low-slung profiles may look more like a puddle of cold molasses than a volcano. But shield volcanoes are every bit as famous. Mauna Loa. Newberry. And in the Cascades, Mount Sheridan,

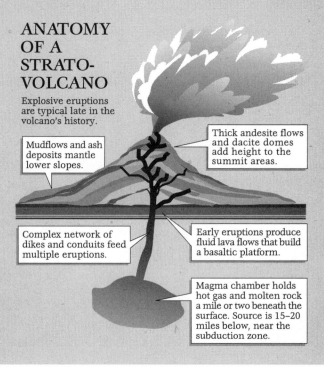

ANATOMY OF A STRATO-VOLCANO

Explosive eruptions are typical late in the volcano's history.

Mudflows and ash deposits mantle lower slopes.

Thick andesite flows and dacite domes add height to the summit areas.

Complex network of dikes and conduits feed multiple eruptions.

Early eruptions produce fluid lava flows that build a basaltic platform.

Magma chamber holds hot gas and molten rock a mile or two beneath the surface. Source is 15–20 miles below, near the subduction zone.

and the base of Mount Bachelor. Shield volcanoes are interplanetary, if not intergalactic, too. The largest known shield volcano is on Mars: Olympus Mons, with a diameter of 370 miles and a summit elevation of 16 miles.

RAMONA FALLS AND SANDY GLACIER VOLCANO

Hike 36

Hike to a scenic waterfall and find the remnants of Mount Hood's predecessor.

DISTANCE ▪ **11 miles round trip**
ELEVATION ▪ **3000–6285 feet**
DIFFICULTY ▪ **Moderate to Ramona Falls; strenuous to Sandy Glacier volcano viewpoint**
TOPOGRAPHIC MAPS ▪ **Mount Hood South, Mount Hood North**
GEOLOGIC MAPS ▪ **22–24**
FEES/REGULATIONS ▪ **Northwest Forest Pass required for trailhead parking.**
PRECAUTIONS ▪ **None**
INFORMATION ▪ **Mount Hood Visitor Information Center: (503) 622-4822**

Directions: To reach the trailhead, from Zigzag on US Highway 26 take USFS Road 18 north about 4.5 miles past Riley Campground to USFS Road 1825. Drive about 1.8 miles and park in the oversized parking lot.

About the Landscape: The relict of the Sandy Glacier volcano protrudes from the west slopes of Mount Hood like a joey peeking from mother kangaroo's pouch. The Sandy Glacier volcano's vent area is exposed as dark orange-brown rocks hidden in the head of the Muddy Creek and Sandy River canyons. Like Hood, the Sandy Glacier volcano was a stratovolcano. Unlike Hood, which has erupted mostly andesite, the Sandy Glacier volcano erupted mostly basalt.

The crags near Mount Hood's summit are easily visible on this hike. They provide proof of Hood's volcanic virility. At Hot Rocks near Hood's summit, boiling water and sulfur-laden gas still escape. Crater Rock, the large knob above Timberline Lodge, is a dacite dome, site of the last major Hood eruption in the 1790s.

Ramona Falls, a scenic waterfall along the way, plunges over an early Pleistocene lava flow that helped form the base of Mount Hood.

Trail Guide: The trail follows a former road, now converted to a hiking trail. Take spur road 1825–100 (Trail 770) to the Ramona Falls (Trail 797) trailhead.

Ramona Falls tumbles over moss-draped andesite at the western base of Mount Hood.

Trail 797 splits, one leg going up the east side of the canyon, the other the west. Take one going up and return along the other. Both explore the stunted forest of lodgepole pine—a disturbance specialist—growing on the Old Maid mudflow of 1782. The western path follows a picturesque andesite cliff that forms the base of Yocum Ridge—and Ramona Falls. The trails meet at the base of Ramona Falls, 2.1 miles into the hike.

At Ramona Falls, the hike joins the Timberline Trail and the Pacific Crest Trail (PCT). The PCT rises up Yocum Ridge through fern-draped forest to the junction with the Yocum Ridge Trail in 0.6 mile. For the best view of Sandy Glacier volcano, continue on the PCT rather than taking the Yocum Ridge spur trail.

The PCT ambles through forest for 2.4 miles, reaching the Muddy Fork at a clearing that permits an outstanding view of the exhumed remnants of the Sandy Glacier volcano as well as the younger vents near Mount Hood's summit. A 1-mile, slow hike up the Muddy Fork and a scrambling climb over talus brings you to the basalt outcrops at the base of Sandy Glacier volcano.

The return route retraces the path along Muddy Fork and the PCT (also called Timberline Trail here) to Ramona Falls. From here, return to the trailhead on the path you didn't hike in on.

TIMBERLINE TRAIL: CLOUD CAP TO TIMBERLINE LODGE

Hike 37

Explore the andesites of Mount Hood and the ghost forests created by Mount Hood's eruption in 1781-82.

DISTANCE ■ 13 miles one way

ELEVATION ■ 4900–8600 feet

DIFFICULTY ■ Moderate to strenuous

TOPOGRAPHIC MAPS ■ Mount Hood South, Mount Hood North

GEOLOGIC MAPS ■ 22–24

FEES/REGULATIONS ■ Northwest Forest Pass required for trailhead parking.

PRECAUTIONS ■ This hike requires a shuttle vehicle at Timberline Lodge. Because of its length, it's best done as an overnight backpack.

INFORMATION ■ Mount Hood Visitor Information Center: (503) 622-4822

Directions: To reach the Cloud Cap trailhead, on Highway 35 14 miles south of Hood River, take the Parkdale exit. At an intersection marked by a blinking light just east of Parkdale, continue straight on Cooper Spur Road, which becomes USFS Road 3512 and reaches the trailhead in about 24 miles.

About the Landscape: One of the most provocative places on Mount Hood lies a mile above Mount Hood Meadows. On this ridge east of the White River, skeletal stumps of whitebark pine convey the agony of their deaths in Mount Hood's eruption in the winter of 1781–82. Like the trees felled more recently by Mount St. Helens, these aged stumps lie parallel, tops pointed away from the mountain's violent blast, weather-beaten roots grasping only air. This eruption of Mount Hood emanated from Crater Rock, a stubby pinnacle—geologically, a dacite plug dome—on the south side of Hood's summit. The force that felled this forest was a hot, dense ash cloud, with temperatures above 700 degrees Centigrade (about 1250 degrees Fahrenheit). Based on the size and form of the trees it felled, its speed has been calculated at 84 mph.

A related ghost forest of fir and pine, now emerging as jagged stumps, is buried in the ash and mudflows of White River canyon.

On the northeast slopes of Mount Hood, Cooper Spur provides an unforgettable view of Eliot Glacier. Eliot is the largest glacier in Oregon. From Cooper Spur you can study the crevasse system and, on a hot August day, listen to the ice groan and crack.

Bleached stumps of trees killed in Mount Hood's last major eruption in 1781–82

Trail Guide: The rocky outcrops at the campground and parking area are andesite, and they provide a first-class view of Mount Hood, Eliot Glacier, Langrille Glacier, and Langrille Crags—the shattered relics of andesite flows.

Take the Timberline Trail south toward Timberline Lodge, heading straight out of the small campground at Cloud Cap through a forest and nicely banded rhyodacite boulders, and skirting the east *moraine* of Eliot Glacier before climbing through a small forest of stunted lodgepole to the Cooper Spur Trail, 1 mile from the trailhead.

The Cooper Spur Trail turns west from the Timberline Trail and climbs steadily across *pumice* and moraine for about 2.3 miles. In early summer, be prepared to cross extensive snowfields on your way up this ridge. The hikers' trail ends at the edge of Newton Clark Glacier's snowfield at about 8600 feet. This windy vantage point provides a tutorial in the complexity of glacial crevasses—and the complexity of glacial noises. The Chimney, a horned crag of dacite and pyroclastic rocks (fragmented rock explosively ejected by a volcano) near Hood's east summit, hovers above. Hood's summit rocks are crumbly and seamed with yellow. They have been altered by steam and sulfur-rich gas over thousands of years. Return the 2.3 miles to the Timberline Trail and rejoin it to continue south and west.

From its junction with the Cooper Spur Trail, the highest part of Timberline Trail crosses a treeless plain of pumice and glacial outwash. It crosses several snowfields, rounds Lambertson Butte, teeters along the brink of Gnarl Ridge and Newton Creek, and dives into Newton Creek's layered canyon, 3.6 miles from the Cooper Spur Trail junction.

On the west side of the Newton Creek canyon, the Timberline Trail crosses rugged and more forested terrain. Good campsites can be found in the headwaters of Heather Canyon, 7.5 miles from Cloud Cap campground. The Timberline Trail ducks beneath the ski lifts of Mount Hood Meadows Ski Area before crossing a Mount Hood Meadows access road and intersecting the Umbrella Falls Trail (Trail 667), where more campsites can be found at 8.9 miles from Cloud Cap.

The forest of whitebark pine killed in the 1781–82 eruption of Mount Hood lies off the Timberline Trail about 0.5 mile above (north of) the Umbrella Falls Trail intersection, at elevations above 7000 feet. Walk across open slopes to these trees, which make Hood's eruptive potential seem very, very real.

Continuing on to Timberline Lodge, now only 4 miles away, the trail crosses the White River canyon. This river is treacherous to cross in the spring and early to midsummer. The White River carves its steep and unstable canyon through ash and mudflows. The layers in the canyon wall are layers of ash, cinders, and mudflows unleashed by the pulses of eruptions two centuries ago. The river is excavating a forest of twisted Douglas-fir stumps, buried by the 1781–82 eruption, from a layer near the canyon bottom. These trees can be viewed from the Lost Forest overlook area.

It is an easy 0.6 mile from the west edge of the White River canyon to Timberline Lodge, where the Timberline and Pacific Crest Trails coincide.

Hike

38

LOST CREEK NATURE TRAIL

Explore the Old Maid mudflows of the most recent eruption of Mount Hood and a lost forest exhumed along Lost Creek.

DISTANCE ▪ 0.5-mile loop

ELEVATION ▪ 2310–2320 feet

DIFFICULTY ▪ Easy

TOPOGRAPHIC MAPS ▪ Government Camp, Bull Run Lake

GEOLOGIC MAPS ▪ 22–24

FEES/REGULATIONS ▪ Northwest Forest Pass required for trailhead parking.

PRECAUTIONS ▪ None

INFORMATION ▪ Mount Hood Visitor Information Center: (503) 622-4822

Directions: From US Highway 26 at Zigzag, turn north onto Lolo Pass Road (USFS Road 18) and continue 4 miles. Turn east on USFS Road 1825. Lost Creek

A cedar stump, exhumed from a mudflow that buried it in the winter of 1781-82, stands in the midst of Lost Creek.

Picnic Area and the trail are 2.2 miles along USFS Road 1825.

About the Landscape: In the middle of Lost Creek, where it borders the trail as well as farther down, rise huge, jagged-topped stumps. In an old-growth forest where large trees and stumps are normal, this situation at first appears quite ordinary—except that trees don't usually grow in the middle of streams.

These stumps are all that remain of trees buried by mudflows during Mount Hood's 1781–82 eruption (the hot, viscous mud prevented the stumps from rotting). The tops of many of these "very old"-growth trees have been snapped off, suggesting that, like the 1980 eruption of Mount St. Helens, the last big eruption of Mount Hood produced explosive blasts as well as speedy mudflows.

Trail Guide: This self-guided, handicapped-accessible trail leads through an old-growth forest stand of cedar and Douglas fir that was largely spared from

catastrophic forest fires of 1893 and 1906. The paved trail passes signed interpretive sites about beaver ponds, wetlands, and forests before threading its way
back to the parking lot.

TABLE ROCK, MOLALLA

*Take a close-up view of the Western Cascades' younger rocks and
the oldest basalts of the High Cascades.*

DISTANCE ▪ **5.2 miles round trip**

ELEVATION ▪ **3625–4880 feet**

DIFFICULTY ▪ **Moderate**

TOPOGRAPHIC MAP ▪ **Rooster Rock**

GEOLOGIC MAP ▪ **1**

PRECAUTIONS ▪ **Beware of cliffs at the summit!**

INFORMATION ▪ **Salem Bureau of Land Management: (503) 375-5646**

Directions: From Oregon Highway 211 in Molalla, turn south on South Mathias
Road, then turn left on South Feyrer Park Road. About 1.7 miles up this road,
cross the Molalla River bridge and turn right on South Dickey Prairie Road. In
5.3 miles cross the river again, then bear left on South Molalla Road, remaining on pavement. After almost 13 miles, bear left on gravel Middle Fork Road.
Then in 2.6 miles, turn right onto Table Rock Road. From this junction drive
5.8 miles to the poorly marked trailhead on the right side of the road.

About the Landscape: Table Rock and Rooster Rock rise above the Molalla
River drainage. This dual-summited plateau is composed of two ages of rocks.
The base of Table Rock is formed of 17- to 10-million-year-old andesites. These
rocks probably once were part of a stratovolcano between Estacada and Mill
City. Today they appear only in a few roadcuts and stream banks.

Basalt forms the summit of Table Rock and Rooster Rock. It may be associated with the High Cascades. Its age is about 4 million years.

Trail Guide: The trail penetrates a forest of large Douglas fir and substantial
understory as it climbs toward the broad summit. This vegetation obscures the
older Western Cascades that form the base of Table and Rooster Rocks. At 1.2
miles the trail emerges from the forest and navigates a talus slope at the base
of a 150-foot-high cliff of columnar basalt. This is the younger basalt that forms
the summit of Table and Rooster Rocks. The well-developed columns and thickness of the flow suggest it is a basalt flow from one of the early High Cascades
shield volcanoes that flowed down a canyon of the ancestral Molalla River
about 4 million years ago.

At 2.1 miles the trail reaches a saddle and a junction. Turn left for the 0.5-mile hike north to the top of Table Rock. (For an optional 1.7-mile [one way] side trip to Rooster Rock, turn right.) From the top of Table Rock—an outcrop of relatively old High Cascades basalt—there are picture-perfect views of Mount Hood, Mount Jefferson, and the wrinkled Western Cascades.

Hike 40 ROOSTER ROCK, MENAGERIE WILDERNESS (VIA THE TROUT CREEK TRAIL)

Peer into the eroded throat of an ancient Cascade volcano.

DISTANCE ▪ **6.6 miles round trip**

ELEVATION ▪ **1240–3567 feet**

DIFFICULTY ▪ **Difficult**

TOPOGRAPHIC MAP ▪ **Upper Soda**

GEOLOGIC MAP ▪ **1**

PRECAUTIONS ▪ **Northwest Forest Pass required for trailhead parking.**

INFORMATION ▪ **Sweet Home Ranger District, Willamette National Forest: (541) 367-5168**

Getting there: From Interstate 5 at Albany, take exit 233 and follow US Highway 20 east 49 miles to Trout Creek Campground on the right (south) side of the highway. Continue just past the entry road, and about 0.1 mile past the campground entrance look for a small pullout and Trout Creek trailhead on the left (north) shoulder of the highway.

About the landscape: This hike takes you into one of the most bizarre landscapes of the Western Cascades—the long vanished and deeply eroded predecessors of the modern range of volcanoes. These once-powerful volcanoes erupted from about 38 to 20 million years ago and produced great volumes of ash (today found in the Painted Hills, see hike 76) as well as powerful mudflows and smaller quantities of basalt. Today all that is left of these vents are spires, such as Tidbits Mountain on the McKenzie River and Iron Mountain, 20 miles west of Rooster Rock. The oddly shaped plugs and spires of the Menagerie Wilderness, including Rooster Rock, are remnants of Oligocene debris flows, mudflows, ash flows, and a few lava flows, as well as a major vent system that was active about 30 million years ago. Ash that erupted here blew east and is found today as the red and ochre bands in the Painted Hills near Mitchell and the gray-green cliffs of the John Day Fossil Beds near Dayville.

Trail Guide: This is a steep and difficult climb, but the view into an ancient volcanic landscape is well worth it. (For a somewhat easier but still scenic 3.4-mile round-trip trek into a more subdued topography, hike the Iron Mountain Trail, which begins near Tombstone Pass, 15 miles east on US Highway 20.) The trail begins at a scramble and then gets steeper, maintaining a steep and steady pace for 2.8 miles. This part of the trip navigates old-growth forest and climbs through a mostly Douglas fir and hemlock stand splotched with rhododendrons and an undergrowth of salal and sword ferns. There are few rocks here, and your principal view will be of the trail immediately in front of you. Take time to enjoy the showy, blooming rhododendrons in the late spring—the best time to take this trail on.

At 2 miles, the trail joins the even rockier and rougher path to the summit of Rooster Rock. The trail continues to steepen in the last mile to the summit. The bedrock here is composed of old Western Cascade mudflows. These rocks, and the soils that develop from them, provide little moisture for vegetation. Look for occasional madrone trees that attest to the quickly draining substrate.

The summit of Rooster Rock provides a great view into an eroded vent complex of a large and long-lived, 30-million-year-old volcano. Many of the spires are composed of multiple blocks of ancient scoria that are glued together with lava and ash. This zone of broken rocks—called *vent agglomerate*—attests to the explosiveness of the eruptions. It's believed that the ancient volcano's summit rose another 3000 feet. Just try to imagine it as you gaze upward. Return as you came.

Hike
41

JEFFERSON PARK VIA SOUTH BREITENBUSH TRAIL

Examine the tracks of the High Cascades' fast-fading glaciers.

DISTANCE ■ **13 miles round trip**

ELEVATION ■ **3200–6040 feet**

DIFFICULTY ■ **Difficult**

TOPOGRAPHIC MAPS ■ **Mount Bruno, Mount Jefferson**

GEOLOGIC MAP ■ **1**

PRECAUTIONS ■ **Northwest Forest Pass required for trailhead parking. Campsites are regulated in this very popular area. Call ahead to determine whether entry permits are required.**

INFORMATION ■ **Detroit Ranger District, Willamette National Forest: (503) 854-3366**

Getting There: From Salem, follow Oregon Highway 22 about 35 miles east to Detroit. Turn left (north) on Breitenbush Road (USFS Road 46). Drive 11

Mount Jefferson and the Jefferson Park Glacier tower above the headwaters of the South Breitenbush River.

miles, and turn right on USFS Road 4685. Drive 4 miles and turn right into the trailhead parking area. Walk along USFS Road 4685 0.2 mile from the parking area to the well-marked trailhead.

About the landscape: Mount Jefferson is a volcano that courageously erupted while swathed in Pleistocene glaciers. Many of the andesite promontories near the peak, including Table Mountain on the north side and Park Butte on the south, are products of those eruptions. Despite Mount Jefferson's efforts to rebuild what the glaciers wore away, the volcano quieted before the last Pleistocene glacial advance 30,000–20,000 years ago. Glaciers of this period wore away much of the mountain's summit area, carved out the lovely basin at The Park, and left polished and grooved andesite bedrock and a variety of boulders to augment the subalpine landscape. The last, fast-fading relics of glacial ice on Mount Jefferson can be seen from The Park. Russell and Jefferson Park Glaciers occupy the north side, and the larger, Whitewater Glacier is perched on the mountain's northeasterly flank.

134

Trail Guide: The hike to Jefferson Park, one of the High Cascades's most scenic spots, is deservedly popular. Lakes and water abound in the alpine landscape. Expect to meet other hikers, even in the off-season. Much of the area is in recovery from past overuse, and campfires are banned. So here, especially, go lightly on the land.

From the trailhead, the South Breitenbush Trail begins an evenly paced, but unrepentant, climb. In the first 2 miles, the path encounters several seasonal creeks, which may be dry late in the fall. At 1.6 miles, the Bear Point Trail turns left; continue slightly right on the South Breitenbush Trail. In about a half mile, the fir and hemlock forest thins as you reach 5000 feet near the base of Park Butte. This butte marks an andesite flow that made little progress as it erupted beneath a cover of ice about 370,000 years ago. The trail here follows a reliable stream around the southern base of the butte.

Once you reach the high ground at 5700 feet, you'll find cedars and small wetlands. There are a few tiny ponds—most of which are now silted-in marshes. The trail hugs the edge of Park Butte, and you can find a number of outcrops (andesites) that provide a nice view of the South Breitenbush River's glacially carved gorge. The trail makes a quick plunge into a small, forested basin, where glacial ice carved out a small tarn. It then climbs out again to find the Pacific Crest Trail and Russell Lake at the base of Mount Jefferson, 5.5 miles from the trailhead.

This is the portal to Jefferson Park. Subalpine firs grow on rock-clad islands amid spongy alpine meadows. After a long hike on gravelly trails, you can exult in the softer footing. Four thousand feet above you are Whitewater Glacier and Jefferson's craggy summit—an andesite flow that resisted glacial erosion and forms a knob near the mountain's summit.

Most of Jefferson's main edifice as well as the rocks that rise just south and east of Jefferson Park are a slightly darker and more crumbly rock than the light gray rocks of Park Butte. Known as the Main Cone Flows, these rocks are basaltic andesites, and most date to more than 200,000 years ago. They covered the first generations of Jefferson's eruptions—a mostly explosive phase that produced ash, scoria, and pumice. These older rocks are exposed today above Russell Glacier.

Turn right at the PCT and follow it about a half mile to Scout Lake at the south edge of Jefferson Park. Look for glacial striations—polished rock and small parallel grooves cut by the rocks held in the bottom of a moving glacier—on the bedrock here. You can scramble farther up toward the Jefferson Park Glacier and explore the remnants of Jefferson's basaltic-andesitic eruptions. Or explore the North Complex—the glaciated and eroded feeder dikes and remnants of a large basaltic vent on the north side of The Park. Return as you came.

SAND MOUNTAIN CINDER CONES

Explore a cinder cone with a lookout on the top.

DISTANCE ■ 1 mile round trip

ELEVATION ■ 5200–5390 feet

DIFFICULTY ■ Easy

TOPOGRAPHIC MAP ■ Santiam Junction

GEOLOGIC MAPS ■ 1, 25

FEES/REGULATIONS ■ Northwest Forest Pass required for trailhead parking.

PRECAUTIONS ■ The Old Santiam Wagon Road and surrounding area swarms with dirt bikes (motorcycles) especially on summer weekends. Watch for fast-moving bikes from all directions! Hiking off trail is prohibited at Sand Mountain.

INFORMATION ■ Sisters Ranger District, Deschutes National Forest: (541) 549-7700

Directions: From Sisters, drive 20 miles west on US Highway 20/Oregon State Route 126 to Santiam Pass. Turn left (south) at the entrance to Hoodoo Ski Bowl (marked also for Big Lake) and drive 3.1 miles on the paved road. Just before you reach Big Lake, turn right on a sandy gravel road (Old Santiam Wagon Road) and follow the main, most worn track 2.8 miles to the road that leads up toward the Sand Mountain lookout. Turn left and follow this road 1.7 miles up to a parking area with a trail that continues 0.5 mile to the summit. The lookout on top is staffed during the summer and fall.

About the Landscape: Some of the most stunning landscapes are the most austere. Sand Mountain, a 3000-year-old cinder cone that, along with others in the area, produced lava flows found at nearby Santiam Pass is a classic example of a cinder cone. En route to Sand Mountain you'll pass Hoodoo and Hayrick Buttes. Both are flat-topped outcroppings of andesite that erupted beneath glacial ice and never made much progress either upward or outward.

Trail Guide: On this short hike to the summit of Sand Mountain you'll find a classical cinder cone crater, as well as small *volcanic bombs* and scoria. Trails lead around the crater rim and duck into the crater.

Sand Mountain is one of an assorted collection of cinder cones—feel free to explore the many cones in this area—there are no formal trails except the path to the lookout. These cones are significant in Cascade geology because this cinder cone, and the twenty-two other cinder cones and forty-one vents in the Sand Mountain "range," erupted lavas that blocked and diverted the original

Mount Washington appears beyond the summit of Sand Mountain.

channel of the McKenzie River, creating Sahalie Falls (a good stop, along Highway 22). Similar flows from nearby Nash Crater dammed the river creating a clear lake and also are responsible for the jagged fields of *aa* lavas (a Hawaiian term for lavas that look like crumb-cakes, with broken or fractured pieces of the flow on their surface) at Santiam Junction, where US Highway 20 and Oregon State Route 22 meet. While signs prohibit extensive hiking and disturbance of Sand Mountain's summit, there are many smaller cinder cones to the west that invite off-trail exploration.

METOLIUS RIVER HEADWATERS

Hike 43

Visit a river that springs from the base of an ancient and unglaciated High Cascades volcano.

DISTANCE ■ **12 miles round trip**

ELEVATION ■ **2730–2880 feet**

DIFFICULTY ■ **Easy**

TOPOGRAPHIC MAPS ■ **Candle Creek, Prairie Farm Spring**

GEOLOGIC MAP ■ **30**

FEES/REGULATIONS ■ **Northwest Forest Pass required for trailhead parking.**

PRECAUTIONS ■ **Cold and swift, the Metolius River is a dangerous place to swim.**

INFORMATION ■ **Sisters Ranger District, Deschutes National Forest: (541) 549-7700**

Directions: From Sisters, drive 9 miles west to milepost 91 on US Highway 20. Turn right (north) on USFS Road 14 and continue 3 miles to the Metolius

The Metolius River's sources are springs at the base of Black Butte, making the Metolius one of Oregon's coldest, swiftest, and cleanest streams.

Headwaters turnout. Park and walk the 100-yard-long trail to the headwaters, then continue for a much more pleasant hike along the river.

From the headwaters parking area, continue 2 miles to USFS Road 1420, marked "Campgrounds." Bear left on Road 1420, following it 2.9 miles to the Canyon Creek Campground entry road, USFS Road 400. Drive 0.8 mile to the trailhead at the end of the loop and park in the designated trailhead parking area. There is no trail connection, unfortunately, to the Metolius headwaters.

About the Landscape: The Metolius River literally springs from the ground beneath Black Butte. The river's abrupt emergence—it actually is fed by several large springs and spring-fed streams but is reputed to emerge from a single major location—is likely due to groundwater that follows an old fracture system beneath Black Butte, a long-inactive 1.4-million-year-old, unglaciated High Cascade volcano. The Metolius is among Oregon's purest rivers and also the shortest, with a length of only 28.6 miles from its source springs to its entry into Lake Billy Chinook—a reservoir on the Deschutes River.

Trail Guide: The Metolius River emerges from springs at the base of Black Butte, a symmetrical volcanic cone that is more than a million years in age. The riverbank trails are practically flat by any hiking measure. Mountain bikes, horses, and many other distractions are banned.

The hike from the lower part of the Canyon Creek Campground follows the west bank of the Metolius closely. It follows the river around a sharp meander, switching directions from almost due south to due north in the first 0.5 mile. About 0.5 mile down the path, several highly productive springs gush water into the river on the opposite bank, creating small waterfalls. From here, the well-worn trail threads along the bank through a narrowing gorge, while the stream frolics through a set of riffles and small rapids, and rushes past several

138

small islands at 1.7 miles into the hike. The river's histrionics culminate in 3-foot-high Wizard Falls at 2.5 miles downstream from the trailhead.

The trail encounters springs and small wetland areas that provide cooling breaks along this stretch where the river is not very accessible. In another 0.2 mile the path enters the Wizard Falls Fish Hatchery parking area. The hatchery, if you like hatcheries, offers an interesting tour.

For a longer hike, continue on the east bank trail for another 3.2 miles. This trail follows the river closely for most of its distance. Although the stream is often obscured by vine maple and small conifers, a quick plunge through the vegetation will bring you to streamside for a scenic break. At 3.5 miles from its start at Canyon Creek Campground, the east bank trail moves away from the river, veering around a piece of private property and crossing the neck of a meander loop. In another 0.5 mile, the path returns to the riverbank and remains close to the stream for its remaining length.

At Lower Bridge, 3.2 miles from the Wizard Falls Fish Hatchery, cross the river and return along the west bank for a change of scenery. The landscape is more open on this trail and the ponderosa pines are perhaps more in their element of flat-sloped, dry-footed, and sunny ground. Remember to cross the stream at Wizard Falls, returning to the west bank where your vehicle awaits at the trailhead.

SOUTH SISTER SUMMIT

Explore this stratovolcano, Le Conte Crater, and Rock Mesa, as well as the pumice desert of Wickiup Plain.

DISTANCE ■ **12.6 miles round trip**

ELEVATION ■ **5446–10,358 feet**

DIFFICULTY ■ **Strenuous**

TOPOGRAPHIC MAP ■ **South Sister**

GEOLOGIC MAPS ■ **27, 28**

FEES/REGULATIONS ■ **Northwest Forest Pass required for trailhead parking.**

PRECAUTIONS ■ **Although no technical skill is required for the climb to South Sister's summit, the last mile is arduous; allow time. Also be aware that weather changes abruptly on the mountain. A special permit may be required to camp at Moraine Lake.**

INFORMATION ■ **Bend–Fort Rock Ranger District, Deschutes National Forest: (541) 383-4000**

Directions: To reach the trailhead, from Bend take the Cascades Lakes Highway (Century Drive) west 25 miles to Sparks Lake. Continue 3 miles west of

Sparks Lake, where the Devils Lake Campground turnoff appears on the left. At the north end of the parking area for Devils Lake Campground, the trailhead is marked "South Sister/Moraine Lake/Climbers Summit Trail."

About the Landscape: The closer one approaches South Sister, the more apparent it becomes that this, like all stratovolcanoes, is not a simple cone. South Sister is a jumble of domes, andesite flows, feeder dikes, and cinder cones that looks like it was assembled by a committee. Glaciers have quarried away the older, softer rocks, with the exception of the dual summit cinder cones. But they were erupted after glaciers ceased to be a serious threat 8000 or 9000 years ago.

The rough-coated rocky features on South Sister's east and west flanks represent the youngest eruptions in this area. Rock Mesa to the west and Devils Hill to the east are dated between 1800 and 2600 years. The pumice that veneers the landscape around South Sister and Broken Top came from the eruption of these domes, which are composed of rhyodacite. This viscous lava cools quickly, creating the glassy rock called obsidian. Le Conte Crater to the west and Cayuse Cone to the east are basalt cinder cones at least 2500 years old. Both erupted basalt lavas from their base.

South Sister is seemingly poised to erupt again sometime soon (geologically), perhaps within this decade. The US Geological Survey has detected and measured a growing bulge on the mountain's western flank about 3 miles from South Sister's summit. While this uplift amounts to only an inch per year, the swelling is geologically significant. Analyses of the air in the vicinity of the bulge also suggest that the mountain is venting minute amounts of volcanic gasses here.

Trail Guide: The Moraine Lake/Climbers Summit Trail leads through a wetland area, crosses the Cascades Highway, and rises through a moss-festooned forest. At about 1.75 miles, the trail climbs steeply and exits the forest, permitting views of South Sister, Broken Top, and the Devils Hill chain of domes to the east. Just beyond the crest, at about 2 miles, the trail intersects the trail to Wickiup Plain and Le Conte Crater (to the west); stay on the Moraine Lake/Climbers Summit Trail. At the next trail junction in 0.3 mile, the Moraine Lake Trail parts company with the Climbers Summit Trail; continue north on the unmarked Climbers Summit Trail. (The Moraine Lake Trail shortly begins a descent to Moraine Lake, a good spot for an overnight camp if you want to make a day-long, leisurely ascent of South Sister.)

Continue north on the Climbers Summit Trail. You can view Rock Mesa and Le Conte Crater by exploring along the west edge of this andesite plateau. The trail continues north for an easy 1.1-mile walk to the base of the South Sister cone. The trail is paved with pumice erupted from Rock Mesa and Devils Hill domes. As you approach South Sister and the Rock Mesa vent to the northwest, this pumice deposit thickens, forming hummocks that resemble low sand dunes.

Rock Mesa was produced by one of South Sister's most recent eruptions, about 1800 years ago.

From the base of the cone to the top, the trail rises 3600 feet in about 2 miles. At the base of South Sister the trail winds through a gray, platy-jointed andesite flow, then climbs 200 steep feet to glassy outcrops of flow-banded rhyodacite. The rock glistens like gray obsidian. It is part of a young dome— a blister of thick lava that never developed into a flow. The rounded gray or pinkish globs and some of the holes in this rock are frozen gas bubbles.

Above the rhyodacite flow at an elevation of 7200 feet, the trail clambers over glacially polished rhyodacite and crawls around a wall of rock. This outcrop is part of a large andesite vent system on the volcano's south flank. In the cliff to the east of the trail, columnar joints at the bottom swirl into platy joints at the top, preserving the downslope direction of the erupting lava flow.

Above this vent system, the trail traverses the upper cinder cone of South Sister. Hiking is slow because of the loose cinders and the steep trail. The hike to the summit (10,358 feet) skirts Lewis Glacier and edges around South Sister's summit crater. From the top, you can enjoy exceptional views of the adjacent peaks. Chambers Lakes, glacial tarns in small valleys on the north side of the mountain, are especially scenic. Teardrop Pool, in the summit crater, is Oregon's highest lake.

When you've finished soaking up the view, return to the junction of the Climbers Summit Trail with the Moraine Lake/Wickiup Plain Trail. Turn west toward Le Conte Crater and Wickiup Plain. This trail leads 1 mile to Wickiup Plain. A 0.5-mile stroll across the "pumice desert" brings you to the youngest volcanic features of South Sister: Le Conte Crater, a cinder cone at least 2500 years old, and Rock Mesa, a rhyodacite dome and stubby flow between 1800 and 2600 years old.

At the base of the Rock Mesa flow, an informal path fades in and out around the perimeter, providing close-up views of all the small-scale features of glassy volcanic rocks. The better trail leads 1.2 miles to the top of Rock Mesa and provides a great view of the ponderous flow patterns now frozen in stone. From Rock Mesa an easy 0.5-mile walk leads across the pumice desert of Wickiup Plain to Le Conte Crater. A frozen basalt flow leaks from the base of this 2500-year-old cinder cone.

Retrace your steps about 2 miles from Wickiup Plain to the trail junction with the Climbers Summit Trail; follow the Climbers Summit Trail 2 miles back to the trailhead.

Hike 45 BROKEN TOP: TODD LAKE TO CRATER CREEK

The anatomy of a stratovolcano is magnificently displayed in the ragged maw of Broken Top.

DISTANCE ▪ 14.2 miles round trip
ELEVATION ▪ 5490–7900 feet
DIFFICULTY ▪ Moderate
TOPOGRAPHIC MAPS ▪ Broken Top, Bachelor Butte
GEOLOGIC MAPS ▪ 27–29
FEES/REGULATIONS ▪ Northwest Forest Pass required for trailhead parking.
PRECAUTIONS ▪ None
INFORMATION ▪ Bend–Fort Rock Ranger District, Deschutes National Forest: (541) 383-4000

Directions: To reach the Todd Lake Campground trailhead from Cascade Lakes Highway, turn north at the entrance to the Todd Lake Campground, a gravel road 2 miles west of the Mount Bachelor Ski Area entrance to Todd Lake Campground. Drive approximately 0.5 mile to the parking area for the walk-in campground. The Todd Lake Trail begins at the campground entrance.

About the Landscape: The gray rocks enfolding Todd Lake, where this hike

Broken Top's ragged profile was carved not by violent eruptions but by glaciers.

begins, are the remnant of Todd Lake volcano. Todd Lake volcano is much older than the Three Sisters and Broken Top, and has been virtually erased by glaciers.

Broken Top provides an intimate view of stratovolcano anatomy. Despite its exploded appearance, this cone was ravaged by glaciers, not a cataclysmic eruption. The ragged spires on the northwest are remnants of Broken Top's central volcanic conduit. The layers are alternating ash, lavas, and cinders, each representing a different eruption. The layers thicken, thin, and feather into one another.

Tiny and rapidly vanishing Crook Glacier, cradled in Broken Top's east face, hides behind its imposing moraine like the shriveled Wizard of Oz behind his gilded curtain. Today, the moraine is far more impressive than the withered glacier that built it. The moraine dates to the Little Ice Age in the late seventeenth century. In 1966 glacial meltwater breached the moraine, creating a flood on Crater Creek and carving a wide notch in the moraine's summit.

Trail Guide: From Todd Lake, the trail leads upslope at an even grade, crossing light-colored rhyodacite and topping out after about 1.2 miles. A mantle of pumice from the eruptions of Rock Mesa, Le Conte Crater, and the Devils

Crook Glacier, on Broken Top's east face, has nearly disappeared.

Hill chain of flows and domes covers the ground. The trail offers several enticing previews of Broken Top as it weaves up and down through forests, alpine meadows, and dry pumice flats.

Follow the signs for Soda Springs Trail, which you intersect in about 2.5 miles. Then continue straight (west) on the trail to Broken Top and Green Lakes, crossing Soda Creek and Crater Creek. At the junction in 1.3 miles, where the Green Lakes Trail leaves the Broken Top Trail, turn north onto the Broken Top Trail.

The trail continues for about 0.8 mile to the crossing of Crater Creek. Broken Top beckons hikers from the trail. A 0.5-mile walk along Crater Creek brings an intimate view of the devastated volcano and the boulder-strewn recessional moraine of Crook Glacier. An informal trail leads up the moraine.

Return from Crook Glacier to the Broken Top Trail, where you continue north to the north side of Broken Top in a 0.8-mile walk. Here you will find Bend Glacier and more elegantly exposed layers of ash and volcanic rock, crosscut by feeder dikes. Return as you came.

For a side trip on your return that will extend your hike by about 2 miles, when you reach the junction of the Broken Top and Green Lakes Trails, turn right (west) on the Green Lakes Trail for 1 mile to get a close-up view of Cayuse Crater. The trail takes you across the side of Cayuse Crater, just above the vent for basalt flows. This large cinder cone erupted a little more than 9500 years ago.

YAPOAH AND COLLIER CONES, THREE SISTERS

Hike 46

View some of the High Cascades' youngest lavas and rapidly disappearing Collier Glacier.

DISTANCE ▪ **14.4 miles round trip**

ELEVATION ▪ **5300–7334 feet**

DIFFICULTY ▪ **Moderate**

TOPOGRAPHIC MAPS ▪ **Mount Washington, North Sister, Black Crater, Trout Creek Butte**

GEOLOGIC MAPS ▪ **27, 30**

FEES/REGULATIONS ▪ **Northwest Forest Pass required for trailhead parking.**

PRECAUTIONS ▪ **Weather can deteriorate quickly at high elevations.**

INFORMATION ▪ **Sisters Ranger District, Deschutes National Forest: (541) 549-7700**

Directions: Begin at Lava Camp Lake Campground, approximately 1 mile east of McKenzie Pass on Highway 242 (McKenzie Pass Highway). The trailhead, to the west of the main campground, is marked for the Pacific Crest Trail (PCT).

About the Landscape: The youthful cinder cones at the northern end of the Three Sisters, including Yapoah, Four-in-One, and Collier Cones, are among the youngest vents in the Cascades. And on this hike, you can peer right into their navels.

Yapoah, a Native American term for an isolated hill, is a high-standing cinder cone between North Sister and McKenzie Pass. It erupted between 2900 and 2500 years ago, producing some of the lavas at McKenzie Pass. On Yapoah Cone, these lavas spill from their vent like jumbled bowels from a gash in the earth's fragile belly. This is a wonderful spot to examine lava *gutters*, pressure ridges, and the frozen relics of a volcanic throat. The rock is crumbly, sharp, and piled in unstable mounds.

Collier Cone may be the youngest lava vent in the Oregon Cascades. It erupted sometime between 2500 and 500 years ago. Collier Cone produced lava flows that extend more than 8 miles east. Post-Pleistocene glacial advances of Collier Glacier have almost overridden the cone and deposited glacial erratic boulders on the cone's south shoulder. Collier Glacier, now in full retreat and virtually invisible except for its ghostly moraines, still holds the official title as Oregon's longest glacier.

Trail Guide: This hike is among the most stunningly beautiful and diverse in Oregon's High Cascades—a region chock-full of scenic hikes. It provides two lakes for cooling, close encounters with one of the youngest lava flows in the Cascades, and provides an up-close view of one of the Cascades' longest glaciers—or at least, the moraine-rimmed valley where Collier Glacier used to be. All this in a 7-mile walk on well-maintained and easy-to-follow trails where there are no lung-numbing climbs. What hiker could ask for more?

As always, you'll need to take a few aspects of this hike under advisement. Although you'll visit two large lakes and a reliable spring, there are long open stretches in the last two-thirds of the hike—some that cross dark cinders or lava—that can be very hot, dry going. Not surprisingly, this is a popular route, so expect plenty of other hikers, as well as llama trekkers and horseback riders.

The hike to Mathieu Lakes and Collier Cone begins along a short path that leads generally south through a forest rich in lodgepole pines from the parking area to the PCT—the main thoroughfare for the hike. Signs help point the way to the PCT. At about 0.3 mile the path runs head-on into a dark, crumpled lava flow—and the PCT.

Turn left (south) on the main PCT. Almost immediately, the path veers away from the rugged lava, entering a cool forest of lichen-draped fir and hemlock. It passes through inviting wetlands—these may be dry in the late summer and fall. At 1 mile from the trailhead the path reaches a well-marked junction. There's a small pond just north of this junction, though it is hard to see among the trees. At the junction, the inviting trail to North Mathieu Lake points straight ahead; the less-traveled path that detours around this first lake turns right. The less-traveled path (the PCT!) climbs around North Mathieu Lake on the shoulder of a cinder cone. If you take—or return via—this route, look for red volcanic bombs and aerodynamic cinders along the trail. You can also scoot to the top, where there are more of these to be found.

The trail past North Mathieu Lake (the path straight ahead) leads through dark hemlock and Douglas fir forest, crawling over outcrops and rocks, then tracks along the edge of the lava flow, encountering a tiny forest pond and wetland in 0.5 mile and then switch-backing up to forest-lined North Mathieu Lake 2.2 miles from the beginning of the hike.

The trail tours along the lakeshore, passing a number of designated camping sites. Then it begins a quick, 0.6-mile ascent to South Mathieu Lake. The difference between the settings of the two lakes is stark. North Mathieu Lake, at

From atop Collier Cone, the glacially ravaged remnants of Mount Washington and Three Fingered Jack, as well as the more active Mount Jefferson and Mount Hood are visible.

5795 feet, is surrounded by forest; the much smaller South Mathieu Lake, elevation 6040, sits in a rock-lined subalpine basin, offering a breathtaking view of North Sister and Collier Cone ahead.

At South Mathieu Lake, a trail leads to the east, connecting with Green Lakes basin between Broken Top and South Sister. However, for this hike, keep straight ahead toward Collier Cone and North Sister on the PCT.

From South Mathieu Lake, the PCT navigates across a lava flow for about 0.7 mile, then steps off into a meadow along the barren side of Yapoah Cone and tiptoes over the top of the very vent that, about 2500 years ago, produced the lava that today clogs McKenzie Pass. From the vent, the path leads downslope to a verdant meadow and another side trail that leads northwest toward Four-in One Cone, about 1 mile to the west.

Follow the PCT south. At 6 miles from the trailhead where you started, and 0.5 mile from the Four-in-One intersection, the trail reaches Minnie Scott Spring, usually a reliable source of backpacker's water.

From the spring, the trail rounds a bend and heads for Collier Cone. About 7 miles into the hike, the PCT climbs to Opie Dildock Pass on the north flank of Collier Cone. This is an inviting place to explore the varied sculptings that lava and cinders can produce. A short climb to the top or south side of Collier Cone's red cinders provides a view of rapidly shrinking Collier Glacier, and the huge gravel moraines it left behind.

To visit the Obsidian Cliffs area, from Opie Dildock Pass, continue another 3 miles southwest on the PCT, then turn right on Trail 3528 at Obsidian Falls and travel west 2 miles to a lava flow and cliffs. Note that this is a popular area, and a special permit is required for hiking and camping in the Obsidian Falls–Obsidian Cliffs area. From Opie Dildock Pass (or the Obsidian Cliffs area if you choose to extend your hike) return as you came, or for variety, at South Mathieu Lake, continue straight on the PCT rather than dropping to North Mathieu Lake. This trail follows the side of a volcanic cinder cone, providing great views and cooler air (but more sun) than the route past North Mathieu Lake, and glimpses of a few volcanic bombs on the trailside. In 2.1 miles from South Mathieu Lake the route meets the North Mathieu Lake Trail. Here, continue along the PCT, returning as you came to the trailhead.

Hike 47 LAVA RIVER TRAIL AND LITTLE BELKNAP CRATER

Explore the desolate, rubbly lava fields of McKenzie Pass.

DISTANCE ■ 0.5 mile, Lava River Trail; 3.8 miles round trip, Little Belknap Crater/PCT

ELEVATION ■ 5350–6250 feet

DIFFICULTY ■ Easy to moderate

TOPOGRAPHIC MAP ■ Mount Washington

GEOLOGIC MAPS ■ 27, 30

FEES/REGULATIONS ■ Northwest Forest Pass required for trailhead parking.

PRECAUTIONS ■ This rugged trail is unshaded to Little Belknap Crater.

INFORMATION ■ Sisters Ranger District, Deschutes National Forest: (541) 549-7700

Directions: From Sisters, drive 14.5 miles west toward McKenzie Pass on Oregon Highway 242. The Lava River Trail is a paved interpretive pathway that begins at the Dee Wright Observatory parking area. The route to Little Belknap Crater follows the Pacific Crest Trail (PCT) and begins at a shaded parking area on the right (north) side of the highway 0.5 mile west of the observatory. To find this trailhead, look for signs to the PCT.

About the Landscape: The black terrain of McKenzie Pass looks bleak. We are accustomed to landscapes smothered in plants. This barren, rocky pass, the lowest Cascade portal from eastern Oregon to the west, ushered pioneer wagons into the Willamette Valley in the 1890s. Disconnected relics of the original road still remain, visible along the Lava River Trail. Geologically, the

Little Belknap Crater provides a close-up view of Mount Washington.

trail reveals long-frozen lava streams that flowed from Belknap Crater and South Belknap and Yapoah Cones, swirling as fiery rivers toward Sisters and the Deschutes plains. The age of these young-looking lava flows ranges from about 3000 to 1500 years.

Belknap Crater is a shield volcano. Little Belknap, on its eastern flank, vented cinders and lavas. The Belknap Crater lava flows to the north and west are about 2900 years in age. They lie atop cinders and flows erupted during the last 8000 years. Lavas from Belknap Crater flowed more than 12 miles westward and probably also covered the McKenzie Pass area.

Trail Guide: Begin by hiking the short, easy Lava River Trail. The pathway begins at Dee Wright Observatory and follows a basalt flow that originated at Yapoah Cone 2600 years ago. The trail engages the lava field, including an elongated lava tube that has collapsed and several small pressure ridges. It climbs to a high point on a lava levee, where the lava spilled out of its main channel and pressure on the levee cracked it open. The trail winds through this cracked levee, revealing the columnar joints and cooling cracks within it. From the top of the levee, the Lava River Trail provides a panoramic view of the dark lava fields of McKenzie Pass and the High Cascades.

Return to the Dee Wright Observatory, and continue to the PCT, 0.5 mile west on Highway 242.

The path to Little Belknap Crater begins deceptively through the tree-shaded terrain of a kipuka—an area that was not covered—but was instead surrounded—by the lava flows of Belknap Crater and Yapoah Cone some 2000 years ago. (*Kipuka* is Hawaiian for "oasis.") The trail heads uphill and in 0.3 mile emerges at the edge of the lava flows, crosses a frozen river of basalt, then skirts the flow on the lava river beach of a second kipuka. From this point, hikers will be crunching across sharp-edged aa rubble all the way to Little Belknap, 1.6 miles across the flows.

En route there are a lot of lava flow features to explore, including lava gutters, small tubes, and pressure ridges. Little Belknap is reached by a very short, obvious spur trail to the right. It offers a nice view of Mount Washington and the surrounding volcanoes, as well as an up-close look at one of the High Cascades' youngest vents.

Hike
48

TIDBITS MOUNTAIN

Examine the eroded remnant of a long-vanished Western Cascade peak.

DISTANCE ▪ **4 miles round trip**
ELEVATION ▪ **4180–5200 feet**
DIFFICULTY ▪ **Moderate**
TOPOGRAPHIC MAP ▪ **Tidbits Mountain**
GEOLOGIC MAP ▪ **1**
FEES/REGULATIONS ▪ **Northwest Forest Pass required for trailhead parking.**
PRECAUTIONS ▪ **Be wary of crumbly cliffs and falling rocks.**
INFORMATION ▪ **McKenzie Ranger District, Willamette National Forest:**
(541) 822-3381

Directions: From Eugene, drive east on Highway 126 (McKenzie River Highway) 42 miles and turn north on USFS Road 15 to Blue River Reservoir. Drive 4.8 miles on this nice paved road, then take graveled USFS Road 1509 for 8.3 miles to the junction with spur road 877. You can park here and walk the next 0.2 mile up the steep and unmaintained road to the official trailhead (or drive and park at road's end).

About the Landscape: The rocks of the Western Cascades form a belt that extends from southwest of Ashland to the foothills of Mount Hood. They represent the first (Eocene to Miocene) volcanoes of that range. Generally, these volcanoes were similar to the modern Cascades, although at the time they first erupted, they were virtually on Oregon's coastline. Their rise contributed to climate change in eastern Oregon—these volcanoes created the first "rain shadow" and, along with global factors, engendered a drier eastside climate. In the 20 million years of their activity, the Western Cascades saw the ecosystems of Oregon shift from subtropical Eocene landscapes of katsura and magnolia trees to a temperate oak-maple-pine savannah with hemlocks at higher elevations by the early Miocene 25 million years ago when the rocks of Eagle Creek (Hike 34) were formed. The volcanoes of the Western Cascades, including the vents near Tidbits, were probably most active in the Oligocene, from 38 to 25 million years ago. Their voluminous, ashy eruptions contributed to the soils now found in the John Day Fossil Beds and Painted Hills (Hikes 74–76). By middle Miocene, the eruptions of the Western Cascades activity had virtually ceased.

Trail Guide: The road to the trailhead provides multiple views of the Western Cascades's rocks. Most are boulder-laden volcanic debris flows that flowed several miles or more from major vents. The colors vary from green to purple, depending upon the degree of alteration by hot waters after they were deposited. Look also for a few volcanic rocks—mostly andesites—and also dikes that cross-cut the volcanic deposits. The amount of ash and unconsolidated material in the Western Cascades indicates that many of the volcanoes erupted volumes of ash and behaved explosively.

The trail to Tidbits Mountain traverses an old-growth Douglas fir forest. Tidbits Mountain is an Oligocene vent surrounded by debris-flow deposits, and the strange pinnacles of these rocks can be seen at several places along the trail. At 1.3 miles there is a trail junction and the tattered remains of a USFS cabin. Continue to the left toward Tidbits' summit.

The final ascent of Tidbits is a scramble up the barren relict of a 30-million-year-old andesitic vent. The views of the Western Cascades from here are astonishingly good. Return as you came.

Hike 49 MOUNT THIELSEN

Gain a close-up view of a glacially sculpted lightning rod.

DISTANCE ▪ **6.5 miles round trip**

ELEVATION ▪ **5430–7600 feet (not to summit)**

DIFFICULTY ▪ **Moderate**

TOPOGRAPHIC MAP ▪ Mount Thielsen

GEOLOGIC MAP ▪ 1

FEES/REGULATIONS ▪ Northwest Forest Pass required for trailhead parking.

PRECAUTIONS ▪ This hike does not include an off-trail climb to the summit. Although informal trails lead to the summit, technical climbing skills are recommended for a safe ascent and descent.

INFORMATION ▪ Diamond Lake Ranger District, Umpqua National Forest: (541) 498-2531

Directions: Go 1.5 miles north of the Highway 230/Highway 138 road junction near Diamond Lake. The trailhead parking lot is located along the east side of

151

Mount Thielsen, a severely glaciated volcano, is known as the Cascades' "lightning rod."

Highway 138. The trailhead can be reached by a mile-long trail from the resort area, too.

About the Landscape: Mount Thielsen is a very, very dormant volcano that ceased erupting probably more than 100,000 years ago and was eroded by ravenous glaciers into its present "lightning rod" shape and deserved reputation (there are fulgerites—rocks melted and fused into lithic glass—near Thielsen's summit). Thielsen displays the gaudy banding of a stratovolcano.

Trail Guide: The trail toward Thielsen's top begins in a hemlock-Douglas fir forest and rises at a steady clip. At 1.6 miles, the trail crosses a side trail and at 2 miles it switchbacks through a denser stand of hemlock.

In about 2.6 miles the trail reaches a ridgeline that offers a fine view of the mountain and its banding. From the viewpoints, the path follows the ridgeline, intersecting the Pacific Crest Trail (PCT) at 2.6 miles. Beyond the PCT, the trail to the summit—another 2000 feet in vertical climb—is informal, though well-worn. A hard hike upwards another 400 feet or so rewards the climber with a close-up view of Thielsen's geology. The trip to the top is recommended only for those with climbing experience.

CRATER LAKE: MOUNT SCOTT

Ascend the oldest (and only) remaining peak of the original multispired Mount Mazama.

DISTANCE ■ 5.1 miles round trip

ELEVATION ■ 7696–8926 feet

DIFFICULTY ■ Moderate

TOPOGRAPHIC MAPS ■ Crater Lake East, Crater Lake West, Crater Lake National Park and Vicinity

GEOLOGIC MAP ■ 31

FEES/REGULATIONS ■ National Parks admission or annual pass.

PRECAUTIONS ■ Use caution around the cliffs at Mount Scott's summit. Carry water.

INFORMATION ■ Crater Lake National Park: (541) 594-3100

Directions: From Bend, drive about 65 miles south on US Highway 97 to Chemult and continue another 10 miles south to the junction with Oregon Highway 138. Turn west (right) and follow Highway 138 12 miles to the park entry road. Turn left on the entry road and continue 2 miles to the Rim Drive. The trail up Mount Scott begins on the far eastern side of Crater Lake National Park's Rim Drive.

About the Landscape: Mount Scott is the highest and oldest part of Mount Mazama. It once stood as a separate, scoria-topped peak on the side of a much larger volcano. Isolation served it well. A major portion of the Mount Scott cone survived both glaciation and the cataclysmic eruption of the larger volcano. Today, Scott still sits apart, but the recluse is king of the mountain.

Like most volcanoes of the High Cascades, including Mounts Jefferson and Hood, Mount Scott is mostly composed of andesite. The eroded sides and slopes reveal layers of tawny gray andesite and reddish cinders. These andesites are among the oldest remaining rocks of Mount Mazama (or Crater Lake), dated at about 420,000 years.

As the trail climbs the southern, exposed side of Mount Scott, both wind and sun apply their energy. On a warm day, this trail may be hot; on a cool day it will be windy.

Trail Guide: The trail begins by dipping across a low, glacially carved depression at Mount Scott's base. It then twists around to the peak's south side and

153

begins a steady, gracefully switch-backed climb toward the summit. On the lower and mid-slopes, glacial polish and scouring have smoothed many outcrops. As the trail nears the summit, scoria and a light cap of Crater Lake pumice, a relatively light dusting from the catastrophic eruption 7700 years ago, blanket rock exposures.

At a little over 2.5 miles, the summit is a platform of glacially scoured andesites with abrupt drop-offs to the rocky slopes below. A lookout roosts on the summit, providing a great overview of the area. Return along the same route.

Hike 51
CRATER LAKE: THE WATCHMAN

Gain a bird's-eye view of the convoluted lavas of Wizard Island.

DISTANCE ■ 1.4 miles round trip

ELEVATION ■ 7400–8056 feet

DIFFICULTY ■ Easy

TOPOGRAPHIC MAPS ■ Crater Lake East, Crater Lake West

GEOLOGIC MAP ■ 31

FEES/REGULATIONS ■ National Parks admission or annual pass.

PRECAUTIONS ■ None

INFORMATION ■ Crater Lake National Park: (541) 594-3100

Directions: Follow the directions in Hike 50 from Bend to Crater Lake National Park's Rim Drive. On Crater Lake's west rim, the trail leaves from a parking lot below The Watchman.

About the Landscape: The Watchman is a thick andesite flow on the west rim of Crater Lake. Its summit provides telling views of Llao Rock, Wizard Island, and, like all high points around Crater Lake's rim, views of the High Cascades, from Mounts Jefferson and Hood in the north to Shasta and Lassen in the south. From The Watchman, views of Llao Rock, Cleetwood Flow, and the lava flows of Wizard Island are especially noteworthy.

Trail Guide: The broad trail—actually an old road—traipses up a gradual slope. Large andesite boulders litter the sides of the path. At 200 yards along this old road the trail turns upslope and winds up at the south side of The Watchman, achieving the lookout station at the top in 1.2 miles without encountering many outcrops.

From the top, the line of crags that represent the feeder dikes for the Watchman flow appears to extend from Wizard Island to The Watchman. But these two rock formations are unrelated, and several hundred thousand years

From near the base of The Watchman, the circular form of Crater Lake is apparent.

different in age. Wizard Island looms beneath The Watchman. Wizard Cone looks as though it erupted yesterday, although its actual age is about 6500 to 7000 years. Return as you came.

CRATER LAKE: THE PINNACLES

Find the towering remnants of Mazama's last gasp.

DISTANCE ■ 0.7 mile round trip

ELEVATION ■ 5450–5460 feet

DIFFICULTY ■ Easy

TOPOGRAPHIC MAPS ■ Crater Lake East, Crater Lake West

GEOLOGIC MAP ■ 31

FEES/REGULATIONS ■ National Park admissions or annual pass.

PRECAUTIONS ■ Steep, unfenced drop into the canyon.

INFORMATION ■ Crater Lake National Park: (541) 594-3100

Directions: Follow the directions in Hike 50 to the east side of Crater Lake National Park's Rim Drive. About 4 miles south of the Mount Scott trailhead,

155

The Pinnacles are the hollow remains of fumaroles, conduits through which gases rose to the surface during Mount Mazama's last eruption.

take the Lost Creek Campground road 5.7 miles to The Pinnacles viewpoint. **About the Landscape:** The Pinnacles are not quite what they seem. You would think that these spires are solid, pointy columns, erosion-proofed by some dark, resistant caprock. In fact, they are hollow, made erosion-proof from the inside out. The Pinnacles represent fumaroles—pipes or conduits through which hot gases trapped in this ash flow rose to the surface. The hot gasses cemented the loose pumice around the flumes through which they rose, forming a very hard, resistant rock around a hollow conduit. This resistant rock remains today as a pinnacle, while the loose pumice and ash around it has been eroded by rain and the action of Sand Creek.

The ash flow in which The Pinnacles developed represents part of the culminating eruption of Mount Mazama. Each pinnacle displays a gradual transition from light-colored base to dark-colored top. This change in color is related to a change in the composition of the erupted pumice. As the frothing magma chamber of Mount Mazama emptied, the ash at the top of the chamber was light-colored and silica-rich; the bottom contained darker minerals and dark basalt magma. The result is the light bottoms—the first ash that fell—and dark tops—the basaltic dregs of the magma chamber bottom—of The Pinnacles.

Trail Guide: This flat hike is more an overview than a hike, although a short, 0.2-mile path continues from the parking area along the canyon rim, providing unfettered views into the odd pinnacles below. This is a great hike for those interested in Mount Mazama's last day. The short walkway along Sand Creek Canyon provides opportunities to peer over the rim, or sit and contemplate the view. Similar fumaroles occupy the canyon of Annie Creek along the south entrance to Crater Lake on Highway 62 at the Annie Falls turnout, about 4 miles inside the national park boundary.

Hike 53
TOKETEE FALLS

Visit one of Oregon's most unique waterfalls, where the North Umpqua River burrows through a columned lava flow.

DISTANCE ▪ 0.8 mile round trip

ELEVATION ▪ 2500–2580 feet

DIFFICULTY ▪ Easy

TOPOGRAPHIC MAP ▪ Toketee Falls

GEOLOGIC MAP ▪ 1

FEES/REGULATIONS ▪ Northwest Forest Pass required for trailhead parking.

PRECAUTIONS ▪ More steps than trail!

INFORMATION ▪ Diamond Lake Ranger District, Umpqua National Forest: (541) 498-2531

Directions: Drive 58 miles east of Roseburg on Oregon Highway 138. Turn left (north) onto USFS Road 34 (Toketee-Rigdon Road) and almost immediately left again. Continue 0.4 mile to the trailhead parking lot.

About the Landscape: The late Pliocene and early Pleistocene lava flows (3

At Toketee Falls, the North Umpqua River plummets through a basalt flow of the early High Cascades.

million to 500,000 years in age) of the High Cascades built a broad platform of basaltic shield volcanoes. These lava flows were subsequently buried beneath younger eruptions as the volcanoes grew. They are visible now in eroded canyons, including the canyon of the North Umpqua where one of the most spectacular waterfalls in Oregon plummets through a columned lava flow of the early High Cascades.

Trail Guide: The trail to Toketee Falls is short and consists more of stairs— metal, wooden, concrete, and stone—than a trail. They lead to an otherwise impossible viewpoint above the waterfall, whose name, which means "pretty" or "graceful" in a Chinook language, is an understatement. The viewpoint is remote from the waterfall, and other than hang gliding or rappelling, there is no way into the steep-sided gorge. But the view of silky water rushing through a perfect U-shaped channel in columnar basalts is spectacular just as it is.

Hike 54 WATSON FALLS

Hike to the base of Oregon's second-highest waterfall.

DISTANCE ▪ 0.8 mile round trip
ELEVATION ▪ 2700–3010 feet
DIFFICULTY ▪ Moderate
TOPOGRAPHIC MAP ▪ Toketee Falls
GEOLOGIC MAP ▪ 1
FEES/REGULATIONS ▪ Northwest Forest Pass required for trailhead parking.
PRECAUTIONS ▪ An informal trail that continues from the base of the falls to its top leads along the slippery edge of perilous cliffs.
INFORMATION ▪ Diamond Lake Ranger District, Umpqua National Forest: (541) 498-2531

Directions: Remarkably close to Toketee Falls, Watson Falls can be reached by driving from Roseburg 60.5 miles east on Highway 138, turning right on Fish Creek Road, and then almost immediately turning right into the trailhead parking area.
About the Landscape: Watson Falls shares the honor of second-highest waterfall in Oregon with Salt Creek Falls. Both are, ostensibly, 272 feet high. But Watson Falls is less tamed, and you can hike right up to its shoelaces, as well as examine the thick basalt flows that it cascades down.
Trail Guide: From the parking area, the trail crosses Fish Creek Road and climbs upslope, curving through a Douglas fir

The second highest waterfall in Oregon, Watson Falls plunges over multiple basalts of the High Cascades.

and cedar forest. It crosses Watson Creek on a spiffy wooden bridge, offering the first good view of the reclusive waterfall, and arrives at a better viewpoint in 0.4 mile from the trailhead. A side trail continues upward and reaches the tiptop of the falls, but this trail is often slippery and is not recommended. Instead, you can clamber over boulders and investigate the waterfall itself, as well as the andesites at its foot.

To return, take the same trail you came on. Or continue on the left side of the creek on an alternative trail. This latter route requires you to walk about 100 yards along the road before returning to the trailhead.

Hike 55 UPPER ROGUE RIVER: NATURAL BRIDGE TO BIG BEND

Explore a site where a giant lava tube swallows a river.

DISTANCE ■ **6.8 miles round trip**

ELEVATION ■ **3200–3740 feet**

DIFFICULTY ■ **Moderate**

TOPOGRAPHIC MAP ■ **Union Creek**

GEOLOGIC MAP ■ **1**

FEES/REGULATIONS ■ **Northwest Forest Pass required for trailhead parking.**

PRECAUTIONS ■ **None**

INFORMATION ■ **Prospect Ranger Station, Rogue River-Siskiyou National Forest: (541) 560-3400**

Directions: Lower trailhead: Near milepost 52 on Oregon Highway 62, turn left (west) at the sign for Natural Bridge Campground. Drive west 0.4 mile and bear left (south) into the parking area for the Natural Bridge Interpretive Trail. The paved interpretive trail here leads toward a bridge across the Rogue. To find the north trailhead of the Upper Rogue River Trail, look for an unpaved trail that ducks left into the forest about 200 feet before the snazzy, arching footbridge across the Rogue River.

Upper trailhead: From Natural Bridge, continue north on Highway 62, then bear left (right) on Oregon Highway 230 in 2.6 miles from the Natural Bridge parking area. Drive north 0.9 mile on Highway 230, then turn left (west) onto USFS Road 6510, marked "Big Bend." Cross the Rogue on this road and drive 0.6 mile to a well-marked Big Bend, Rogue River Trail trailhead.

Trail Guide: Natural Bridge evokes a mental image of soaring arches of red

The Rogue River carves its way through lava flows and lava tubes at Natural Bridge and at the Rogue Gorge.

sandstone, à la Arches National Monument. But there is no sandstone within a hundred miles or so of this spot. Instead, this "natural bridge" is a lava tube that swallows the Rogue River whole, then disgorges it a hundred yards or so downstream. The Rogue Gorge, about 4 miles upstream, is a former lava tube that probably contained the river underground until the top of the lava tube gradually collapsed, leaving the river visible and confined to a narrow but rather deep and incredibly swift channel.

To reach the northbound trail from the Natural Bridge Interpretive Trail, follow the paved and developed trails northward, along the east bank of the

161

Rogue, bypassing the Natural Bridge Campground and keeping to the riverbank behind the campsites. Cross the footbridge to the west bank of the Rogue about 1 mile from the trailhead at the Natural Bridge Interpretive Trail.

Once you are across the river and away from the chatter of campers, the trail follows the river quite faithfully for another 1.5 miles. The west side trail bypasses a set of cabins and yurts along the river's east bank—part of Union Creek and the Union Creek Campground. The hike here moves through stately yellow and sugar pines, crosses a footbridge over Flat Creek, and follows a river bend to the east. You will have to endure another mile of hiking along the west bank with views of cabins and campers as the river bends north and then east.

At 2.8 miles from the trailhead, the trail begins to climb up the bank to avoid steep shores along the river and the Rogue Gorge. A side trail leads to an optional overlook. The digression from the river rises about 100 feet in a gradual switchback, then winds back to the river in another 0.3 mile.

After a fleeting glimpse of the water, the trail moves away again, and then upslope, this time climbing well above the river and into a Douglas fir–dominated forest along fairly steep slopes. This part of the trip is cool, even on hot summer days.

Hike 56

UPPER ROGUE RIVER: TAKELMA GORGE

View a scenic river canyon cut through lavas and mudflows.

DISTANCE ■ **8 miles round trip**

ELEVATION ■ **2815–2960 feet**

DIFFICULTY ■ **Moderate**

TOPOGRAPHIC MAPS ■ **Whetstone Point, North Prospect**

GEOLOGIC MAP ■ **1**

FEES/REGULATIONS ■ **Northwest Forest Pass required for trailhead parking.**

PRECAUTIONS ■ **Gorge rimrock may be crumbly and undercut.**

INFORMATION ■ **Prospect Ranger District, Rogue River-Siskiyou National Forest: (541) 560-3400**

Directions: Lower trailhead/beginning: River Bridge: Drive north on Oregon Highway 62 to milepost 49 and turn left (west) on USFS Road 6210, marked for River Bridge Campground. Drive 0.5 mile on Road 6210 to the trailhead.

Upper trailhead/end: Woodruff Bridge: Drive north on Oregon Highway 62 to milepost 68 (also 0.75 mile north of the Mammoth Pines Picnic Area).

UPPER ROGUE RIVER: TAKELMA GORGE

Turn left (west) on USFS Road 68, marked for Woodruff Bridge Picnic Area. Drive 1.75 miles on this paved road—it seems as though you will never get to the river, but eventually the picnic area appears on the right, the bridge

At Takelma Gorge the Rogue River has eroded deeply into volcanic mudflows and debris flows.

and river are straight ahead, and the trailhead parking is on the left.

About the Landscape: This hike reveals the High Cascades underpinnings of the Upper Rogue River: debris flows and ropy *pahoehoe* basalt.

Trail Guide: This segment of the Upper Rogue River Trail is among the most scenic. It follows the river closely for its entire length, and although for 0.7 mile or so the stream runs through narrow and steep-walled Takelma Gorge, while the trail follows along the top, making water inaccessible (or virtually inaccessible), for the remainder of the trip the river is an affable companion. You will also encounter a set of buildings and likely some people at the Rogue Baptist Camp.

From the River Bridge trailhead, the path follows a broad, calm, and almost quiescent river. This is, however, only a river resting from its labors upstream where it has notched a 100-foot-deep canyon through young lava flows and mud flows that blocked its way about a million years ago. Many of the boulders along the stream here have been quarried from the gorge walls. Their relatively angular shapes indicate that they have not been carried far by the bouncing, rolling, and rounding power of high-energy river water.

Along the pumice-soiled flats near the trailhead, huge ponderosa pine and sugar pine vie for sky-space, dwarfing the fir and understory of vine maple and alder. This portion of the trail really glows with almost fluorescent reds, oranges, and yellows when frost kindles fall colors in October.

At the end of the first mile of nearly level hiking, you'll catch a glimpse of low-slung buildings ahead through the thinned forest. The trail hugs the river, but still sideswipes the Rogue Baptist Camp—a facility that is unoccupied for much of the year. Beyond the camp, the trail enters a section that appears wild and pristine, although it is never very far from the gravel entry roads that lead to the camp. The river's pace quickens a bit; the forest closes its canopy, and even the trail picks up its pace, steepening ever so slightly (though it is still, by most hiking standards, flat).

About 0.7 mile beyond the Rogue Baptist Camp the trail moves away from the river as the stream recedes into Takelma Gorge.

This gorge is a channel cut by the Rogue through a relatively young lava flow and into the underlying and quite unconsolidated debris flows. The gorge is at most about 100 feet deep and about 1 mile in length. The path along its rim offers occasional glimpses into the chasm. For the best views you will have to leave the trail. The gorge walls, especially in the middle of the hike along the vertical-walled section, reveal a sequence of rubbly basalt flows as well as more fragile mud flows. Because the relatively thin lava flows were underlain by soft and unconsolidated mudflow deposits, the river was able to erode its channel easily once it had worn its way through the harder basalts.

Near the north end of the hike along the gorge, the trail steps over ropy, pahoehoe basalt—now relatively subtle after a million years of rain and organic acids—and 20 years of human feet—have weathered it.

After exploring the rim of Takelma Gorge, the trail remains remote from the river for another 0.5 mile, then plays tag with the stream, dropping to a wetland area in 3 miles from the River Bridge trailhead, and reaching the Woodbridge trailhead in 4 miles from the start of the hike. Return as you came.

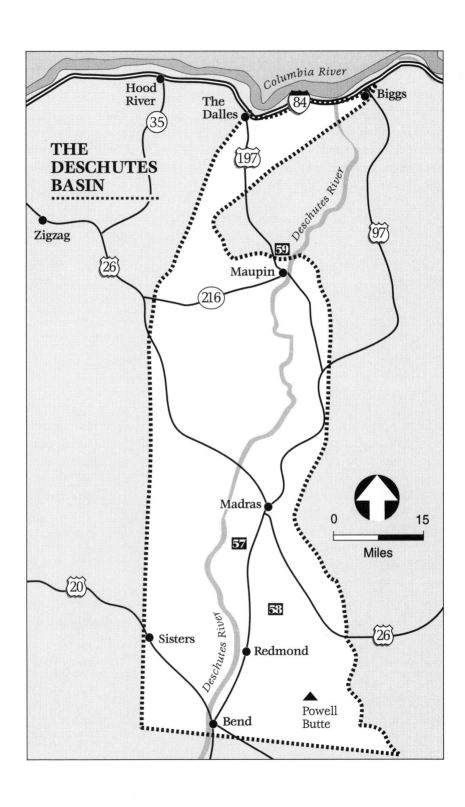

THE
DESCHUTES
BASIN

Columbia River

Hood
River

The
Dalles

Biggs

84

35

197

Deschutes River

97

Zigzag

59

26

Maupin

216

Deschutes River

Madras

57

0   15

Miles

58

20

Sisters

Deschutes River

26

Redmond

Powell
Butte

Bend

Chapter 6

THE DESCHUTES BASIN

Above its foundation of Columbia River basalt and older, Oligocene volcanoes (Hike 59), the Deschutes Basin provides a record of explosive eruptions from vanished volcanoes: the flat, explosive volcanoes of the Cascades that erupted from about 7 to 2 million years ago, and which are now covered by the High Cascades peaks (Hike 57).

Several older rhyolite domes and vents, including Smith Rock (Hike 58) and Powell Butte (east of Redmond), while geographically in the Deschutes Basin, have different geologic genetics. Technically, these Miocene and Oligocene rocks seem closely related to the Western Cascades. Their eruptions of ash may have contributed to the John Day Fossil Beds and Painted Hills, and their

Oligocene contemporaries constructed the Western Cascades. But who would ever look for them in that category? So they have been adopted by adjoining regions, much like a neighbor might adopt the cat of a family that moved away. Some geologists toss them into the High Lava Plains. Others, including this one, consider them part of the Deschutes Basin's history.

These rocks, especially the layers of tuff near Cove Palisades State Park, hold the remains of ancient, streamside forests. Collected and analyzed by Mel Ashwill of Madras, the vegetation found in these rocks shows a wetter climate here in the Late Miocene.

Cross-bedding, Deschutes Basin sediments, Cove Palisades

JOINTS

They seem to be the most insignificant things: Cracks in the rock.

Geologists call them joints. Like gray hairs or wrinkles, though, joints are an outcrop's biographer. They tell the story of the stresses the rock has experienced throughout its life—the tension, compression, heat, burial, *intrusion,* folding, faulting, and weathering that have affected it through tens of millions of years.

Basalts usually display columnar joints, which grow as lava cools. Basalts solidify from the bottom upward and also from the top down. As the flow cools into solid basalt, joints grow simultaneously from the bottom upward and the top down, meeting in the middle.

Platy jointing in andesite

Columnar joints in basalt

Granites and other plutonic igneous rocks also crack as they cool, producing widely spaced sets of joints that permeate the entire solidified *batholith.* Unlike the basalts' columnar style, joints in intrusive bodies do not create columns. Instead, they create angular patterns of cracks, often at angles of 90 or 45 degrees to one another.

Joints or cracks in the rocks may develop as the earth shifts. The pattern of joints reveals the direction and magnitude of the stresses that have acted on an outcrop, betraying an otherwise invisible pattern of folding. However, when stress becomes more than a rock can endure, it breaks—often transforming a simple joint into a fault.

Hike 57 COVE PALISADES

Visit a spectacular canyon cut into colored and columned cliffs, with a lake in the bottom.

DISTANCE ▪ 2 miles round trip

ELEVATION ▪ 2400–2500 feet

DIFFICULTY ▪ Easy

TOPOGRAPHIC MAPS ▪ Round Butte Dam, Culver

GEOLOGIC MAPS ▪ 32–34

FEES/REGULATIONS ▪ Oregon State Parks day fee or annual pass.

PRECAUTIONS ▪ As in all park areas, collecting rocks requires a permit and is for scholarly study only.

INFORMATION ▪ Oregon State Parks: (800) 551-6949

Directions: To reach Cove Palisades, from Redmond take US Highway 97 north 5 miles. Near the bottom of the north-facing downgrade from Juniper Butte,

The Ship, at Cove Palisades, is a stack of ash flow tuffs, ignimbrites, sediments, and thin basaltic lava flows.

Layers of ash, sediments, and ignimbrites, about 5-7 million years in age, are truncated by younger, 1.2 million-year-old basalts from Newberry volcano (right).

take the road to the left marked "Culver and Cove Palisades." In downtown Culver, turn left on Main Street and follow signs for Cove Palisades State Park, 3 miles west. Drive through the park to the headquarters and camping area at the base of The Ship. The trailhead for day hikes is at the main park campground just below The Ship. At the registration kiosk, cross the road and turn right to head downhill.

About the Landscape: Tucked into the backcountry between Madras and Mount Jefferson is a raw wound slashed by the Deschutes and Crooked Rivers into the fragile, stacked bedrock of the Deschutes Basin. The canyon's layered walls are composed of alternating ash beds, gravels, and lava flows.

The most spectacular features of this 300-foot-deep canyon are the intra-canyon flows of basalt, about 1.2 million years in age. These basalts form the high columned cliffs that veneer the canyon's sides and also form The Island, a high, isolated finger of basalt that juts south from the center of Cove Palisades. The Island interests ecologists because it is among the few places in central Oregon never grazed by domestic livestock, except briefly in the 1920s by a band of sheep whose owner kept them—and a whiskey still—active for several years atop this tiny plateau.

Near the campground, a spectacular, layered rock formation known as The Ship displays pastel layers that are ash-rich gravels, river sands, and welded ash-flow tuffs (*ignimbrites*). The sands and gravels were deposited by braided streams from the Cascades. The pinkish layer is an ash-flow tuff that erupted as a hot cloud of molten ash and gas that probably moved at speeds in excess of 100 mph.

While Cove Palisades is largely a boaters' state park, with few trails, much of the pleasure in the place stems from its layered scenery and the younger

170

basalts. On days when there is little traffic, one of the best places to view the varied formations is a walk along the road at the park's west side. This hike reveals the variety of tuffs, gravels, and lava flows that emanated from the earliest High Cascade volcanoes.

Trail Guide: Along the trail and to the left at the trail's beginning, coarse columnar jointed basalts of the young basalt flows can be examined. The trail begins to drop toward Lake Billy Chinook, with a view of the columnar cliffs of The Island several hundred yards to the right. Note the 30- to 50-foot-long dome-shaped arches of the columns in the upper part of the island. These are good examples of inflated basalt—basalt that was supported by gas pressure as it cooled.

The trail system on this side of the road is a network of wide, easy paths. Most provide views of the surrounding canyon walls. Note especially that the column-rich basalt flows are simply stuck on the sides of the canyon walls.

An informal trail leads to the top of The Island. It is steep, rugged, undeveloped, and hazardous. Inquire at the Cove Palisades State Park Headquarters about the trail condition and access before exploring this area. Return as you came.

Hike 58 SMITH ROCK

Walk among tuffs, columned basalts, and rhyolite in a climbers' paradise on the Crooked River.

DISTANCE ▪ 5.5-mile loop

ELEVATION ▪ 370–2800 feet

DIFFICULTY ▪ Moderate

TOPOGRAPHIC MAPS ▪ Redmond, Opal City, Gray Butte, O'Neil

GEOLOGIC MAP ▪ 35

FEES/REGULATIONS ▪ Oregon State Parks annual pass or day fee.

PRECAUTIONS ▪ Stay on the route described; other routes may result in being cliffed out or requiring technical skills and equipment to descend rock ledges. Collecting rocks requires a permit.

INFORMATION ▪ Oregon State Parks: (800) 551-6949

Directions: To reach Smith Rock State Park, from Redmond drive about 5 miles north on US Highway 97 to Terrebonne, and turn east onto B Street. Cross the railroad tracks, go down a hill, and then turn left on First Street. In 0.5 mile turn right onto Wilcox, drive 1 mile, and turn left onto Smith Rock Loop. Reach the park in about 2 miles. From the parking lot, asphalt paths lead to the trailhead.

At Smith Rock State Park, rimrock on the south side of the Crooked River is 1.2 million-year-old basalt, while the tan rocks on the north side of the river are part of a 14 million-year-old tuff cone and its vent system.

About the Landscape: Smith Rock is a climbers' mecca. These gritty tuffs invite handholds and hammered supports. The scope of the rocks and of the Crooked River's winding course through the area provide a perspective that is both humbling and full of grandeur.

Smith Rock is only part of a much larger volcanic and sedimentary complex centered around Gray Butte to the northeast. The tan and buff Smith Rock tuff erupted about 14 million years ago. This small volcano coughed up a hot, pasty mixture of ash and steam that formed and flowed in thin layers before it cooled and solidified. The vent area may have been near today's popular Smith Rock climbing area.

The gas-charged eruptions carried chunks of the underlying bedrock up the volcanic conduit. The holes in the rock walls today are cavities left when these chunks of rock erode, and/or when gas pockets where frothy tuff col-

A climber finds a handhold on Smith Rock.

lected are hollowed out by water and wind. In many parts of Smith Rock State Park the crude layering created by multiple eruptions of sticky tuff is evident.

The darker red rock that forms a picturesque maroon spire and magenta laces across the vertical walls is rhyolite. It intruded through the tuff cone. Close examination reveals vertical banding in this rhyolite—a relic of its upward flow.

A dark-rimmed basalt plateau frames the riverbank on the south side of Smith Rock. These basalts likely flowed from near Newberry Crater, filling the ancestral Crooked River Canyon about 1.2 million years ago. The Crooked River recarved its channel through these thick basalts during the Pleistocene (Ice Age).

Trail Guide: The hike around Smith Rock explores the Smith Rock tuff. The overlook where the trail plunges down to Crooked River provides a vista of the tawny Smith Rock tuffs just across the river, of the red spire of rhyolite dike—the dark pinnacle at the first river bend—of the Newberry basalts that the overlook is built on, and of the oldest rocks here—the 18-million-year-old rhyolite of Gray Butte just below the basalt at this overlook.

The trail leads downslope and across the Crooked River. Just across the bridge, follow the trail upstream along the Crooked River. The buff and magenta

The Crooked River flows past the rhyolite dike that intrudes Smith Rock tuff.

cliffs that rise to your left are Smith Rock tuff laced with veins of red rhyolite. At 0.75 mile the main trail continues upslope past basalt rimrock to the right. On this slope the trail is a scramble that leads to a roadway (locally called the Burma Road) which briefly follows an irrigation canal (the North Unit canal) and provides a switch-backed path to the Smith Rock ridge crest, about 2 miles from the bridge crossing.

The ridge crest rewards the hiker with a climber's-eye view. Along this ridge you can glimpse streaks of iron oxide that tint the rocks red and examine the inclusions that create knobs and holes. To the north, 1 mile across Sherwood Canyon, multiple horns of Smith Rock tuff emerge from the ridge.

From this point, an informal climbers' trail plunges down the rocky but hikable back side of Smith Rock. In 0.5 mile look carefully for a spur trail to the north. This unmarked trail provides a rough but hikable 1-mile route back to the Crooked River and the main trail along the base of Smith Rock. The river trail leads from the west side of Smith Rock back to the bridge and trailhead.

Hike 59
WHITE RIVER FALLS

On this short hike the White River tumbles over a double falls.

DISTANCE ■ 0.5 mile round trip
ELEVATION ■ 875–1040 feet
DIFFICULTY ▲ Moderate
TOPOGRAPHIC MAP ■ Maupin
GEOLOGIC MAP ■ 1
PRECAUTIONS ■ Be prepared for a rugged, informal trail.
INFORMATION ■ Oregon State Parks: (800) 551-6949

Directions: From The Dalles, drive south 28 miles on US Highway 197. Turn left (east) onto Oregon Highway 216 (marked for Sherrars Bridge). Drive 4.1 miles and turn right into the park entrance.

About the Landscape: Flows of Columbia River basalt are found throughout the Deschutes Basin. The 90-foot double waterfall seen from this trail plunges over two of them. A now-abandoned power plant at the base of the falls provided electricity to The Dalles from 1910 until 1960 when The Dalles Dam was completed on the Columbia.

Trail Guide: From the parking area, the trail leads to commanding overviews of the White River and the falls, which tumble over two Columbia River basalt flows. These flows may mark part of the ancestral Columbia drainage. About 16 million years ago when these basalts flowed across the landscape the Columbia's course ran slightly south of today's Mount Hood.

An informal and rough path leads to the abandoned power plant below the

The White River plummets over basalt flows at White River Falls before it joins the Deschutes River near Sherrars Bridge.

falls. Flumes and power-generating equipment are still evident here. The view of the falls from the trail and power plant is more compelling than the view from the overlook at the top.

Return as you came.

Chapter 7

THE HIGH LAVA PLAINS

In Oregon, the High Lava Plains is the land of the laconic geologist. Out here, just two words will get you by: rhyolite and basalt.

The High Lava Plains is, very simply, a wide belt of small rhyolite and basalt volcanoes that stretch from south of Burns to south of Bend. Most Oregonians call the area the High Desert. It follows the Brothers fault zone at the northern edge of the Basin and Range.

The most curious thing about the High Lava Plains volcanoes is their age. Generally, the oldest ones (Duck Butte and Beatty's Butte, 10.4 million years) are on the east end. The ages of the volcanoes and eruptions grow progressively younger to the west. The youngest vent system is Newberry Volcano, just south of Bend, which birthed the Big Obsidian Flow only 1200 years ago. Geologists are unsure of the reason for this neat progression of volcanism across Oregon's midriff. The best explanation seems to be that the Brothers fault zone has opened access to the earth's mantle, rather like a zipper opening steadily from Burns to Bend.

The most visible rocks of the High Lava Plains are basalt flows and rhyolite domes. The domes include Glass Buttes (6 million years old), Quartz

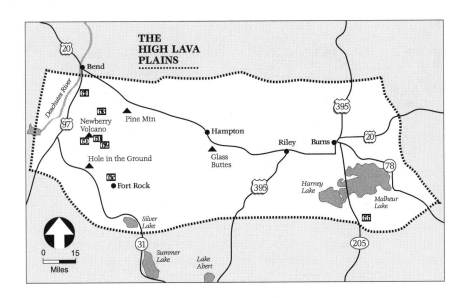

177

Fort Rock, once a tuff cone amidst a Pleistocene lake, now rises from a sea of sagebrush.

Mountain and Pine Mountain (about 1 million years old), and China Hat (800,000 years old). Gas-laden rhyolite tuff eruptions produced Fort Rock and Hole in the Ground less than 1 million years ago.

LOOKING AT LAVAS: THE BIOGRAPHY OF
A VOLCANIC ROCK

The colors and textures of a volcanic rock can tell you a lot about its history. Three things in particular to look for:

Vesicles: Tiny holes in most volcanic rocks are the heritage of gas bubbles—like the bubbles in soda pop or beer. As the lava solidifies, gas is trapped as bubbles and creates small holes that remain after the fluid lava has solidified. Vesicles are often more abundant at the tops of lava flows. They may be elongate—stretched in the direction the lava was moving at the instant it solidified. In rare cases where the flow did not move much, the gas holes may be elongate upward—formed as the gas rose through the molten rock.

Pillows: When hot basalt lava flows into water, it chills rapidly into rounded shapes called pillows or pillow lava. Pillows—even the 55-million-year-old pillow lavas on Marys Peak—usually have a glassy rim and radial cracks. Pillow lavas may be far from water today, but when they were molten they flowed into the sea or a large lake where they chilled into balls and solidified.

Phenocrysts: Volcanic rocks are very fine-grained. It's hard to find identifiable minerals in them because they often chill quickly with no time for crystals to grow. But sometimes, a larger crystal—or many—is evident. These bigger crystals in a fine-grained matrix are called phenocrysts (from the Greek meaning "visible crystals"). The presence of these larger crystals suggests a two-stage cooling process for the lava. The phenocrysts began growing slowly while the lava was still far below the surface. When the lava rose and erupted, it carried these larger, already-formed crystals with it, a bit like an early spring flood carrying bits of ice. Once the lava reached the surface, it chilled rapidly without time for more large crystals to grow, but leaving the phenocrysts as a reminder of its past life deep in the earth's warm womb.

Vesicles in basalt

Hike 60

PAULINA PEAK TRAIL

Ascend to the rim of Newberry Volcano for views of the High Cascades, Paulina and East Lakes, and the Big Obsidian Flow.

DISTANCE ▪ 5 miles round trip

ELEVATION ▪ 6400–7484 feet

DIFFICULTY ▪ Strenuous

TOPOGRAPHIC MAPS ▪ Paulina Peak, East Lake

GEOLOGIC MAPS ▪ 36, 37

FEES/REGULATIONS ▪ Northwest Forest Pass required for trailhead parking.

PRECAUTIONS ▪ This trail follows cliff edges.

INFORMATION ▪ Lava Lands Visitor Center: (541) 593-2421

Directions: From Bend, drive south 20 miles on US Highway 97. Turn left (east) on USFS Road 21, marked "Newberry National Volcanic Monument." Drive 13 miles to the Paulina Lodge Road, then continue 0.5 mile to Paulina Peak Road and turn right. About 0.7 mile along this road, turn left into a small gravel parking area marked "Paulina Peak Trailhead."

About the Landscape: Newberry Volcano, a classical basaltic shield volcano within geologic spitting distance of the High Cascades, is a product of High Lava Plains volcanism. It fits nicely into the pattern of younger vents to the west. It first erupted 1.2 million years ago. Some lava may have flowed more than 40 miles to the north to Cove Palisades State Park.

Newberry Volcano's crater was created by a collapse of the shield volcano's summit area about 200,000 years ago. Since then, the volcano has sporadically tried to fill in the hole with rhyolite, obsidian, and tuff. The eruptions built up the land area in the central part of Newberry Crater, dividing what had been one lake into two. The area between Paulina and East Lakes is the product of eruptions that lasted from 7300 to 7100 years ago. These eruptions produced the central cone and several rhyolite domes and obsidian flows. Two obsidian flows (Game Hut and Crater obsidian flows) emanate from this cone and are the same age (about 7300 years). The Interlake obsidian flow occupies the north end of this area and extends to both Paulina and East Lakes. It is the youngest part of this central area, erupting 7100 years ago.

Paulina Peak also affords a view of the Big Obsidian Flow just to the east. This flow is dated at 1200 years—Oregon's youngest known lava flow. Semicircular pressure ridges and elongate flow gutters indicate the direction of the flow and its complex patterns.

Trail Guide: The trail rises sharply for 100 yards, then eases along a ridge crest. Red tuff, a product of very old (300,000 years?) Newberry eruptions, appears in low outcrops along the trail's edge. At about 1 mile into the hike, the trail crosses into a gray rhyolite unit. This rock forms the cliffs of Paulina Peak and supports its steep slopes. For the next mile, the trail rises steeply, veering occasionally to the edge of cliffs for a view of East Lake and the imposing sides of Paulina Peak. The trail flattens near the crest of the peak and crosses thick accumulations of pumice deposited by the eruption of the Big Obsidian Flow. At 2 miles into the hike, the trail intersects the Paulina Road Trail (Trail 58). Keep straight ahead on the North Paulina Peak Trail, another 0.5 mile to the summit.

When you have had your fill of scenery, return as you came. (For a longer walk on a gentler grade, hike along Paulina Peak Road 4 miles to the trailhead.)

Newberry Volcano. The Big Obsidian Flow is visible at upper right. (Photo courtesy Oregon Dept. of Transportation)

Hike 61 BIG OBSIDIAN FLOW

A short, well-developed path reveals the texture, colors, and origin of this glassy volcanic flow.

DISTANCE ■ 1 mile round trip
ELEVATION ■ 6400–6500 feet
DIFFICULTY ■ Easy
TOPOGRAPHIC MAPS ■ Paulina Peak, East Lake
GEOLOGIC MAPS ■ 36, 37
FEES/REGULATIONS ■ Northwest Forest Pass required for trailhead parking.
PRECAUTIONS ■ Volcanic glass is very sharp! At the beginning of the climb, there is a 30-foot-high metal staircase.
INFORMATION ■ Lava Lands Visitor Center: (541) 593-2421

Directions: See Hike 60 for driving directions to Newberry Volcano. To reach the trailhead, drive to the official entry station for Newberry National Volcanic Monument at Paulina Lake. Continue on County Road 21 around the south shore of Paulina Lake. The marked turnoff is on the right about 1 mile east of the entry station.

About the Landscape: This trail takes you on an Alice in Wonderland–like trip through the fifth-largest obsidian flow in North America. The rocks are glassy and extremely variable. The glassy nature of obsidian is created by the very rapid solidification of a pasty, gas-laden and often very foamy rhyolite. When the rhyolite erupts, the gas escapes and the

Flow banding imparts a pattern to the dark, glassy rocks of 1200-year-old Big Obsidian Flow—Oregon's youngest volcanic rock.

flow solidifies so quickly that no crystals have time to form. Instead, the rock chills as glass.

Trail Guide: The trail leads about 30 feet up a sturdy metal staircase to the top of the flow's steep front. Once you have scaled the stairs, the rest of the hike is easy, relatively level, and on a well-developed trail complete with benches and interpretive signs. There is a lot to see on this short hike: The color of the obsidian varies from black to light gray as more water—in the form of microscopic bubbles—was incorporated in the rock. Where steam surged through the glassy flow, oxidizing the microscopic iron particles in the cooling obsidian, the rock is a red-brown color. In places along the trail, swirls that look like patterns in taffy show the direction the lava was flowing when it chilled abruptly into solid glass. When you reach trail's end, return along the loop to the trailhead.

THE DOME

A breached cinder cone clings to Newberry's south flank.

DISTANCE ■ **3 miles round trip**

ELEVATION ■ **6950–7150 feet**

DIFFICULTY ■ **Easy**

TOPOGRAPHIC MAP ■ **East Lake**

GEOLOGIC MAPS ■ **36, 37**

FEES/REGULATIONS ■ **Northwest Forest Pass required for trailhead parking.**

PRECAUTIONS ■ **None**

INFORMATION ■ **Lava Lands Visitor Center: (541) 593-2421**

Directions: See Hike 60 for driving directions to Newberry Volcano. To reach the trailhead, from the official entry station for Newberry National Volcanic Monument at Paulina Lake, drive about 5 miles to the end of Newberry Crater Road (County Road 21), turn east, uphill, on USFS Road 21 (China Cap Road), and drive 2.5 miles. The trailhead is on the right at a subtly marked turnout.

About the Landscape: The Dome is a young cinder cone near the summit of a 300,000-year-old volcano. It represents Newberry Volcano's first eruptive episode after the Ice Age, dated about 11,500 years in age. Like a young child afraid of heights or open places, The Dome teeters on the brink of the desert, clinging to the sparsely forested side of its Mother Newberry.

The Dome opens to the east, allowing basalt lavas to flow from the open side. This opening, or horseshoe shape, is called a breach. The Dome, technically, is a breached cinder cone. A hike around The Dome's rim reveals the

183

cinder cone's interior—layers of red-brown lava, volcanic bombs, and unconsolidated cinders. The dark surface of The Dome is veneered with gray pumice from Big Obsidian Flow's eruptions—providing a deceptively light color to
this basaltic cinder cone.

Trail Guide: The 0.75-mile trail to the top of The Dome rises in short switchbacks through sparse vegetation. The barren, crescent-shaped summit of The
Dome invites a 0.75-mile walk around the rim. A few examples of aerodynamic
geology—volcanic bombs—lie on the rim's surface. Other bombs tempt from
below. But remember that an easy hike down in these unconsolidated cinders
requires a difficult struggle to regain the summit. After your circuit of the rim,
return the way you came.

Hike 63 LAVA CAST FOREST TRAIL

*This fossil forest is a rather Zen concept—a forest represented by
the vacant hollows where there used to be trees.*

DISTANCE ▪ 2-mile loop

ELEVATION ▪ 4750–4800 feet

DIFFICULTY ▪ Easy

TOPOGRAPHIC MAP ▪ Lava Cast Forest

GEOLOGIC MAPS ▪ 36, 37

FEES/REGULATIONS ▪ Northwest Forest Pass required for trailhead parking.

PRECAUTIONS ▪ Entry road is washboarded by midsummer; allow plenty of
time (30 minutes) for the drive on USFS roads.

INFORMATION ▪ Lava Lands Visitor Center: (541) 593-2421

Directions: From milepost 153 on US Highway 97 at the turnoff to Sun River
(west), turn east on USFS Road 9720, marked "Lava Cast Forest." Follow this
gravel road 8.5 miles to USFS 9720-950—Lava Cast Forest Road—and drive
another 0.5 mile to the parking area and trailhead.

About the Landscape: Lava Cast Forest is a misnomer—these are hollow molds
of tree trunks. Lava molds form when lavas are cool enough to flow around and
chill (solidify) against a tree, but still so hot that they set the tree on fire. Considering that this basalt solidified at about 1000 degrees Centigrade (about 1900
degrees Fahrenheit), it is no wonder that nearly solid lava could ignite anything
that it touched. This forest burned as the lava flowed through it.

This missing forest is the product of a basalt flow from Newberry Volcano's
Northwest Rift zone. The age of this flow is about 6000 years, based on carbon
14 dates of charcoal from the burned trees. The direction that the lava moved

184

is preserved in many vertical molds. The lava piled up on the upstream side of the trees, leaving a mold that is slightly higher and thicker on the uphill side of the tree toward the lava's vent. The horizontal tree molds here most likely developed as the trees fell from their burned stumps into the flowing lava below.

Trail Guide: This handicapped-accessible walk is a 2-mile loop on a paved trail. It is interesting to compare the diameter of the trees standing at the time of the lava flow with the size of the present old-growth trees, and to close your eyes and visualize what the forest must have looked like before and during the eruption.

Basalt preserves the form of a tree inundated by lava about 6000 years ago.

TRAIL OF THE MOLTEN LAND: LAVA BUTTE AND LAVA LANDS VISITOR CENTER

Stroll a paved path to examine the navel of Lava Butte's eruption.

DISTANCE ■ 1-mile loop

ELEVATION ■ 4500–4650 feet

DIFFICULTY ■ Easy

TOPOGRAPHIC MAP ■ Lava Butte

GEOLOGIC MAPS ■ 36, 37

FEES/REGULATIONS ■ Northwest Forest Pass required for trailhead parking.

PRECAUTIONS ■ None

INFORMATION ■ Lava Lands Visitor Center: (541) 593-2421

Directions: The trail begins from the Lava Lands Visitor Center—headquarters for Newberry National Volcanic Monument—on US Highway 97 11 miles south of Bend.

About the Landscape: Lava Butte is part of Newberry Volcano's Northwest

185

Lava Butte and the 6500-year-old "aa" basalt at its base, are closely linked to Newberry Volcano's eruptions.

Rift zone. Although very close to the High Cascades, this cinder cone is a child of the High Lava Plains, not the Cascades.

About 7000 years ago, fissure eruptions (lava fountains) developed along the line of faults known as Newberry's Northwest Rift zone. By about 6500 years ago, the Lava Butte cinder cone was built. Then another pulse of fluid basalt magma about 6200 years ago burst through the side of the cinder cone, creating the Lava Butte flow. This basalt flow extends to the Deschutes River. It dammed the ancestral river, creating a lake that backed up the Deschutes past Sun River almost to La Pine. As the lake drained, the Deschutes cut a new channel which it now follows.

Trail Guide: The visitor center provides background information about the geology, ecology, and human history of the area. During the summer, competent volunteers provide hourly tours and geologic interpretation. The bus ride up Lava Butte offers a good overview of the lava flow.

From the visitor center, the handicapped-accessible loop trail winds through the 6200-year-old lava flow that erupted from the base of Lava Butte. It showcases features of the flow (lava balls, pressure ridges, columnar joints, gutters, levees, and others) through a series of well-placed interpretive signs.

FORT ROCK STATE NATURAL AREA

Hike 65

Explore a desert volcano whose most important ingredient was water.

DISTANCE ▪ 1-mile loop
ELEVATION ▪ 4350–4500 feet
DIFFICULTY ▪ Easy; moderate for informal trails
TOPOGRAPHIC MAP ▪ Fort Rock
GEOLOGIC MAP ▪ 1
PRECAUTIONS ▪ A few brave or foolish rattlesnakes may lurk among Fort Rock's ledges.
INFORMATION ▪ Oregon State Parks: (800) 551-6949

Directions: To reach Fort Rock, from US Highway 97 near La Pine, take Highway 31 approximately 20 miles east and turn north onto County Road 5-12C (Cabin Lake Road). Drive 3 miles to downtown Fort Rock. Follow signs 1.5 miles to Fort Rock State Natural Area.

Fort Rock is a tuff cone that erupted into a Pleistocene lake.

From the parking area, informal trails lead through Fort Rock. The most obvious path provides a quick scramble up to the flat wave-cut bench just above the kiosk. The notch here was carved by the waves of the huge Pleistocene lake that once surrounded this horseshoe-shaped relic.

About the Landscape: While Newberry Volcano looks suspiciously like the Cascades, its younger cousin, Fort Rock, is unmistakably part of the High Lava Plains. This ring of volcanic tuff rises 300 feet, a monument to fire and water. Its

Wave-cut bench above the parking area at Fort Rock State Park

circular structure was hewn into today's familiar semicircle by the unrelenting action of a huge lake. In the Pleistocene, Oregon's desert floor was awash in six huge lakes from Fort Rock east to the Owyhees. The lake that surrounded Fort Rock covered 585 square miles and was about 100 feet deep. The tuff ring rose as an island in 50 feet of water. The prevailing southeast winds drove against the soft tuff, wearing away the wall and creating the semicircular opening.

Today, wave-cut terraces surround Fort Rock, and even appear in its interior. The terraces are especially notable on the south and east sides near Fort Rock State Natural Area. The lake waters were at their highest level about 20,000 years ago, and water lapped at Fort Rock's feet until about 13,000 years ago. Fort Rock Cave, in a nearby tuff ring, has yielded human artifacts (sandals) dated at 13,200 years in age.

Based on its form and degree of erosion, Fort Rock is probably between 50,000 and 100,000 years old (Pleistocene). Like other tuff rings on Oregon's High Lava Plains, Fort Rock was built by explosive, gas-charged eruptions of frothy lava and water-laden ash. Instead of producing a solid flow (like Big Obsidian Flow), the frothy lava erupted hot, gooey ash. This ash plopped out of a ring-shaped circular vent, creating a ring of porous tuff. The fine bedding in Fort Rock's walls represents layers of sticky tuff.

Trail Guide: From the wave-cut bench a 1-mile-long loop follows the interior of Fort Rock. At the beginning of this walk, large, oddly shaped holes are evident on the north wall; these are mostly enlarged, eroded gas pockets, although a few once housed angular stones that the explosive magma ripped from underlying bedrock.

About 0.25 mile farther along the northwest wall, the steep interior cliffs showcase the layers left by the repeated belches of gloppy gas-laden ash and lava (about the same consistency as fresh cow pies) that built Fort Rock. The layers indicate that a rapid succession of coughs and belches, not just one traumatic upheaval, created Fort Rock. Note that the layers slope down toward the center, or vent area, of Fort Rock. In some areas, especially on the north and west interior walls, the layers display droops, bends, folds, cross-bedding, and other "sedimentary" structures, which indicate each was deposited as a very thick, plastic mass that deformed under its own weight and the dictates of gravity.

About 0.5 mile from the parking area, the path reaches the west side of Fort Rock. Here several earlier wave-cut benches are evident, as well as more strongly layered tuff. Water once reached high in the interior of Fort Rock, creating huge piles of rubble. From the west side, a road heads downhill, and branches to the south, reaching the southeast bench in about 0.25 mile. After touring the well-developed terraces on the southeast side, where at least three different lake levels can be deciphered, follow the roadway 0.25 mile back to the trailhead and picnic area.

DIAMOND CRATERS NATURAL AREA

Hike 66

Explore a landscape of spatter cones and craters bedecked in glassy, ropey pahoehoe.

DISTANCE ▪ **4 miles round trip**

ELEVATION ▪ **4900–5200 feet**

DIFFICULTY ▪ **Easy**

TOPOGRAPHIC MAPS ▪ **Diamond Swamp, Diamond**

GEOLOGIC MAP ▪ **1**

PRECAUTIONS ▪ **Do not collect or damage plants, animals, or rocks in this BLM natural area. Bring plenty of water. This is a desert area with no trees—and no toilet facilities, either. Some cross-country hiking is necessary to see all features; a detailed brochure is available at the Burns District BLM office in Hines, 5 miles west of Burns, or at a kiosk at Lava Pit Crater.**

INFORMATION ▪ **Burns Bureau of Land Management: (541) 573-4400**

Directions: To reach Diamond Craters Natural Area, from Burns take US Highway 20 east 2 miles to Highway 205, then drive south 40.5 miles to the Diamond

A pressure ridge at Diamond Craters lifts sagebrush and rabbitbrush like a huge, barnacled whale.

Grain Camp Road. Drive east 6 miles, then turn north and drive 2 miles to Diamond Craters Natural Area. The hike around Diamond Craters begins at the Lava Pit Crater parking lot 0.6 mile into the Diamond Craters Natural Area.

About the Landscape: Along much of Highway 205 east of US Highway 20, the red-brown, coarsely columned cliffs are Devine Canyon ash flow, a 9-million-year-old ignimbrite that erupted from vents near Burns. At Lava Pit Crater, note the flow patterns frozen into the lavas, including exquisite lava gutters, tubes, and ropy pahoehoe festooned and wrinkled as the flowing lava formed a glass skin and solidified.

Trail Guide: Begin your hike with a tour of the multiple lava pits at the first stop. The surface of this pahoehoe lava is fragile, so please be careful. Also, the rims of these craters are undercut and unsupported; stifle the urge to run to the edge and peer over, or you could become the latest addition to the rubble on the crater floor. Continue another 0.6 mile along the road to Red Bomb Crater. This cone is constructed of red cinders, or scoria. Many volcanic bombs are scattered here. Remember this is a geologic catch-and-release area: don't take any souvenirs home with you.

Continue 2.7 miles along the roadway to Twin Craters. These symmetrical craters are *maars*—blowouts created by an eruption or explosion of steam. The road ends at Dry Maar at the edge of the Central Crater Complex about 0.6 mile farther. This complex was a main part of the collapse as lava escaped from

190

under the inflated dome at the eruption site—Lava Pit Crater. This crater complex is really a collapsed caldera, similar to Newberry Volcano but smaller (200 feet deep and 3500 feet wide), with many smaller nested craters.

To return, retrace your steps or scale the central ridge and return cross-country along the north side of the Central Crater Complex and then head 0.25 mile west along the margin of a narrow valley, the graben created by the collapse of the basalt crust of Diamond Craters.

A driblet spire at Diamond Craters rises where hot lava was forced up and out of a cooling lava flow, building a monument of fluid, oozing, and glassy basalt.

Chapter 8
THE BASIN AND RANGE

Oregon's Basin and Range specializes in open space, an arid climate, and huge fault-block mountains: Steens Mountain, Abert Rim, Hart Mountain, and the Pueblos. Thermal springs and earthquakes energize this region, which extends from Klamath Falls almost to the Idaho border, hanging like a skirt below the High Lava Plains volcanics. There are few marked trails in the vast open region. But who needs trails when you can see for miles in a 360-degree circle? Part of the beauty here is the region's quiet vastness—what writer John McPhee has called "a soundless immensity with mountains in it."

This is the home of the young and the restless, where the mantle rises closest to the surface and the continent moves and stretches. The uneven tableau of basins and flat-topped ranges are the stretch marks of a continent birthing new land—a stretching landscape built on a thin-skinned carapace of ancient terranes (Hike 68). The basalts that cap Steens Mountain, Abert Rim, Poker Jim Ridge, and other ranges are contemporaries of the Columbia River flood basalts, erupted about 16 million years ago. The basalts share a similar source—the first eruptions of lavas known as the Yellowstone hotspot. The hotspot is a plume of hot magma that stays in one spot while the earth's crust moves over the top of it. As North America moved west, the eruptions effectively

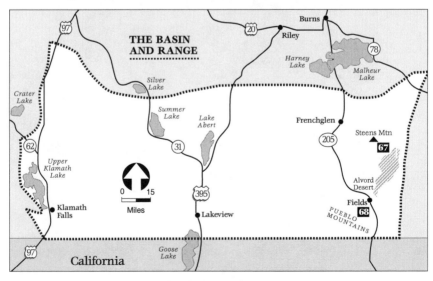

The Alvord Desert is part of the expanding Basin and Range.

moved east. Today this same source of magma has hardly moved, but in the last 16 million years, North America has inched some 350 miles westward. The plume that fed the Steens and Columbia River basalts today drives the geysers—and possible future eruptions—at Yellowstone National Park.

Until about 10 million years ago, this was a flat, arid, basalt-drowned landscape. Then, gradually, the faults of the northern Basin and Range in Oregon became active. In the Basin and Range, major faulting and uplift began in earnest less than 9 million years ago. Steens Mountain, rising to 9774 feet above the Alvord Desert, is a major Basin and Range escarpment. Hot springs mark the Alvord fault, one of the tension gashes across southeast Oregon that stretch the continent westward. In about 9 million years, the summit of Steens Mountain was uplifted 7000 feet. While this seems like a lot of uplift, it works out to

9 inches per 1000 years, or the equivalent of one magnitude 7 earthquake per 1000 years. Not as earthshaking as it first seems. For 9 million years the Basin and Range has been pulling apart, leaving fragments of crust floating on the mantle like ice on a rolling spring sea. Mantle fluids—the young basalt flows of Jordan Craters (Hike 71) and a hundred other nameless vents—have oozed to the surface as the crust thins.

Hike 67
STEENS MOUNTAIN RIM WALK

Hike at the rim of Oregon's largest fault block mountain.

DISTANCE ■ **12 miles one way**

ELEVATION ■ **8400–9774 feet**

DIFFICULTY ■ **Moderate to strenuous**

TOPOGRAPHIC MAPS ■ **Wildhorse Lake, Alvord Hot Springs, Mann Lake, Big Pasture Creek**

GEOLOGIC MAPS ■ **39–42**

PRECAUTIONS ■ **The summit of Steens Mountain can attract and hold severe weather year-round; be prepared for snow, rain, high wind, and/or intense heat. There is no water on this route; carry plenty. The Steens Mountain Loop Road is open from July 1 to October 31; the best time to try this hike is usually from July 15 to September 15. The hike can be done using a shuttle vehicle at the Kiger Gorge viewpoint.**

INFORMATION ■ **Burns Bureau of Land Management: (541) 573-4400**

Directions: To reach the trailhead at Wildhorse Lake, from Burns take US Highway 20 east to Highway 205. Drive 75 miles south on Highway 205 to Frenchglen. From Frenchglen, take the Steens Mountain Loop Road 25 miles to the summit of Steens Mountain. From the summit, continue south to Wildhorse Lake trailhead.

About the Landscape: Steens Mountain, a layer cake of rock, is uplifted along the Alvord fault. Steens Mountain stands high above the desert not because it was built by lava flows, but because faults and earthquakes uplifted its east side almost 1 mile long after the eruptions ceased.

The oldest rocks of Steens Mountain are the 20- to 25-million-year-old light-colored rocks exposed in its base. They jut from the Alvord Creek drainage, form the bottom of Devine Rock, and are best exposed along the eastern face of Steens. These rhyolites, dacites, and lakebed sediments (known as the Alvord Creek Formation, Pike Creek Formation, and Steens Mountain Volcanics) formed a low-slung complex of domes, andesites, stubby rhyolite flows, and thick layers of tuff. The sediments of small lakes reveal plant fossils of early Miocene age. The older rhyolites and andesites brought mineralization and ores with them. Gold, silver, and mercury have been mined from these rocks, especially where they are well exposed south of Steens Mountain.

The dark flows of Steens basalt form the top two-thirds of Steens Mountain's escarpment. Steens erupted rapidly about 16.6 million years ago; most basalt flows welled to the surface and then spread. The Steens basalts are flood basalts that erupted from fissures; the roots of these fissures are exposed as vertical dikes in the mountain's steep face. The Steens basalts appeared during a reversal of the earth's magnetic field. The changing direction of magnetic north and south are preserved in one single flow, about halfway down Steens Mountain's face.

Many basalts on Steens Mountain bear interesting textures. Near Wildhorse Lake and elsewhere, basalt outcrops and boulders sport large rectangular white or gray crystals of feldspar. They often cluster in clumps, prompting the informal name "turkey-track" basalts for rocks with this distinctive texture. Other basalts display rounded holes, both large and small,

View of Wildhorse Lake, Steens Mountain

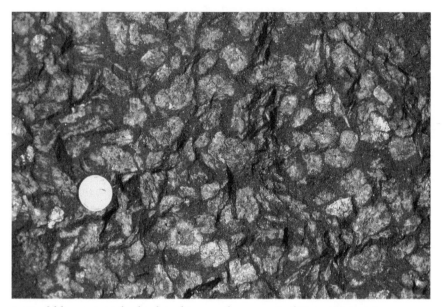

Large feldspar crystals clog basalts near the summit of Steens Mountain.

which are the bubbles created by gas trapped in the cooling basalt lava.

The spectacular canyons of Steens Mountain were carved by glaciers. Big Indian, Kiger, and Blitzen Gorges display classic broad-bottomed U shapes. Wildhorse and Little Wildhorse Lakes are glacial cirques. During the Pleistocene, Steens Mountain sported an extensive ice cap. Glacial moraine extends 10 miles down Steens' gentle west slope. Polished and striated (scratched) bedrock surfaces are abundant from Fish Lake to the summit of Steens Mountain.

Trail Guide: Most people drive to the top of Steens Mountain, peer over the rim, express some degree of awe or humility, and drive away, thinking they've seen the place. And they have seen some of it. But they have not felt Steens Mountain, not breathed its wind, felt its heat, or touched its brooding, basaltic heart. This hike covers the descent to Wildhorse Lake and back, then walks along the rim of Steens Mountain to Kiger Gorge, examining rocks and landscape along the way. There is no developed trail; you can make the hike longer or shorter. Or you may drop a vehicle at Kiger Gorge, the farthest point on the hike, and drive a second to the Wildhorse Lake trailhead to begin a one-way hike. No developed trails connect the top and bottom of Steens Mountain, although the Desert Trail route extends from Frog Springs up along ridges above Wildhorse Canyon to the Wildhorse Lake parking lot.

Begin at the Wildhorse Lake and Steens Summit parking area at the end of Steens Mountain Road. You may want to hike the 1-mile round-trip trail to the summit first for a breathtaking view (literally, at 9774 feet). The 3-mile round-trip trail from the parking area down to Wildhorse Lake and back, while an undeveloped path, is easy to follow and the only trail to be found on the top of Steens Mountain. This small, turquoise lake is tucked into austere basaltic surroundings.

Ascend back to the parking area and head upslope to the rim of Steens Mountain. There is no trail along the rim; however, the view from the top changes at every promontory and every canyon. At the south end of this walk, look for the older, lighter-colored volcanic rocks beneath the Steens basalts. Toward the developed East Rim overlook parking area, 2 miles north, feeder dikes of Steens basalt become more abundant. These vertical forms contrast markedly with the horizontal pancake-stack of basalt flows that compose the mountain. Many dikes create a linear spine. Dikes also cut through the headwall of Kiger Gorge and the narrow divide between Kiger Gorge and the east face of Steens Mountain.

This walk ends at the Kiger Gorge viewpoint, about 0.25 mile north of the main Steens Mountain loop road. This vista showcases a classic U-shaped glacial valley. Glacial polish has smoothed the outcrops at the head of Kiger Gorge. When you have had all the views, wind, cold, or heat you can handle, return along the top of Steens Mountain or shuttle back to the Wildhorse Lake parking area.

Hike
68

PUEBLO MOUNTAINS

Hike into an exotic terrane of ancient greenstones, the remnants of Jurassic islands..

DISTANCE ▥ **9 miles round trip**
ELEVATION ▥ **4300–7200 feet**
DIFFICULTY ▥ **Moderate**
TOPOGRAPHIC MAPS ▥ **Ladycomb Peak, Van Horn Basin**
GEOLOGIC MAP ▥ **43**
PRECAUTIONS ▥ **Carry water. Watch out for rattlesnakes. The weather is capricious; be prepared for extreme heat, violent thunderstorms, and summer snow. Portions of the road are impassable when wet.**
INFORMATION ▥ **Burns Bureau of Land Management: (541) 573-4400**

Directions: To reach the trailhead, from Fields take Highway 205 south for 9.2 miles to Arizona Creek Road (BLM Road 82551-1-A0). Follow this unmarked dirt track east for 0.5 mile until you reach the BLM Wilderness Study Area sign at the mouth of Arizona Creek canyon.

Rhyolite outcrops loom above Arizona Creek

About the Landscape: The 170- to 200-million-year-old rocks along Arizona Creek are very different from the rocks of Steens Mountain. They are much older, and like the rocks of the Blue Mountains and the Klamaths, they are part of an exotic terrane. These were once volcanoes. But their compositions suggest that unlike the island terranes of the Blue Mountains or Klamaths, the ancient rocks of the Pueblos developed on the western edge of the continent and likely have been moved more than 150 miles north from their original location by faulting.

Trail Guide: The hike follows the road for the first 1.5 miles, rising through soft slopes cut into the young Miocene gravels and tuffs. The bedding is best exposed in the slopes south of the road and in several steep exposures just above it.

About 1 mile up the canyon, a track veers upslope to the right. This path leads, in another mile, to several abandoned mines and glory holes (open pits) in the Jurassic rocks and to a fine view of the valley to the west. Return to the main road and continue to the crossing of Arizona Creek. The road continues left, switch-backing up Pueblo Mountain; follow the path straight ahead instead. This hikers' trail/cow path leads, in 2.5 miles, to inviting pinnacles and jagged outcrops of Jurassic rhyolite. Detailed examination of these rocks, and the talus along the trail, reveals the characteristic angular clasts (fragments)

198

of volcanic breccia and, in the darker rocks, the yellow-green of epidote.

Above the pinnacles the trail meets a jeep track. Continue along the path through outcrops of metamorphosed rhyolite along the creek. About 3.5 miles into the walk, emerge from the canyon and note that the bedrock changes. From here to its end in Stergen Meadows, at 4.5 miles, the hike traverses Miocene Steens basalts and slightly older ash-flow tuffs. Ambitious hikers may want to scale the back side of Pueblo Mountain. Return as you came.

THE EXPANDING BASIN AND RANGE

If you'd like to invest in real estate and know that your holdings will grow, then buy property at Adel or Plush, Fields or Frenchglen. For in remote southeast Oregon, where there seems to be plenty of landscape already, the continent is stretching. Beneath the Basin and Range a restless mantle is forcing the earth's crust to expand ever westward. The growth rate is about the same at which a fingernail grows—about a centimeter per year for the last 20 million years.

The stretching mantle and crust of the Basin and Range has shoved parts of Oregon farther to the west. In particular, it has rotated the Cascades, Klamath Mountains, and Coast Range rather like the swing of a huge pendulum, with the pivot point somewhere in north-central Washington. This same stress has rotated the Blue Mountains a bit northward. The tilted and faulted basalt near Mosier and The Dalles are the result of this motion. But the most obvious results of motion in the Basin and Range are the region's huge fault-bounded rims—including Steens Mountain, Abert Rim, and Hart Mountain, along with the basins between them—a landscape that will continue to grow for a long time to come.

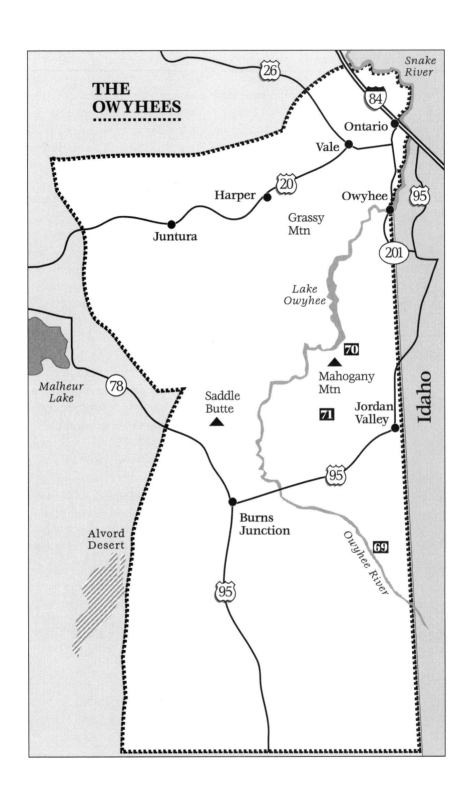

THE
OWYHEES

Snake
River

26

84

Ontario

Vale

20

Harper

Owyhee

95

Juntura

Grassy
Mtn

201

Lake
Owyhee

70

Mahogany
Mtn

Malheur
Lake

78

Saddle
Butte

71

Jordan
Valley

Idaho

95

Burns
Junction

Alvord
Desert

95

Owyhee River

69

Chapter 9

THE OWYHEES

The Owyhees are tucked absent-mindedly into Oregon's back pocket like a rumpled dollar bill. Many dusty roads, but few trails, navigate their wrinkled landscape. Few hikers explore their canyons. The Owyhees remain a faraway, forgotten desert landscape, whose loudest voice is silence.

The Owyhees are the domain of calderas—flat-lying, explosive volcanoes that produced ash and gas and gold. Owyhee geology is distinct from the High Lava Plains or the Basin and Range, although the rocks are similar in age.

The volcanoes of the Owyhees first erupted 17 to 15 million years ago. Mahogany Mountain and Three Fingers Rock represent two of these old volcanoes. The principal products of these two major calderas were gas and ash and explosive eruptions of hot, thick, sticky ash-flow tuffs. Today these rocks form the cliffs of Leslie Gulch and Succor Creek.

The second period of geologic activity followed closely on the heels of the calderas. The scene of action shifted west. From 14.5 to about 12 million years ago, the central part of the Owyhees began to pull apart, forming a north-south fault-bounded valley (the Oregon-Idaho graben) that today extends through the town of Harper. Parts of this valley contained lakes. Volcanic eruptions poured into these shallow lakes, producing layered ash and pillow basalts.

The third period of volcanic activity persisted from 10 to about 6 million years ago. The spotlight shifted west again. Several large volcanic centers, including Saddle Mountain, Star Butte, and Mustang Butte, erupted. Basalts and rhyolites poured out of these rhyolite volcanoes.

As these eruptions dwindled, a new chapter in Owyhee geologic history began. Faulting created a broad valley. Water from the southward-draining Snake River collected in a deepening valley, creating a lake. This lake, called Lake Idaho, persisted from about 7 until 2 million years ago. The fragile sedimentary rocks of this lakebed stand as stark white cliffs north of Harper. About 2 million years ago, broad regional tilting drained Lake Idaho and helped create the present northward course of the Snake River.

The last eruptive episode lasted from about 2 million until only 4000 years ago. These relatively young lavas include the flows at Jordan Craters (about 4000 years in age) and the basalts that surround Saddle Butte (about 100,000 years old).

OWYHEE RIVER, THREE FORKS

Hike

69

Hike along the Owyhee River bank to a relaxing hot spring.

DISTANCE ■ 4 miles round trip

ELEVATION ■ 3850–3980 feet

DIFFICULTY ■ Moderate

TOPOGRAPHIC MAP ■ Three Forks

GEOLOGIC MAPS ■ 1, 51

PRECAUTIONS ■ This is prime rattlesnake territory, though snakes are not often seen here. Temperatures are torrid on hot summer days. This hike requires wading the river: hike at low water in fall. Roads may be impassable in spring or rainy weather. It's a 60-mile round trip from Jordan Valley to Three Forks and back, so fill gas tanks at Jordan Valley.

INFORMATION ■ Vale Bureau of Land Management: (541) 473-3144

Directions: From Jordan Valley, where US Highway 95 makes a 90-degree turn near a service station at the north end of town, turn east on Juniper Mountain Road (Mud Flat Road). The road is paved here and eventually turns south. At about 2 miles, the road enters Idaho. At about 7 miles the pavement ends near Pleasant Valley School. Bear right and continue on unpaved Juniper Mountain Road for 14 more miles to Three Forks Junction. Turn right and travel 10 miles to Three Forks Road. Turn left and travel 3 miles to the rim of the canyon. Follow the steep road down to the river 1.5 miles and 800 feet elevation drop.

About the Landscape: The Owyhee River and the North Fork of the Owyhee River meet at Three Forks. This is also the site of the Three Forks Dome, a large rhyolite extrusive center that disgorged thick, viscous flows of silica-rich lava here between 14 and 10 million years ago. Its summit, 4755 feet, towers 1000 feet above the river here. Younger faults that are part of the Oregon-Idaho graben have provided pathways for the Owyhee River's erosion. They also permit warm water to surface at hot springs, including the multiple hot springs found about 2 miles upstream along the Owyhee from its confluence with the smaller North Fork.

Trail Guide: From a generous parking area and informal campground at the bottom of the road down from the Owyhee Canyon's rimrock, a well-developed road leads 0.2 mile to the confluence of the North Fork and main-stem Owyhee. The trail to the hot springs is very informal but well-trodden—once you find it. Ford the North Fork at this confluence and continue on a very

The rhyolite at Three Forks forms daunting, rosy cliffs with broad, awkward columnar joints along the Owyhee River.

diffuse pathway through reeds and cottonwoods. (There are nettles here, too.) Your goal is to make your way to the base of the much drier slope about 100 yards to the west. The trail begins at the base of the slope.

Follow the path to the west (right). In another 100 yards it crosses a barbed-wire fence gate. Then your hike is in the clear for the next 1.7 miles. The path follows the river, providing exceptional views of massive rhyolite columns above and sandy beaches on the river below.

1.8 miles from the North Fork, the trail arrives at the Owyhee River. To reach the hot springs, you'll need to ford the river at this point. In June, the Owyhee is about thigh-deep and quite warm. By August, it is knee-deep or less.

The trail rambles through the riverbank willows, heading for the drier terrain along the river's north shore. Follow this path an additional 0.2 mile to the hot springs. There are pools here for soaking in. This is a popular spot for river-runners as well as hikers, so expect company while you're soaking. Return as you came.

LESLIE GULCH AND JUNIPER CREEK TRAIL

Hike through the sculpted outpourings of a caldera's eruption.

DISTANCE ▪ 4–7 miles round trip

ELEVATION ▪ 3100–3700 feet

DIFFICULTY ▪ Moderate

TOPOGRAPHIC MAP ▪ Rooster Comb

GEOLOGIC MAPS ▪ 46, 50

PRECAUTIONS ▪ Summer weather is torrid and dehydration is a serious threat; take twice the water you would in the mountains. Rattlesnakes abound; be watchful and remember that a calm, quick retreat is the safest way to deal with a snake. Roads are muddy to the point of impassability in the early spring (March) and in wet weather.

INFORMATION ▪ Vale Bureau of Land Management: (541) 473-3144

Directions: The most scenic route to Leslie Gulch Road begins in Idaho. Take US Highway 95 south from Interstate 84. Two miles after US Highway 95 crosses into Oregon, turn west on Succor Creek Road. Follow Succor Creek Road west and north 6 miles and turn west onto the broad, inviting surface of Leslie Gulch Road. After 7 miles, Upper Leslie Gulch canyon opens to the south. To find Juniper Creek Trail, look to the right side of the road for a parking area and rest area at about 10 miles along the Leslie Gulch Road.

About the Landscape: The tawny, 15.5-million-year-old rocks of Leslie Gulch erupted from the Mahogany Mountain caldera just to the south. This caldera is the oldest known in the Owyhees. Part of the vast caldera vent system is

Odd forms are sculpted from ash flow tuffs along Juniper Creek near Leslie Gulch.

exposed about 7 miles down the Leslie Gulch Road, near the cabin at Mud Spring (Diablo Canyon); dark red rhyolite dikes that carried lavas to the surface cut through the tawny canyon walls. The Leslie Gulch ash-flow tuff was only one product of the Mahogany Mountain caldera's eruption. Ash from this volcano covered thousands of square miles. A variety of rhyolite domes and flows also scatter across the landscape here. By 14.9 million years ago, the caldera quieted and eruptions from the main vent complex ceased.

Trail Guide: One of the best hikes in Leslie Gulch is the hike up Juniper Creek. This well-developed trail begins at a rest area about 10 miles along the Leslie Gulch Road. In 2 miles of walking up the trail, the pockmarked tuffs never fail to astound hikers with their colors and forms. All were deposited as hot, sticky, wet ash erupted from the Mahogany Mountain caldera about 15.5 million years ago. Wind and rain have sculpted the soft, gas-pocketed stones.

You can also hike to Mahogany Mountain along Dago Gulch. The informal trail fades after the first 0.5 mile, but the open canyon is easily navigated on animal trails. Cavities in the tan to yellow Leslie Gulch tuffs were created by gas bubbles; a few are the casts of other rocks carried along in the powerful ash flow. In about 2 miles, reach Upper Leslie Gulch, which leads to Mahogany Mountain—the source of the Leslie Gulch ash-flow tuff that dominates the landscape here. A relict stand of ponderosa pine—old growth about 400 years in age—hides on north-facing slopes about 3 miles along the canyon. Look for desert bighorn sheep in late fall. When you've gone as far as you'd like, retrace your steps back down the gulch.

Hike

71 JORDAN CRATERS

Explore a vent complex with frozen, glassy lava that looks as though it erupted yesterday.

DISTANCE ▪ 1 mile or more round trip

ELEVATION ▪ 4550–4670 feet

DIFFICULTY ▪ Easy to moderate

TOPOGRAPHIC MAPS ▪ Jordan Craters North, Jordan Craters South

GEOLOGIC MAPS ▪ 48–50

PRECAUTIONS ▪ The location is isolated and the drive long and bumpy but well worth it. Parts of this road can be muddy. This area is torrid in the summer; the trip is best attempted in May or September. No services after US Highway 95.

INFORMATION ▪ Vale Bureau of Land Management: (541) 473-3144

Directions: From Interstate 84 in Idaho, take US Highway 95 south about 60 miles. Turn west on Jordan Craters Road, about 2 miles past an old schoolhouse.

Drive west a total of 35 miles on Jordan Craters Road, which becomes Blow Out Reservoir Road. Jordan Craters' Lava Field becomes visible in the last 7 miles of the drive. As you pass most of the flow, the road curves and rises up a hill. An unmarked road to the left takes you to the Jordan Craters Lava Field, Coffeepot Crater, and the beginning of the hike.

About the Landscape: Jordan Craters are among the youngest and youngest-looking basalts in Oregon. They are part of a group of basalt cinder cones and vents, including nearby Clarks Butte and Rocky Butte, that erupted a very fluid alkali *olivine* basalt lava. Jordan Craters erupted 4000 years ago. The ropy pahoehoe textures of Jordan Craters basalts contrast with rubbly aa lavas common in the Cascades. The smooth flows from Jordan Craters belie their rugged topography. Collapse pits, small spatter cones, lava gutters, and lava tubes challenge the cross-country hiker.

Trail Guide: From the parking lot, a 1-mile trail leads around Coffeepot Crater. It offers memorable views of the stratified lava flows inside this vent. Trace a counterclockwise path around the loop to encounter a wonderland of lava flow forms. The gutters, or lava flow paths, as well as ropy pahoehoe surfaces and thinly surfaced lava tubes, are plainly evident. The layers on the crater walls are built of successive flows. Continue around the crater to the cindered slope. The trail gains strength up this slope, and leads to another overview of Coffeepot Crater. From the top you can see the flow patterns of the basalt as it moved toward Cow Lakes. The spatter cones and hoodoos on the west side of the crater are classic examples of blowouts, or cones built of spattered, hot, gooey lava bombs.

A cinder cone rises above the dark, ropy, pahoehoe flows typical of the Jordan Craters basalts.

206

CALDERAS

A caldera is among the most deceptive type of volcano. Its landscape is generally flat. There is no menacing peak. In fact, there is usually a scenic lake (Crater Lake, Yellowstone Lake) or flat, unbothersome basin (Pueblo Valley, Leslie Gulch). But these places are geologic wolves in geographic sheep's clothing. They have—or will—produce the most violent volcanic eruptions on the planet.

There are three types of calderas: (1) those that, like Crater Lake and Krakatoa, produced the final extremely explosive eruptions of stratovolcanoes or shield volcanoes. (2) vast depressions, like the summit of Mauna Loa, that are caused by the collapse of a volcanic summit as the supporting lava erupts, and (3) the hugely destructive volcanoes that combine the worst of both worlds: explosive eruptions of ash and gas, that covers hundreds or thousands of square miles, followed by collapse of the low, flat summit into the evacuated magma chamber below.

The third type of massive eruption produced much of the Owyhees' landscape, including the tuffs of Leslie Gulch, the Honeycombs, and Succor Creek. The ornate holes in many of these rocks are a vestige of the gas trapped by sticky ash-lava explosive mixes and frozen in place as the hot, frothy eruptive mass solidified quickly. These huge volcanoes also contributed to the gold deposits of Grassy Mountain, Red Mountain, and other claims in the Owyhees.

Chapter 10
THE BLUE MOUNTAINS AND THE COLUMBIA PLATEAU

The Blue Mountains were built with a foundation of exotic terranes overlain by native volcanic rocks from Eocene to Miocene in age (55 to 15 million years). The remnants of islands that developed about 400 to 170 million years ago—off the coast of Idaho—and were accreted to the continent beginning about 120 million years ago—are well exposed in Hells Canyon, the Wallowas, Elkhorn, Greenhorn, and Strawberry Mountains, where they have been uplifted by faulting and folding. These rocks are similar to the rocks of the Klamath Mountains in Oregon and northern California. They are known, collectively, as the Blue Mountain island arc, and they seem to represent a single, though complex and multigenerational, system of island arc volcanoes.

On a cold August day in the Wallowas, it is hard to realize you are walking in what once was a tropical sea some 235 million years ago. Yet with a little

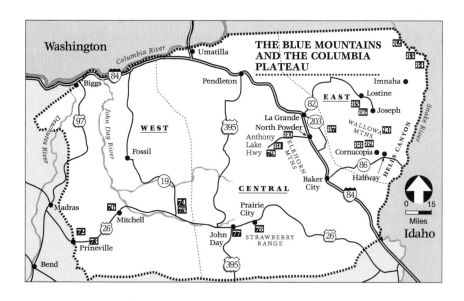

imagination, you can be in Tahiti. For the Wallowa Mountains' rocks, like those of neighboring Hells Canyon, originated as reef-fringed volcanic islands—about the latitude of modern Hawaii. Hells Canyon is carved mostly from the volcanoes (Hike 83); the Wallowa Mountains feature coral reefs and the adjacent seafloor (Hike 88). Together, these are the Wallowa terrane of the Blue Mountain island arc.

Hells Canyon displays the twisted wreckage of ancient volcanoes (Hike 83). Like a double-decker bus, there are two generations of volcanoes here, one built atop the other.

Triassic sedimentary rocks compose much of the Wallowa Mountain landscapes along Hurricane Creek.

The oldest volcanoes (275 million years in age, or Permian) stretch along the Snake River from Oxbow north to Hells Canyon Dam. The tattered remnants of younger (Triassic) rocks, 235 million years old, extend from the dam north to Asotin, Washington. All these volcanic rocks—originally andesite and basalt—bear the greenish hue of age and abuse. They have been altered to greenstone, a low-temperature metamorphic rock. In the Wallowa Mountains, more green-hued volcanic rocks frame the Wallowa River, proving the link between Hells Canyon and the Wallowas. Similar rocks occur in the North Fork of the John Day River (Hike 79), while the roots of ancient volcanoes now reside atop Canyon Mountain (Hike 77).

Most of the Wallowa Mountains' layered rocks are coral reefs and sediments that fringed and ultimately covered the island volcanoes. Some 235 million years ago, tropical fish swam at Sacajawea Peak and ichthyosaurs played on its flanks. The soft gray limestone of Sacajawea Peak, Marble Mountain, and Hurwall and Hurricane Divides was a flourishing coral reef complex (Hike 86). Similar limestones occur at Summit Point in the southeast Wallowa Mountains (Hike 88). These rocks preserve a fossil ecosystem of clams, brachiopods, corals, and sponges. Because this region was a series of small islands far from a major landmass during most of the Mesozoic, four-footed dinosaurs probably

209

never roamed the ancient, tropical beaches of the Blue Mountains, although remains of both swimming (ichthyosaurs) and flying (pterosaurs) dinosaur relatives have been found.

Hard, white rock cores the Wallowa Mountains, Elkhorn Ridge, and parts of the Greenhorn Mountains. These rocks look like granite, feel like granite, and break like granite. But they are not granite. Though they are similar, subtle differences in minerals and chemical compositions distinguish them from classic granites. Geologists call these rocks granitic rocks (Hikes 80, 81, 85–90). These bland white rocks provided Oregon's richest and longest-lasting gold mine, at Cornucopia (Hike 89), and many other gold mines in the Wallowa, Elkhorn, and Greenhorn Mountains.

Once the exotic islands of the Blue Mountain island arc docked with North America, two generations of volcanoes contributed to Blue Mountain landscapes. The earliest, the Clarno Formation, built volcanoes similar to Mount Hood from Prineville to John Day and north to Fossil and Condon about 45 million years ago during the Eocene period. The exceptional fossils in the John Day Fossil Beds near Dayville provide a record of the animals and semitropical vegetation that thrived here in a warmer and wetter climate (Hike 74).

By 35 million years ago, in the Oligocene period, the first volcanoes of the Cascades were active, and ash from their eruptions covered much of the cooler eastern Oregon landscape (Hikes 74, 76). This time is recorded in the colorful banded soil deposits of the Painted Hills and Sheep Rock units of the John Day Fossil Beds (Hikes 74–76).

The Columbia River basalts cap these rocks and, in fact, cap the geology of the Blue Mountains. While the linear vents and shield volcanoes erupted to the south at Steens Mountain (at the time, it was Steens plateau), similar basaltic lavas covered much of northeast Oregon. Their continuing and voluminous eruptions stacked basalt more than 15,000 feet deep in the center of the Columbia Basin and sent lava flows all the way to the sea, 300 miles away (Hikes 16, 18, 20, 82, 84).

During the last 10 million years, the Wallowa Mountains have been uplifted more than 7000 feet by the Wallowa fault (and other faults on the south and west sides of the range). Faulting began about 13 million years ago and still uplifts the range today.

The Wallowas' most recent chapter was written by glaciers. Nine major alpine glaciers chiseled the Wallowas into their present form during the Pleistocene, finally retreating (melting) completely back into their mountain stronghold about 10,000 years ago. Wallowa Lake, swaddled in gravelly moraine, is Oregon's second-deepest lake.

Hike 72

TWIN PILLARS, MILL CREEK WILDERNESS

Hike into the remnants of a 23-million-year-old vent.

DISTANCE ■ **10 miles round trip**

ELEVATION ■ **3750–5360 feet**

DIFFICULTY ■ **Moderate**

TOPOGRAPHIC MAP ■ **Steins Pillar**

GEOLOGIC MAP ■ **60**

FEES/REGULATIONS ■ **Northwest Forest Pass required for trailhead parking.**

PRECAUTIONS ■ **None**

INFORMATION ■ **Lookout Mountain Ranger District, Ochoco National Forest: (541) 416-6500**

Directions: From Prineville, drive 8 miles east on US Highway 26. Turn left (north) on Mill Creek Road (which becomes USFS Road 33) and follow it for 10.7 miles to Wildcat Campground. The trailhead parking for the Mill Creek–Twin Pillars hike is just before the campground entry. (To find Brennan Palisades, drive about 5 miles down Mill Creek Road, turn left onto Forest Road 3370, and in 0.9 mile bear left on an unsigned road. Brennan Palisades is less than a 0.25 mile down the road on the right.)

About the Landscape: This hike follows Mill Creek for much of its distance, then strikes off across country to visit an ancient, 23-million-year-old volcanic vent—now a rock outcrop known as Twin Pillars. It also tours the recovery of the area burned in August 2000, as part of the 18,000-acre Hash Rock Fire. En route to the trailhead, you'll see Steins Pillar—a narrow

Steins Pillar is a remnant of Oligocene volcanoes.

211

spire composed of debris-flow deposits that possibly originated from the Twin Peaks vents long, long ago. A trail, accessible from Forest Service Road 3300-500, leads to the pillar's base. You may also want to explore Brennan Palisades, a macabre landscape of a sculpted and eroded 31-million-year-old rhyolite flow nearby.

Trail Guide: The Mill Creek Trail begins at the parking lot on the right just before you enter Wildcat Campground. Walk down the road and just across the bridge the trail follows the creek to the left. Another trailhead also leaves from the campground. Both spurs join 0.4 mile from the bridge.

For its first 2.5 miles, the nearly flat trail meanders back and forth across Mill Creek. Hikers must ford the stream at several crossings, and a pair of Gore-Tex-lined boots is a boon here. In spring, Mill Creek can be a raging torrent, so be prepared to contend with a vigorous stream from late March through mid-June.

The first portion of the hike leads through the Hash Rock Fire's outer fringes, where many trees survived and the landscape is little-changed. You may not notice the fire scars at first, but by 2.5 miles into the hike, as you approach the junction with Belknap Trail, it's obvious that a fire has affected the landscape.

At 2.5 miles, the trail splits—the Belknap Trail heads up the hill to the right; the Twin Pillars Trail continues straight, along the creek. As you continue on the Twin Pillars Trail, evidence of the fire increases.

At 3 miles, the trail climbs away from the creek and enters an area where the fire burned hotter, a stand-replacement blaze that killed 80 percent to 100 percent of the older pines and tamaracks. This gaunt but recovering landscape is fascinating. Grass, some seeded after the fire, some native, flourishes on the nitrogen-enriched soils. Native bull thistle, aster, and snowberry have sprouted. Ceanothis, a nitrogen-fixing shrub whose seeds sprout only after being heated by fire, is beginning to grow. And in places where the ground might seem completely bare and sterile, mosses and lichens are restoring the forest's macrobiotic crust. Woodpeckers, including black-backed and flickers, are busy drilling the trees (woodpecker, nuthatch, and chickadee populations increase dramatically after fires), while rufous-sided hummingbirds patrol the creek banks for mint, columbine, shooting star, and fireweed.

The 2-mile trek from the creek to Twin Pillars (a very obvious landmark now, given the absence of trees) has only a few spots of good shade and little water, save in one small creek crossing, so plan accordingly and carry water for this stretch.

You reach Twin Pillars 5 miles from the trailhead. To explore these dual rocks, you will have to leave the trail and scramble upslope a bit. The rock here is crumbly. Note the layers in the smaller pillar and on the flanks of the larger spire. Here, there are light-colored volcanic rocks that erupted in layers of hot, pasty lava, accompanied by blasts of steam from the vent. It's hard

212

to imagine this as a volcanic vent, but 23 million years ago this spot may have resembled the slopes of a modern Mount Hood.

The Mill Creek Trail continues past Twin Pillars, but there is no water farther along the path—and very little shade in the burned-over forest. This is a good place to turn around and return as you came.

LOOKOUT MOUNTAIN: SUMMIT AND INDEPENDENT MINE LOOP

Hike **73**

Explore basalts atop one of the Ochoco's grandest peaks.

DISTANCE ■ 5 miles round trip

ELEVATION ■ 5810–6920 feet

DIFFICULTY ■ Moderate

TOPOGRAPHIC MAP ■ Lookout Mountain

GEOLOGIC MAPS ■ 60, 61, 64

FEES/REGULATIONS ■ Northwest Forest Pass required for trailhead parking.

PRECAUTIONS ■ Old mine tunnels and adits honeycomb the area near the trailhead. Please keep out of areas marked as dangerous by USFS signs.

INFORMATION ■ Lookout Mountain Ranger District, Ochoco National Forest: (541) 416-6500

Directions: From Prineville, drive 14.7 miles east on US Highway 26 and bear right (east) on County Road 123 (Lookout Mountain Road). Continue 8 miles to Ochoco Ranger Station. Just past the ranger station, bear right on USFS Road

Columbia River basalt caps Lookout Mountain.

42 and drive 6.3 miles to the junction with spur road 4205 and a parking lot for the Independent Mine Trail. To shorten your hike by almost 2 miles, continue on gravel road 0.9 mile to the real trailhead.

About the Landscape: This hike takes you past an old mine that produced mercury and a bit of gold until about 1950. It follows a trail to the top of Lookout Mountain with outstanding views of the Cascades and Ochocos.

Trail Guide: There are three routes to Lookout Mountain's summit that leave from the trailhead. Trail 808, which heads out toward the north provides a slow but easy and shaded ascent 4 miles to the top—and it's the trail you'll return on. Begin the loop hike on Trail 808A. This path tackles Lookout Mountain directly, after circling past a danger zone underlain by abandoned mine shafts that are prone to collapse. Heed the USFS warning signs here! The Independent Mine scratched mercury and gold ores from 40- to 45-million-year-old Clarno volcanic rocks—mostly debris flows that absorbed mineral-rich fluids from nearby vents on Round Mountain. In 0.2 mile, the trail joins an abandoned road that leads almost straight to flat meadows on Lookout Mountain's southern end. Here you can catch a first glimpse of the view in about 0.9 mile.

As it nears the summit, the trail encounters the first outcrops of Columbia River basalt. This is one of the westernmost exposures of Columbia River basalt in central Oregon, and it is responsible for Lookout Mountain's flat top and barren red soils. The trailside ground where the trail finds its first clearing is wet and marshy in the spring and in late summer is occupied with false hellebore (skunk cabbage) and silver sage, stunted rabbitbrush, lupine, and tarweed. There is virtually no grass, except for rip-gut brome and bottlebrush squirreltail—both are grasses designed with strong defenses against being eaten by sheep. The absence of normal bunchgrass and domination by unpalatable shrubs is the result of severe overgrazing of Lookout Mountain (and most eastern Oregon alpine area) by sheep in the late nineteenth and early twentieth centuries. In such a harsh, thin-soiled alpine environment, restoration takes a very long time. Most of the topsoil on Lookout Mountain's summit was eroded along with overgrazing.

In 1.5 miles, the trail reaches a junction with Trail 808. For a short loop, you can return downhill here—but once you have made it this far, you should explore the true

The Independent Mine extracted mercury ore from the base of Lookout Mountain until the 1950's.

summit areas of Lookout Mountain that still lie ahead. At 1.8 miles, there is a snow shelter, built in 1989 by the USFS. Continue north along the trail, and in 0.6 mile, you will reach the true summit area of Lookout Mountain, with views of the Cascades to the west and the Ochocos to the north and east.

Then return as you came to the junction of Trails 808 and 808A. Here, turn downslope on Trail 808—a path much easier on the knees. This trail heads gently downhill, then turns in a very wrong-headed direction to the north, when your instincts scream for you to hike to the south. It crosses a bog and leads along a stream. And after 0.5 mile of hiking, the trail switchbacks and turns toward home.

In another 1.4 miles, after crossing two more streams, it brings you into sight of the stamp mill and refinery of the Independent Mine—a long abandoned operation. In 0.5 mile from your first view, you pass just below the mine and also pass an adit (mineshaft); follow the main trail uphill about 0.1 mile and find the short spur trail connecting to the trailhead.

BATHOLITHS

The interiors of Oregon's oldest mountains harbor large bodies of white-colored, coarse-grained igneous rock that looks like granite. These rocks represent huge chambers of once-molten rock that lies far below the earth's surface. They are called batholiths—from the Greek *bathos*, or "deep," and *lithos*, or "stone."

There are several ways to generate a batholith. Smaller versions— a few miles across—may once have been the magma chamber beneath a volcano—or several volcanoes. Larger batholiths, including the Wallowa batholith of the Blue Mountains and Grayback pluton of the Klamaths, more likely represent crust and upper mantle melted during the collision of North America and island arc terranes. It is unlikely that these rocks represent the magma chambers beneath a volcano.

Big batholiths originated as complex and long-lived chambers of molten rock. Usually, they contain multiple generations of intrusions. The Wallowa batholith records at least four major periods of intrusion. The Grayback pluton records at least three. These large bodies of molten rock take tens of millions of years to cool and solidify. Their huge reservoir of heat metamorphoses the surrounding "country" rock that houses the molten material. Batholiths often melt and incorporate adjacent solid rocks, including sandstones, shales, and other crustal rocks, into their melts.

JOHN DAY FOSSIL BEDS: BLUE BASIN LOOP

Enter the domain of the oreodont, rhinos, and mouse-deer.

DISTANCE ▪ 3-mile loop

ELEVATION ▪ 2490–3000 feet

DIFFICULTY ▪ Moderate

TOPOGRAPHIC MAPS ▪ Clarno, Porcupine Butte

GEOLOGIC MAPS ▪ 60–62

FEES/REGULATIONS ▪ Northwest Forest Pass required for trailhead parking.

PRECAUTIONS ▪ Collecting fossils, or any other materials, in the national monument is illegal without a permit; permits are available only for research collection; inquire at the Cant Ranch headquarters about participating as a volunteer.

INFORMATION ▪ John Day Fossil Beds National Monument: (541) 987-2333

Directions: From John Day, drive west on US Highway 26 to Picture Gorge. Elegant exposures of the 16-million-year-old Picture Gorge basalt line the highway

View into Blue Basin

through the gorge; the ridge cut by Picture Gorge is capped by the 7.2-million-year-old Rattlesnake ignimbrite. In Picture Gorge, turn right on Highway 19 and cross the bridge over Rock Creek. A multilayered pinnacle known as Sheep Rock appears on the north side of the road along Highway 19. One mile from the Hwy 26–Hwy 19 junction, the new Paleontological Museum and Research Center appears on the left (south) side of the road—a great place to learn the local geology and examine fossils. To reach the trailhead, continue 4 miles west on Highway 19 to the Blue Basin turnoff and trailhead.

Bands in Blue Basin tuffs were produced by weathering and alteration.

About the Landscape: The Blue Basin, named for the aquamarine color of the fragile tuff beds, is a deeply eroded badland circumnavigated and invaded by a developed trail. The bluish tuffs are 28.9 million years old (Oligocene). These tuffs were deposited as ash erupted from volcanoes to the west (and possibly from Tower Mountain volcano to the east) and blown here by prevailing winds. The ash settled into shallow lakes, wetlands and forests—as did the remains of many large animals, as well as turtles and rodents.

In this basin, pioneer paleontologist rivals Edward Cope and John Marsh collected fossils competitively in the 1870s. The fossils recovered here more recently include turtles, opossums, dogs, bear-dogs, bears, horses, rhinoceros, giant pigs, oreodonts, and mountain beaver, as well as a variety of rodents and a tiny animal known as a mouse-deer.

Trail Guide: The loop trail around Blue Basin (also known as Turtle Cove) is easiest if hiked clockwise. Begin along the trail to the left that skirts the grassy backslope of the basin. The trail leads to sculpted cliffs on the east side of the basin, and after 1 mile climbs for a prolonged overview as it navigates the top of the basin.

The gravel trail finally descends steeply to the interior of the Blue Basin. Turn right along the paved side path to explore the badlands topography. This 0.5-mile portion of the trail leads into the interior of the Blue Basin. Several large fossils, including a turtle and an oreodont, are preserved in place and identified along the trail. Interpretive signs explain the rocks and the processes of fossil preservation and fossil discovery. Return to the main trail and the trailhead.

FOREE PICNIC AREA, FLOOD OF FIRE

Hike 75

Get an up-close look at the contact between Oligocene fossil beds and Columbia River basalt.

DISTANCE ▪ 0.5 mile round trip

ELEVATION ▪ 3000–3100 feet

DIFFICULTY ▪ Easy

TOPOGRAPHIC MAP ▪ Mount Misery (site and trails not shown on this map)

GEOLOGIC MAPS ▪ 60, 62

FEES/REGULATIONS ▪ Northwest Forest Pass required for trailhead parking.

PRECAUTIONS ▪ Collecting fossils, or any other materials, in the national monument is illegal without a permit; permits are available only for research collection; inquire at the Cant Ranch headquarters about participating as a volunteer.

INFORMATION ▪ John Day Fossil Beds National Monument: (541) 987-2333

Directions: From John Day, drive west on US Highway 26 about 20 miles to Picture Gorge. Turn right (north) on Oregon Highway 19. The new park headquarters are located 1 mile past this intersection on the left and are worth stopping at to explore the displays and learn more about the geologic and human history here. To reach the Foree Picnic Area trailhead, continue north on Highway 19 about 7 miles and turn right at the marked entry road. (At 4 miles, you pass the Blue Basin trailhead and parking area. See Hike 74.)

About the Landscape: This area contains Oligocene rocks, 30 to 25 million years old and similar in age to those of the Blue Basin (Hike 74). These soft-appearing, ash-rich exposures are part of the John Day Formation. They represent soils, stream beds, and lake bottoms. At the time they were deposited, the climate was temperate, with much more rainfall than the area experiences today. Rhinos and huge, boarlike enteleodonts roamed a savannah-like grassland that included maple, oak, and alder. Metasequoia, a tall, deciduous conifer, grew along streams. The entire landscape here was covered by Columbia River basalt flows about 16 million years ago. Subsequent up-lift and faulting tilted the basalts. The John Day River subsequently has carved a cross section through this landscape, revealing its complex history.

Trail Guide: Two very short trails begin at the Foree Picnic Area parking lot. One, called the "Flood of Fire," leads 50 yards or so uphill along a canyon rim, providing an overview of cream-colored spires below and the more distant John Day River. You also get a close-up view of the 16-million-year-old Miocene Columbia River basalt flow that overlies the tawny cliffs. An informal trail continues beyond

The short hikes at Foree Basin explore an environment that supported forests and lakes about 30 million years ago.

the pavement, leads almost to the ridge top here, and doubles the hiking distance.

The other trail heads off through a landscape barren of plants but rich in fossils. The Fossil Beds paleontologists have provided a few interpretive signs, as well as a few sample fossils for you to observe and touch—but not take! Like the Blue Basin's Island in Time Trail, this path (Story in Stone) displays past life, including (as of this writing) fossils of ancient antelope and rodents, as well as an oreodont. While the turtle-rich fossil fauna in the Blue Basin represent a wetland environment, this path traverses a site that was likely drier. The light-colored rocks here have a distinctly blue-green hue (from the mineral celadonite and reduced iron in the clays), but their colors are not as intense as the better-known and more history-laden Blue Basin.

Hike 76 PAINTED HILLS

Four very short hikes explore the features and fossils of a colorful badlands.

DISTANCE ▪ 2.6 miles round trip

ELEVATION ▪ 2060–2200 feet

DIFFICULTY ▪ Easy to moderate

TOPOGRAPHIC MAPS ▪ Sutton Mountain, Painted Hills

GEOLOGIC MAPS ▪ 60–62

FEES/REGULATIONS ▪ Northwest Forest Pass required for trailhead parking.

PRECAUTIONS ▪ Park regulations forbid pedestrian traffic (or vehicles) except on developed trails; do not walk on the Painted Hills's fragile surfaces.

INFORMATION ▪ John Day Fossil Beds National Monument: (541) 987-2333

Directions: To reach the Painted Hills Unit, from John Day take US Highway 26 west to Mitchell. Continue 5 miles west of Mitchell and turn north on Bridge

Bands in the Painted Hills represent 35-25-million-year-old soils that developed in a temperate climate and supported a largely deciduous forest, including walnuts, alder, and Metasequoia, a deciduous conifer.

Creek Road. A well-preserved woolly mammoth tusk was found in the stream bank along Bridge Creek about 1.2 miles downstream from the road junction. Follow the Bridge Creek Road 6 miles to the end of the pavement and turn west (left) onto the gravel entrance road to the Painted Hills Unit.

About the Landscape: The Painted Hills look like enormous yellow- and red-striped piles of dirt. And they are. But it is very old dirt, mixed with volcanic ash. Beneath the soft exterior lies much harder bedrock. A few of these old soil layers, especially deeply colored red ones in the western part of the Painted Hills, are Eocene in age, and 50–45 million years old. Most rocks of the Painted Hills are Oligocene in age, about 39 to 25 million years old. They are part of the John Day Formation, an accumulation of volcanic ash from the Western Cascades. When this ash fell, it gradually began to support plants and gradually turned into soil. Today, the bands in the Painted Hills mark ancient soil horizons.

Trail Guide: Drive past the picnic area to the overview. The first trails begin here.

The 0.5-mile round-trip Overlook Trail leads to an overview of the Big Basin tuff. The Painted Hills are composed of siltstones, accumulations of volcanic ash deposited in shallow lakebeds. The textured surface of the Painted Hills is composed of highly expandable clays that weather quickly from the solid ash-rich stone beneath. These clays absorb water so thoroughly that the clay literally out-competes plants for water. Not even a cactus can survive on the hill's unshaded, popcorn-textured surface. The red bands in the Painted Hills are sedimentary layers and old soil horizons that incorporated iron-rich clays from adjacent Clarno Formation rocks. Most black streaks are local concentrations of manganese oxide; a few are organic material—mostly lignite.

The 1.5-mile round-trip Carroll Rim Trail leads to an overview of the Painted Hills region. The trail climbs slopes of John Day tuff (the Turtle Cove member) and emerges atop the resistant ash-flow tuff (ignimbrite) at the Carroll

Rim summit. This hard rock is the Picture Gorge ignimbrite, dated at 28.7 million years. To the east, Sutton Mountain is John Day tuff capped by Columbia River basalt. The top of Carroll Rim and the surrounding colorful soft sediment are in the John Day Formation. And to the north and west, the older Clarno Formation supports rugged hills.

For the next short hike, turn left on the main Painted Hills Road, drive 0.2 mile, and turn right at the sign for Painted Cove. The 0.3-mile loop Painted Cove Trail provides an intimate view of the popcorn textures and intensely colored beds of the Painted Hills. Halfway around the flat loop, a John Day Formation rhyolite flow juts from an eroded slope.

To reach the next hike, return to the main Painted Hills Road, turn right and drive 0.2 mile to a well-marked turnout on the right. The 0.3-mile round-trip Leaf Hill Trail exposes a classic leaf-fossil collecting locality. The tuffs and lakebed sediments of the Painted Hills have yielded 107 species of leaves and 64 species of coniferous trees and herbaceous plants. The plants include maple, walnut, alder, beech, mulberry, elm, sycamore, hawthorn, metasequoia, pine, fir, hydrangea, pea, and fern. Animal fossils from this area include caddis flies, frogs, salamanders, fish, and a bat.

Hike 77 CANYON MOUNTAIN TRAIL: PINE CREEK TRAIL, STRAWBERRY WILDERNESS

Visit ancient seafloor and upper mantle now sequestered in the Strawberry Mountains.

DISTANCE ▪ 17.4 miles one way

ELEVATION ▪ 5920–7790 feet

DIFFICULTY ▪ Moderate to strenuous

TOPOGRAPHIC MAPS ▪ Canyon Mountain, Pine Creek Mountain, Strawberry Mountain

GEOLOGIC MAPS ▪ 58, 59

FEES/REGULATIONS ▪ Northwest Forest Pass required for trailhead parking.

PRECAUTIONS ▪ This is bear (and cougar) country. Be sure to secure food at night. Trailhead access requires 4WD or high-clearance vehicles.

INFORMATION ▪ Prairie City Ranger District, Malheur National Forest: (541) 820-3800

Directions: To beginning trailhead: From John Day, take US Highway 395 south for approximately 2 miles. Turn right onto County Road 52 (Marysville

Road) in Canyon City. Travel approximately 2 miles, then take a right on County Road 77 for approximately 0.25 mile, then take another right on Forest Service Road 7700-333 and follow the road approximately 2 miles to the trailhead. Note that the last 0.5 mile of this road may be rough or ungraded and is recommended for higher clearance or 4WD vehicles only.

To ending trailhead: (recommended for 4WD vehicles only). From John Day, drive east on US Highway 26 6 miles to Pine Creek Road (Grant County Road 54). Turn right (south) on Pine Creek Road and follow it 4 miles to the junction with Grant County Road 5401. Bear uphill (left) on 5401 toward the Chambers and Celebration Mines. Follow this very rough, narrow, and winding road, which becomes USFS 811, for 7.5 miles from the 54-5401 junction to the trailhead at the road's end.

About the Landscape: Canyon Mountain is a collection of rocks known as an ophiolite: ultramafic peridotites, overlain by gabbro. The rocks here are Permian in age and date to about 275 million years. Their chemical composition suggests they formed the foundation and magma chambers of an island arc volcano. Look for interesting textures—banded peridotites on ridge crests especially in the easternmost part of the hike. This area supported several chrome mines during World War I.

Trail Guide: This 17.4-mile-long (one-way) trail tours the high and generally dry summit ridges of the Western Strawberry Range, connecting peaks from Canyon Mountain on the west with Pine Creek Mountain on the east. There are limited camping opportunities, but some sites are available along the headwaters of streams at 6 miles and 11 miles into the hike. Several side trails lead down to good campsites along Pine Creek, north of the main Canyon Mountain Trail.

From the trailhead, the Canyon Mountain Trail heads around the north shoulder of Canyon Mountain, flirts with the ridge crest, and then drops into a dense forest dominated by Douglas fir and mountain hemlock. At 1.3 miles it switchbacks along Pine Creek. From the creek, it rises into more open glades of mountain mahogany and kinnikinnick, then drops back into a basin at 3 miles, crossing the upper reaches of Dog Creek. Once past Dog Creek, the path maintains an almost flat grade

Layered igneous rocks—peridotites and gabbro—occur on the open ridges north of Pine Creek Mountain.

From the top of Canyon Mountain and Pine Creek Mountain you can see the surrounding Blue Mountains landscape.

for the next 3 miles, staying on the cool, well-forested upper slopes of Canyon Mountain. Look for a few spreading yew trees in the coolest, moist spots and near springs.

At 6 miles from the trailhead, the path begins a descent into the basin of Norton Creek. This glacially carved drainage contains many polished outcrops of gabbro, including many interesting layered and folded rocks. If you are looking for a good off-trail jaunt, these rocky pinnacles make inviting places to explore. There are also good creekside campsites off the trail here.

After dropping 1500 feet into Norton Basin, the trail scrambles 1500 feet back to the ridge crest again, topping out after a 2-mile ascent. Here, vistas of the surrounding mountains and the John Day valley to the north open up. The ridge crest is dominated by scrubby mountain mahogany. Lodgepole pine and some whitebark pine also struggle to survive in this arid, subalpine climate.

At 10 miles from the trailhead, the Canyon Mountain Trail meets the Joaquin Miller Trail, coming in from the south, and for the remainder of this hike it remains at or just below the ridge crest. Peridotite, and layered peridotite and gabbro, dominate the geology from here to the hike's end. At 11 miles into the hike, the trail crosses the shoulder of Pine Creek Mountain and attains its highest elevation (7790 feet) and best views.

To continue on, turn left (a sharp turn, to the northwest) on the Pine Creek Trail. The path leads gently downslope to several springs and campsites along forested north slopes at Indian Creek's headwaters for the next 3 miles. In 0.5 mile from the junction, the headwaters of the West Fork, Indian Creek offer water and reasonable camping sites. In 2 miles from the junction, springs and headwaters of another branch of Indian Creek offer another sheltered camping option.

From these sites, the trail climbs easily to Table Camp, offering great cross-country hikes to Baldy Ridge, a mountain composed mostly of peridotite— especially the olivine-rich variety called dunite. The trail drops to the trailhead along Pine Creek, 4 miles from the junction of the Pine Creek and Canyon Mountain Trails, and 17.4 miles from the hike's beginning.

Hike 78

STRAWBERRY LAKE AND LITTLE STRAWBERRY LAKE

Explore a glacial basin quarried from a 15-million-year-old volcano.

DISTANCE ▪ **6.5 miles round trip**

ELEVATION ▪ **5790–6900 feet**

DIFFICULTY ▪ **Moderate**

TOPOGRAPHIC MAP ▪ **Strawberry Mountain**

GEOLOGIC MAPS ▪ **58, 59**

FEES/REGULATIONS ▪ **Northwest Forest Pass required for trailhead parking.**

PRECAUTIONS ▪ **None**

INFORMATION ▪ **Prairie City Ranger District, Malheur National Forest:** (541) 820-3311

Directions: From Prairie City, drive south on Main Street and in four blocks, just past the museum, jog left and then right onto Bridge Street. This road continues as Forest Service Road 6001 and is marked for Strawberry Lake. Follow this road for 13 miles to the campground and trailhead. The first 11 miles are well maintained, the last 2 miles are steeper, narrower, and may be rutted, but are suitable for slowly driven passenger cars.

About the Landscape: Strawberry Lake is located in a glacial basin quarried from the innards of a 15-million-year-old stratovolcano. The Strawberry Volcanics are contemporaries of the Columbia River basalts. The lake is dammed by glacial moraines. The hike provides nice views of the alternating lavas and cinders in the old volcano.

Trail Guide: From the campground and trailhead, the path to Strawberry Lake departs to the south, making one big switchback and then maintaining a steady pace as it climbs over the gravelly glacial moraines left behind by Ice Age alpine glaciers. The forest here is dominated by Douglas fir and lodgepole pine, with tamarack adding to the mix. Look for snowberry and red huckleberry along with kinnikinnick as the understory.

In 0.5 mile, the path makes another long switchback to climb the second moraine, then turns for the lake. It meets the Slide Basin Trail in 1 mile from the trailhead. Continue toward Strawberry Lake as the Slide Basin Trail traverses an area severely burned in 1998 and again in 2000 by stand-replacement forest fires. The Slide Basin Trail offers little shade and no water. Instead,

Crude columnar jointing is visible in Strawberry Volcanics andesite.

continue along the trail to Strawberry Lake, where, in a hundred yards or so from the Slide Lake Trail, you'll encounter wetlands.

The trail reaches Strawberry Lake in 1.3 miles from the trailhead, and here the fun begins. There are two different trails to explore here.

First, take the trail that circumnavigates the lake. You can go either direction, but for this guide, begin in a counterclockwise direction (to the right). This is an easy hike, with plenty of water and shade. Look for Clark's nutcrackers along the way. In some years, a pair of osprey has set up housekeeping along the lake. Ducks and other waterfowl also make their home here.

Just before you arrive back at the point where you began to circumnavigate the lake, another trail heads sharply to the right. This trail is marked for Little Strawberry Lake. It hangs above the main lake for 0.5 mile, then follows Strawberry Creek almost to Strawberry Falls—a veiled 70-foot drop. From this falls overlook, the path switchbacks upward, reaching Little Strawberry Lake in 1.2 miles of a tour through mostly lodgepole pine. The small, green lake cupped in stark, dark basaltic cliffs was once stocked with trout, but stocking has fallen out of fashion, and the fish have declined markedly in numbers. Return as you came.

NORTH FORK JOHN DAY RIVER: GRANITE CREEK TO BIG CREEK

Hike a wild canyon through the wreckage of ancient tropical islands.

DISTANCE ■ 14 miles round trip to Dixon Bar; 24 miles round trip to Big Creek trailhead

ELEVATION ■ 3370–4270 feet

DIFFICULTY ■ Difficult

TOPOGRAPHIC MAPS ■ Olive Lake, Silver Butte, Kelsay Butte

GEOLOGIC MAP ■ 63

FEES/REGULATIONS ■ Northwest Forest Pass required for trailhead parking.

PRECAUTIONS ■ This is bear country. Do not leave food available at night.

INFORMATION ■ North Fork John Day Ranger District, Umatilla National Forest: (541) 427-3231

Directions: From exit 285, North Powder, on Interstate 84 drive west on County Road 101 marked for Anthony Lake. In 3.5 miles, turn left (south) at a four-way intersection, drive 0.6 mile, and turn right (west) on the Elkhorn Scenic Byway. This road meets the Wallowa-Whitman National Forest and becomes USFS Road 73. Continue on USFS Road 73 past Anthony Lake ski resort (elevation 7500 feet) 28.5 miles to the junction with USFS Road 51 at North Fork Campground. Continue left (south) on USFS Road 73 another 8 miles to Granite. There is a store and gasoline at Granite. From Granite, take Grant County Road 24 (also USFS Road 10) west 1.5 miles to USFS Road 1035. Bear right on USFS Road 1035, drive 4.5 miles to spur 1035. Drive 0.2 mile to the trailhead.

About the Landscape: The rocks exposed in the North Fork Canyon are mostly altered volcanic rocks, part of the ancient volcanoes that formed the Blue Mountain island arc. They are mostly Triassic. Locally, granitic intrusions cut through these dark greenstones. The intrusions are mostly Jurassic, about 140 million years in age. They emplaced the gold deposits that were mined here in the late 1800s and early 1900s—and are still, in some cases, mined today in very small quantities.

Trail Guide: This hike tours the rugged and remote canyon of the North Fork, John Day River. This is true wilderness, with craggy scenery and solitude. There are also old mines and plenty of wildlife. Expect bears. You may hear a wolf—one of Oregon's first documented wild wolves was captured here and returned to Idaho in 1998. Since then, the policy has changed and wolves

The rugged canyon of the North Fork of the John Day River exposes altered Triasssic volcanic rocks (greenstones) and sedimentary formations (argillite)— part of the exotic terranes of the Blue Mountain island arc.

that come here are allowed to stay. Good campsites are rare in this narrow canyon but can be found at Granite Creek (3.5 miles), Silver Creek (5.4 miles), Dixon Bar (7 miles), and Fitzwater Gulch (10 miles) as well as Big

Creek, at the downstream trailhead. For a fast-paced day hike or an overnight backpack trip, Dixon Bar makes a good destination.

From the trailhead the narrow path leads along south-facing slopes high above Granite Creek. At 0.7 mile the trail crosses a small tributary stream. At 0.8 mile the trail joins with a path from the creekside road—and also permits access to Granite Creek. For the next mile the trail continues far above the creek on south-facing slopes, then finds a bridge and crosses to the cooler north slope. Here it is quite rough, pushing through bogs and a small grove of willow, then rising onto drier ground. It finds a junction with the Trail 3018 at mile 2 and a small spring (and spring box) at Snowshoe Spring—a good place to replenish water supplies. In 2.3 miles the trail crosses a major bridge and finds the confluence of Granite Creek and the North Fork, John Day River. Here, the Granite Creek Trail (3016) joins the North Fork Trail (3022).

To continue downstream to Dixon Bar, cross the bridge over the North Fork and turn left. This portion of the trail explores the most remote and rugged parts of the North Fork Canyon, and also contains several rocky and narrow segments. There are more rock outcroppings, including Wind Rock, a looming dark crag of greenstone about 2 miles downstream from the North Fork–Granite Creek junction. The trail stays on the south side of the river to Dixon Bar (in fact, for the remainder of its distance) but provides a crossing to flat forested areas and small meadows suitable as camping sites near Dixon Bar. Side trails lead to the canyon rim (Paradise Trail, 3022 to the east; Glade Creek Trail, to the west. Both climb about 2000 feet to reach campgrounds at USFS roads). There are campsites on both sides of the river, with a bridge to facilitate the crossing. Tributary streams provide additional water. At Dixon Bar, the river trail becomes slightly broader and slightly more traveled, at least for the next mile.

Downstream from the broad, pine and fir glades at Dixon Bar, the canyon narrows again, traversing outcrops on the trail while the river rushes past. The trail also narrows here, becoming quite rocky in places. However, the trail keeps close to the river, and also crosses eight more side streams between Dixon Bar and the trail's end at Big Creek trailhead, so there is adequate opportunity to keep cool. Watch for snakes along the rockier lower stretches of the trail.

A mining cabin appears along the river about 4 miles downstream from Dixon Bar, a reminder that this wilderness has not been free of human disturbance for very long. More evidence—piles of gravelly mining tailings— appear along the open riverbanks just a few hundred yards above the trail's end at Big Creek trailhead and USFS Road 5506. From this trailhead, return as you came.

228

HOFFER LAKES AND ANTHONY LAKE

 Hike 80

A short gambit finds classical alpine meadows and glacially scoured "granite."

DISTANCE ■ 2-mile loop

ELEVATION ■ 7150–7430 feet

DIFFICULTY ■ Easy

TOPOGRAPHIC MAP ■ Anthony Lake

GEOLOGIC MAPS ■ 55, 56

FEES/REGULATIONS ■ Northwest Forest Pass required for trailhead parking.

PRECAUTIONS ■ None

INFORMATION ■ Baker Ranger District, Wallowa-Whitman National Forest: (541) 523-4476

Directions: From exit 285, North Powder, on Interstate 84 drive west on County Road 101 marked for Anthony Lake. In 3.5 miles, turn left (south) at a four-way intersection, drive 0.6 mile, and turn right (west) on the Anthony Lake Highway (Elkhorn Scenic Byway). This road meets the Wallowa-Whitman National Forest and becomes USFS Road 73. Continue 20 miles to Anthony Lake Campground. At the main campground intersection, turn right (past the gazebo) to the day-use area. Continue 0.3 mile to road's end. Follow the path past campsites 0.1 mile to the trailhead on the right.

About the Landscape: The northern end of the Bald Mountain batholith is composed of granitic rocks about 140 million years in age, generated as the Blue Mountain island arc began its collision with North America. Their compositions indicate that the granitic magmas were formed from melted volcanic rocks and some sediments of the island arc.

Trail Guide: This is a short and popular hike to scenic lakes that are quite wild and very alpine. Expect dogs and children here. It's a great hike for both. In early summer the soft alpine meadows are ablaze with wildflowers, including dogtooth violet, shooting star, and paintbrush.

From the trailhead parking lot follow the broad path that leads around the lakeshore. In about 100 yards, a side trail, marked "Hoffer Lakes," leads to the right (south). The path quite purposefully leads upslope, past huge boulders as it parallels Parker Creek, crossing on several bridges. You reach the lake in 0.5 mile. Informal trails continue to a waterfall and rock outcropping on the east shore. This is a good opportunity for a rock scramble and an up-close look at the granitic rocks (granodiorites and tonalities) of the Elkhorn Mountains.

If you want to make this a loop hike, when you reach the lake, bear right

Gunsight Butte, a mountain composed of the granitic rocks of the Bald Mountain batholith, overlooks Anthony Lake.

along a well-worn path that follows the shoreline. In 0.3 mile the trail emerges from the lodgepole pines and subalpine fir into alpine meadows, then at 0.6 mile it joins a gravel roadway that turns right and leads back to the Anthony Lake Picnic Area in another 0.4 mile. At the picnic area and gazebo, turn right again and follow the paved road 0.3 mile along the shore of Anthony Lake and back to the trailhead parking area where you began.

ELKHORN CREST TRAIL, ANTHONY LAKE TO MARBLE CANYON

Hike

81

Hike along an ancient sea bottom now perched on the skyline at 8000 feet.

DISTANCE ■ 20 miles one way

ELEVATION ■ 7220–8200 feet

DIFFICULTY ■ Moderate

TOPOGRAPHIC MAPS ■ Elkhorn Peak, Bourne, Mount Ireland, Anthony Lake

GEOLOGIC MAPS ■ 54–57

FEES/REGULATIONS ■ Northwest Forest Pass required for trailhead parking.

PRECAUTIONS ■ A shuttle vehicle is required; at the Marble Canyon end, the road to the west looks enticing but is not maintained; it is steep and washboarded and has several locations where slides and washouts are a hazard even to 4WD vehicles. The Elkhorn Crest Trail is usually open from late June to October.

INFORMATION ■ Baker Ranger District, Wallowa-Whitman National Forest: (541) 523-4476

Directions: To reach the north trailhead at Anthony Lake, from Baker City drive north to Haines on old Highway 30. Turn left (west) in Haines and take

Elkhorn Scenic Byway (USFS Road 1146), following Anthony Lake Ski Area signs, to Anthony Road and the well-marked trailhead parking area about 1 mile east of the ski area, about 30 miles from Baker City. To drop a shuttle vehicle at the south end of the trail, from Baker City drive west on Pocahontas Road. Turn left onto Marble Canyon Road. The aptly named road tours past several limestone outcrops and through a limestone quarry that once supplied a large cement plant in Baker Valley. (Technically this slightly recrystallized limestone is a marble.) This road is easy and well graded for the first 5 miles, but it deteriorates as it rises steeply at about mile 6. Four-wheel-drive vehicles are recommended for the trip to the ridge crest at 7400 feet, 15 miles from Baker City.

About the Landscape: The granitic rocks of the northern Elkhorn Mountains—mostly granodiorites—are cut by a multitude of parallel cracks called joints. The outcrops appear angular and broken. In a granite batholith, joints occur on large and small scales, cutting not only through mountaintops but through microscopic mineral grains as well. The notches at the summits of Gunsight Mountain and Van Patten Peak are joints.

Two features typical of granodiorites occur in rock along the trail: dark blobs of the surrounding rock, assimilated into the batholith's hot magma, occur as irregular, rounded dark shapes called xenoliths (from the Greek *xeno* meaning "strange" and *lithos* meaning "stone"). Subtle layering is present also, especially in the light-colored granodiorite rocks in the Dutch Flat basin and along the base of Mount Ruth, several miles to the south. This layering develops as the magma cools, with darker minerals crys-

Rugged alpine landscape of the Elkhorns and Wallowas is carved from granitic batholiths.

231

tallizing and settling slowly into a layer, or being swept along magma channels and slowly deposited.

The thinly bedded sedimentary rocks abundant along the southern Elkhorn crest, including Elkhorn Peak, are a silica-rich sedimentary rock known as *chert*. Chert develops as the small, silica-rich skeletons of single-celled marine animals called radiolarians accumulate on the deep ocean floor. These skeletons partly dissolve and then solidify to form layer after layer of the 1-inch-thick chert beds.

Many old gold mines cluster near the contact between Baker terrane rocks and the Bald Mountain batholith. Gold was discovered near Auburn, on the south end of Elkhorn Ridge, in 1861, and gold mines flourished in the Elkhorn and Greenhorn Mountains from the early 1860s into the 1890s. The mines of the Bourne district, just west of the Elkhorn Crest Trail here, produced gold worth more than 150 million dollars. Several mines in this district were still active in the 1980s.

Trail Guide: From the Anthony Lake trailhead, the Elkhorn Crest Trail goes south through lodgepole pine forest. This trail skirts Black Lake, a small, forest-choked glacial lake on the east side of Gunsight Mountain. The main Elkhorn Crest Trail climbs easily across granodiorite to the whitebark pine-laden passes above Antone and Dutch Flat Creeks, offering a distant view of the fault-controlled topography of the Grande Ronde valley 20 miles to the north. South of Dutch Flat Pass, at 6 miles a short trail leads east to Lost Lake, a good campsite and one of the few with water available along the high, dry Elkhorn Crest Trail.

From the junction with the Lost Lake Trail, the Elkhorn Crest Trail skirts Mount Ruth. This peak wears a cap of fine-grained, light-colored granitic rock (leucogranodiorite) that is a slightly younger part of the large, composite Bald Mountain batholith. In another mile, the trail crosses the contact between the Bald Mountain batholith's granitic rocks and the older rocks of the Baker terrane. This contact is abrupt. The argillite—a shalelike sedimentary rock—has been hardened and deformed. This effect is called contact metamorphism. As the trail continues south away from the batholith, the textures of the sedimentary rocks change to a more normal appearance.

The Elkhorn Crest Trail continues south across dark, deformed gabbro and greenstone of the Baker terrane. It also encounters several light-colored limestones and younger intrusive dikes. About 15 miles into the hike, the trail crosses the ridge between Rock Creek basin and the Twin Lakes basin. This cliff-infested area is a favorite hangout for Rocky Mountain goats. To the southwest, Twin Lakes provide a good camping site.

The Elkhorn Crest Trail continues another 5 miles across exposures of argillite and chert—both deep-water sedimentary rocks that are part of the Baker terrane's jumbled, subduction-zone geology—to the Marble Canyon road and trailhead.

COON HOLLOW, WITH A SIDE TRIP TO BUCKHORN OVERLOOK

Explore the bottom of the shallow ocean basin that separated Oregon from the Idaho shore about 140 million years ago.

DISTANCE ■ 16 miles round trip

ELEVATION ■ 890–4260 feet

DIFFICULTY ■ Difficult

TOPOGRAPHIC MAP ■ Jim Creek Butte

GEOLOGIC MAPS ■ 52, 54

FEES/REGULATIONS ■ Northwest Forest Pass required for trailhead parking.

PRECAUTIONS ■ The bottom of Hells Canyon is extremely hot during summer months and commonly reaches temperatures of 100 degrees Fahrenheit; this hike is best during spring or fall. Poison oak and ivy infest the bottom of Hells Canyon.

INFORMATION ■ Hells Canyon National Recreation Area: (541) 426-4978

Directions: From Enterprise, drive 2.8 miles south on Oregon Highway 82. Turn left (east) on Crow Creek Road, marked for Buckhorn Overlook, and follow the paved road 3 miles to a junction. Turn right, and follow this paved road 3 miles to a Y junction. Bear right on Zumwalt Road. In 2.5 miles the pavement changes to gravel. This road tours Zumwalt Prairie, one of the Columbia Basin's most beautiful and threatened grasslands. While most is in private ownership, the Nature Conservancy's Zumwalt Preserve permits hiking, and is located between miles 19 and 23 along the east side of the road. (Dogs are not permitted on Nature Conservancy properties, even on a leash.)

At 28 miles, the road becomes USFS Road 46. At 32 miles into the drive, a spur road (USFS Road 780, marked "Buckhorn Overlook, Buckhorn Campground") turns right. This road leads past a USFS camping area, and by bearing right at all road intersections (right on USFS spur 860 to the overlook), you reach an astounding view of the Imnaha River's canyon—a highly recommended stop en route to the Coon Hollow hike. For a hike off the beaten path, hike out the ridge above the Imnaha or follow the Forest Service spur road that leads to the same. In 6 miles, this road leads to the Snake River and Eureka Bar (see Hike 83). To find this spur, retrace your path along the road and turn right just past the cluster of radio towers about 0.2 mile from the Buckhorn Overlook.

Back on the main road, continue 7 miles to an intersection and turn right on Cold Springs Ridge Road, USFS Road 4680. This road provides more heart-stopping views of Hells Canyon to the east.

Continue on Cold Springs Road 13 miles to the gated spur road to Cache

Creek. You'll find this road on the right, 0.3 mile past a set of hairpin turns as Cold Springs Road begins to descend, and just before the road reenters private land and becomes County Road 699. Park here and begin the hike.

About the Landscape: Throughout Hells Canyon, the older rocks of the Blue Mountain island arc are overlain by Columbia River basalts. Below these 16-million-year-old basalts, Coon Hollow exposes relatively young, and often fossil-rich, sedimentary rocks that were deposited long after the old island arc volcanoes became dormant about 180–175 million years ago.

The rocks of Coon Hollow (the Coon Hollow Formation) represent a shallow marine basin that lay between the rocks of the Blue Mountain island arc and North America. Fewer than 20 miles may have separated continent and rocks of the islands. The sediments record remnants of a gingko-and-conifer-rich forest, as well as abundant fossil ferns. Occasionally in Coon Hollow's sediments there is a granitic pebble—possibly a small piece of nearby North America deposited by a major North American river into the shallow seaway. Somewhat younger rocks of the Coon Hollow Formation exposed at Pittsburg Landing, about 30 miles upstream along the Snake River from Coon Hollow, are even more fossil rich.

Trail Guide: This hike follows a good but gated Forest Service road along Cache Creek for 6 miles to a Forest Service station staffed year-round by volunteers, then continues 3 miles along roads and the Snake River to explore fossil-rich Jurassic rocks found in Coon Hollow. There are many additional opportunities for energetic hikers to roam Hells Canyon and the Coon Hollow area.

From the gate on the Cache Creek road, follow this roadway 7 miles to the Cache Creek Ranch on Snake River. The road climbs 1500 feet in a long switchback to reach the ridge top and a great view of Hells Canyon in 2 miles. Look for abandoned homestead and sheepherders' cabins on slopes along the way.

From the ridge top, the road descends purposefully along another long

Sedimentary rocks of Coon Hollow contain scattered fossils of a Jurassic forest that grew on islands just off the coast of Idaho. Trees included gingko and palms.

switchback. Roadcuts provide a nice up-close view of the basalts and occasional old soils (paleosols) between them. In 2 miles and another 1500 feet (down this time!) you cross imperceptibly from 16-million-year-old basalts to 175-million-year-old sedimentary rocks. Here the Coon Hollow Formation is a strongly folded low-grade slate, and fossils are rare. The road continues 2.8 miles, reaching the Snake River and Cache Creek Ranch house about 5 miles from the ridge crest and 7 miles from the start. Watch for wild turkeys, mule deer, and bighorn sheep along the way. Cougars have been reported in this canyon (and everywhere else in Oregon) as well.

There are good camping areas along the river and friendly caretakers at the house. Watch for occasional yellowstar thistle plants (a non-native noxious weed) and report the locations of any you notice to the caretakers.

To see Coon Hollow and the volcanic and sedimentary rocks there, follow an old wagon road upstream 0.9 mile along the Snake River. This path bypasses an historic sheep-shearing pen. The road continues into Coon Hollow proper just beyond the sheep sheds. Explore the open terrane here at your leisure. Return as you came.

Hike 83
IMNAHA RIVER TRAIL TO EUREKA MINE AND EUREKA BAR

Explore a deep river canyon and a long-defunct gold mine.

DISTANCE ■ 12 miles round trip

ELEVATION ■ 1050–1125 feet

DIFFICULTY ■ Moderate

TOPOGRAPHIC MAPS ■ Cactus Mountain, Dead Horse Ridge

GEOLOGIC MAPS ■ 52, 54

FEES/REGULATIONS ■ Northwest Forest Pass required for trailhead parking.

PRECAUTIONS ■ The unpaved portion of the Imnaha River Road is rough; it may be muddy and impassable for passenger cars in early spring (February to April); 4WD is strongly recommended. The road is narrow and curvy; use caution; allow at least 2 hours to drive from Joseph to the trailhead. The bottoms of the Imnaha and Hells Canyons are extremely hot during summer months and commonly reach temperatures of 100 degrees Fahrenheit; this hike is best during spring or fall. Poison oak and ivy infest the bottom of Hells Canyon. Rattlesnakes, poison ivy, and prickly pear cacti abound.

INFORMATION ■ Hells Canyon National Recreation Area: (541) 426-4978

Directions: From Joseph, take County Road 350 (Little Sheep Creek Highway) to Imnaha. Turn north on Imnaha River Road. Follow this road to the end of pavement and continue cautiously, going another 20 miles on gravel and dirt roads. Just before you cross the Imnaha River at the Cow Creek bridge, the trailhead is straight ahead. There's a small parking area. (The left trail follows the Imnaha River through a canyon cut into the Imnaha pluton, an 8-mile round trip to Eureka Bar and the historic Eureka Mine on the Snake River.) **About the Landscape:** The lower end of the Imnaha River cuts its gorge through an old magma chamber of the ancient arc. This hard, greenish white diorite forms rugged outcrops that are ideal habitat for Rocky Mountain sheep. This rock is 260 million years old, Permian in age. It fed the eruptions of the first generation of volcanoes in the Wallowa terrane. Then, uplifted and eroded, it served as a solid foundation for the second generation of Wallowa terrane eruptions 40 million years later.

Similar rocks appear along the Snake River near Dug Bar and form the steep terrane along the Snake at the mouth of Deep Creek. At Deep Creek, the dark rocks are mostly gabbro. They are crosscut by light-colored dikes of rocks similar to granites. The age of the Deep Creek plutonic complex is 231 million years. **Trail Guide:** This hike along the Imnaha River tours the rocks of the Imnaha pluton in a scenic, albeit poison ivy-lined gorge. The *plutonic rocks* are gray and somber-looking. They are deformed in many places and crosscut by somewhat younger dikes.

In the Imnaha River Canyon, en route to the Nee Mee Poo trail, Miocene Columbia River basalts about 16 million years in age lie directly above 230-million year old Triassic rocks of the Blue Mountain island arc.

At several places along the trail you can catch furtive glimpses of the overlying Columbia River basalts—mostly on the opposite side of the Snake River.

The best part of the hike is the trail's junction with the Snake River. Here, at Eureka Bar, a short bridge crosses the Imnaha, allowing you to explore the Eureka Mine (but the mine may be gated, as it is now habitat for Townsends big-eared bats). The mine was developed in the 1880s and never produced any gold; however, rumors still abound that it was a scam to lure Eastern investors hungry for a new gold rush. The trail down the Snake River leads to the huge stone foundation of a stamp mill and also a town site. The paddlewheel steamer *Imnaha* sank just downstream here when delivering machinery for the stamp mill—which was never built.

Return as you came.

NEE ME POO NATIONAL HISTORIC TRAIL, HELLS CANYON

Hike 84

Follow the footsteps of Chief Joseph's retreat across Columbia River basalts to the Snake River.

DISTANCE ▪ **14-mile loop**

ELEVATION ▪ **1005–2380 feet**

DIFFICULTY ▪ **Moderate**

TOPOGRAPHIC MAPS ▪ **Cactus Mountain, Dead Horse Ridge**

GEOLOGIC MAPS ▪ **52, 54**

FEES/REGULATIONS ▪ **Northwest Forest Pass required for trailhead parking.**

PRECAUTIONS ▪ **The unpaved portion of the Imnaha River Road is rough; it may be muddy and impassable for passenger cars in early spring (February to April); 4WD is strongly recommended. The road is narrow and curvy; use caution; allow at least 2 hours to drive from Joseph to the trailhead. The bottoms of the Imnaha and Hells Canyons are extremely hot during summer months and commonly reach temperatures of 100 degrees Fahrenheit; this hike is best during spring or fall. Poison oak and ivy infest the bottom of Hells Canyon. Rattlesnakes, poison oak, and prickly pear cacti abound.**

INFORMATION ▪ **Hells Canyon National Recreation Area: (541) 426-4978**

Directions: From Joseph, take County Road 350 to Imnaha. Turn north on Imnaha River Road. Follow this road to the end of pavement and continue cautiously, going another 20 miles on gravel and dirt roads. Cross the Imnaha River and at the Cow Creek trailhead, follow the trail (which begins as a rough road that you can drive for the next 2.5 miles if you want) to the right. (The left trail follows the Imnaha River through a canyon cut into the Imnaha pluton, an 8-mile round trip to Eureka Bar and the historic Eureka Mine on the Snake River.)

About the Landscape: The Imnaha River has sliced its canyon through a layer cake of Columbia River basalts. The basalts at the bottom of this canyon are the oldest and most primitive, or mantlelike, Columbia River basalt and are known as the Imnaha basalt. These flows erupted about 16.6 million years ago. The Imnaha area was a lowland at that time, and many flows simply pooled here, filling the depression. The Imnaha flows do not cover a very wide area and are best exposed in this canyon. The large crystals evident in many of these dark flows are the hallmark of the Imnaha basalts.

This hike travels the Nee Me Poo Trail to the Snake River, then follows a road back for a loop trip. The Nee Me Poo Trail to Dug Bar follows the path of Chief Joseph's band as they fled their homeland in 1877, pursued by the US Cavalry. The Nez Perce, including women, children, the elderly, and all their livestock, forced from their homeland in the Wallowa Valley, followed this trail, crossed the Snake River at Dug Bar when the Snake was at its peak flow in mid-May, and fled toward Canada.

Trail Guide: The road to the right climbs gradually out of the canyon and up the flank of Cactus Mountain. This road weaves along the contact of the Imnaha pluton and Columbia River basalt. At a weathered sign about 2.5 miles into the hike, the road intersects the Nee Me Poo (Nez Perce) National Trail. Follow this trail, which branches to the right, as it heads directly up the small canyon toward Lone Pine Saddle. The basalts here are Imnaha type, with large crystals of feldspar. Grande Ronde basalt appears at Lone Pine Saddle and on Cactus Mountain immediately north.

From Lone Pine Saddle, the Nee Me Poo Trail drops through Columbia River basalts to the Snake River at Dug Bar. There are opportunities to camp along the river. Two miles to the south, rugged topography along the Snake displays the Deep Creek pluton, a magma chamber of the old island arc. Only informal trails provide access to the steep terrain.

To return to the trailhead from Dug Bar, follow the road north along the river. This part of the hike encounters older, highly deformed rocks before turning upslope and returning through basalts to the trailhead at Cow Creek, 8 miles from Dug Bar.

Hike 85 MAXWELL LAKE

Visit a quiet lake tucked into a basin of craggy granitic volcanoes.

DISTANCE ▪ 7 miles round trip

ELEVATION ▪ 5450–7730 feet

DIFFICULTY ▪ Difficult

TOPOGRAPHIC MAP ▪ North Minam Meadows

GEOLOGIC MAP ▪ 1

FEES/REGULATIONS ▪ Northwest Forest Pass required for trailhead parking.

PRECAUTIONS ▪ None

INFORMATION ▪ Eagle Cap Ranger District, Wallowa-Whitman National Forest: (541) 426-4978

Directions: From Lostine, turn south on Lostine River Road. Drive 17 miles to Shady Campground and the Maxwell Lake trailhead on the right (west) side of the gravel road.

About the Landscape: This hike takes you up a moraine, through part of the Wallowa batholith's granitic rocks, and into a glacial basin with an azure lake.

Trail Guide: This is one of the least-hiked paths that lead up from the Lostine River. The trail begins at the west side of a large parking area that serves both campers and hikers. It crosses the Lostine River on a sturdy wooden footbridge and leads through a small wetland before crossing Maxwell Creek, hitting the side of the valley in 0.3 mile and beginning a well-graded, switch-backing ascent. Maxwell Creek can be boisterous in early summer, and there is no bridge here, though stepping across the water on several of the large rocks can help

Granitic peaks, part of the Wallowa batholith, surround glacial tarn, Maxwell Lake.

keep your feet dry. This is the last real and reliable water until the trail's end, so be sure to take advantage of it here, especially in warm weather.

For the next 2 miles the trail maintains a steady pace as it climbs long loops of switchbacks. The trail occasionally emerges from the Engelmann spruce- and Douglas fir–dominated forest into sunlit meadows, and in early summer, most of these are fairly moist, with glowing blooms of mule ears, lupine, and paintbrush. Occasionally you can catch a fleeting view of the high Wallowa peaks to the south, including Eagle Cap.

At 2.6 miles from the trailhead, the path reaches the top of the gravelly moraine and its switchbacks and abruptly changes its character from Dr. Jekyll to Mr. Hyde. It turns west and begins a rough, serious crawl up the last 1000 feet to the Maxwell Lake basin. As the trail ascends, it crosses springs and wet meadows, though by midsummer these may be dry. At 3 miles it enters alpine meadows where it leads around huge, glacially sculpted outcrops and *rouche mounenee*, or glacially polished sheep-shaped rocks, before descending to Maxwell Lake at 3.5 miles and its cool, gray basin lined with 130–140 million-year-old granitic rocks (tonalite and granodiorite). The views from the meadows and out- crops above the lake are mostly to the Lostine Canyon and peaks carved from Triassic sedimentary rocks and capped by Columbia River basalt on the west side of the river, including Sawtooth Peak and Twin Peaks. Return as you came.

Hike 86
HURRICANE CREEK TRAIL TO LAKES BASIN

Tour the Wallowa Mountains' most spectacular scenery.

DISTANCE ■ 6.4 miles round trip to Slickrock Creek (day hike); 24 miles round trip to Lakes Basin/Mirror Lake

ELEVATION ■ 5020–7700 feet

DIFFICULTY ■ Moderate

TOPOGRAPHIC MAPS ■ Chief Joseph Mountain, Eagle Cap

GEOLOGIC MAP ■ 1

FEES/REGULATIONS ■ Northwest Forest Pass required for trailhead parking.

PRECAUTIONS ■ Early in the hiking season (June, early July) Hurricane Creek and Fall Creek may be difficult to ford.

INFORMATION ■ Eagle Cap Ranger District, Wallowa-Whitman National Forest: (541) 426-4978

Directions: From Joseph, turn west on Wallowa Avenue, which becomes Hur- ricane Creek Road. In 3 miles, at the white Hurricane Creek Grange building,

Peaks visible from the lower part of the Hurricane Creek Trail are carved from Triassic sedimentary rocks and topped by Miocene Columbia River basalt.

turn hard left on gravel road. Continue 2.9 miles to the parking area and trailhead at the end of the road.

About the Landscape: The core of the Wallowa Mountains is granitic rock. Altogether, twelve separate intrusions comprise the Wallowa batholith. Most are similar in appearance and age—about 145 to 160 million years. These rocks are mostly tonalite and granodiorite. The black, iron-rich minerals in these rocks are mostly hornblende—a hard, prismatic or rectangular mineral. *Biotite*— a flaky, soft, dark brown mica—is less abundant.

Although granites in Oregon are often associated with gold deposits, the Wallowas are notoriously gold-poor. This paucity of precious metal is probably due to the surrounding sedimentary rocks which, as former coral reefs and shallow seafloor, had little gold to share with the invading granitic magmas. The sole exception is the Cornucopia stock, at the southeast edge of the Wallowas (Hike 88). Cornucopia hosted Oregon's largest lode gold mine, which operated until 1948.

Trail Guide: This trail leads into the Lakes Basin of the Eagle Cap Wilderness.

241

It is less crowded than the trails up the Lostine River or the path from Wallowa Lake. There is some use by horses and riders. You may glimpse mountain goats on the slopes high above you.

From the trailhead, the path moves through lodgepole, tamarack, and grand fir forest for 0.3 mile to an unbridged crossing of Falls Creek—getting across can be a challenge in early summer. Just upstream is a 70-foot-high waterfall. Informal trails lead up to the base of this inviting cascade. This destination alone makes Hurricane Creek a good walk.

Beyond this detour, the trail crosses a treeless expanse that appears to be a clearcut. But it is a natural clearcut—a forest mowed down by snow avalanches in the 1960s and storms more recently. Beyond this natural and brushed-over area, the trail slips into lodgepole-larch woodland, then emerges into subalpine meadows at Deadman Creek, 1.5 miles from the trailhead. The meadows offer views of Twin Peaks to the west and Sacajawea Peak to the south. If you watch the ridges to the west closely, you may see white dots—mountain goats frequent the rocky upper slopes.

Beyond Deadman Creek the trail reenters a lodgepole-dominated forest for another 1.7 miles, switch-backing along outcrops and tiptoeing at the edge of an abrupt drop into Hurricane Creek and emerging into the open as it nears Slickrock Creek. This stream comes by its name honestly. The bedrock is coarse marble—a soft stone that has been polished and smoothed by running water. Approaching the Slickrock crossing (elevation 5780 feet), the trail teeters above cliffs, then minces across the slippery outcrops at the creek's junction with Hurricane Creek. It's a nice watering spot, and also a popular destination for day hikes.

At Slickrock Creek the trail steepens slightly, continuing through a forest increasingly composed of grand fir and Engelmann spruce along with logdepoles. Tamaracks are less abundant at this higher altitude. As you proceed up the trail, look for spindle-topped subalpine fir to increase in numbers.

At 5.1 miles from the trailhead the path meets the junction of USFS Trail 1824 to Echo Lake. This trail is steep and very rough, climbing about 2500 feet in 3.1 miles to the rocky alpine environment of Echo Lake (elevation 8372 feet). If you want to put some grunt and challenge into your trip, this trail provides it.

Just past the junction with Trail 1824, the Hurricane Creek Trail jogs left and crosses Hurricane Creek. There is no bridge, and few stepping stones, so expect to wade through cold, knee-deep water. In early summer this crossing may be hazardous. There are numerous good camping sites near this junction and crossing, and many hikers make this crossing, combined with the crawl to Echo Lake, an early summer backpacking destination.

After plunging across Hurricane Creek, the trail steepens and strays away from the stream, though it crosses two hefty tributaries in the next mile. It encounters several abandoned and decaying cabins at about 8.3 miles from the trailhead, where the path tempers its uphill pace and encounters pretty, paintbrush- and lupine-laden meadows as it climbs from 6800 to 7000 feet. Look for Clark's nutcrackers here, and a stunning view up the adjacent, rugged, glacially polished marble slopes of Sacajawea Peak. At the end of this series of meadows the path steepens again for its final climb to the Lakes Basin.

At 9.4 miles the trail crests at 7700 feet, and then drops for 0.3 mile to meet the well-worn trail to Douglas Lake to the left (east). This trail, which heads for Douglas Lake and the Wallowa River, is also the beginning of a 4.3-mile Lakes Basin Loop hike that makes a superb day hike during your stay here. To hike the loop, turn east on this trail for 1.6 miles past Douglas Lake to a junction with Trail 1810. Turn right (west) at this sharply angled junction and follow this trail to Moccasin Lake at 2.6 miles and back (west) to Mirror Lake.

To reach campsites near Mirror Lake, continue straight here, toward Eagle Cap and the Lakes Basin 1.2 miles ahead. The Lakes Basin is an overused area, with many areas roped off for restoration. Choose campsites well away from lakeshores and enjoy the stunningly beautiful landscape. Return as you came.

BURGER PASS TO TOMBSTONE LAKE

Hike 87

Explore remote lakes, glacial valleys, and 100-million-year-old river channels.

DISTANCE ■ **14.4 miles round trip**

ELEVATION ■ **5840–7860 feet**

DIFFICULTY ■ **Difficult**

TOPOGRAPHIC MAPS ■ **China Cap, Steamboat Lake**

GEOLOGIC MAP ■ **1**

FEES/REGULATIONS ■ **Northwest Forest Pass required for trailhead parking.**

PRECAUTIONS ■ **None**

INFORMATION ■ **La Grande Ranger District, Wallowa-Whitman National Forest: (541) 963-7186**

Directions: From Union, drive 11.3 miles south past Catherine Creek State Park on Oregon Highway 203. Turn left (east) on USFS Road 7785, Catherine Creek Road. Drive 4.3 miles, past a bridge and spur road 700 up the South Fork, to USFS Road 7787. Turn right (south) and follow the road 6 miles uphill to the Buck Creek trailhead.

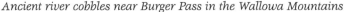

About the Landscape: This hike offers an intimate and extensive view of the 140- to 130-million-year-old granitic rocks of the Wallowa batholith. It also provides glimpses of Columbia River basalt feeder dikes (those broad red streaks that cut through the white granitic rocks), the dikes of a basalt feeder system that are clustered together on Burger Butte, and alpine glacial features, including the small lakes carved in headwalls and cirques.

Trail Guide: This hike has a lot of up and down to it, but the small alpine lakes at the end are worth the trip. Trail maintenance is limited from Buck trailhead to Burger Pass. There is not much water along the first 2 miles of the trail, especially in late summer.

The jaunt to Tombstone Lake begins inauspiciously. The trail leads across an overgrown clearcut, then parallels an abandoned road for 0.7 mile. The path encounters the edge of a second clearcut in 1.2 miles, then turns back into the forest and unpillaged landscapes for the remainder of the hike. This forest is dominated by Douglas fir and grand fir, with a few tamarack and ponderosa pine for variety. Snowberry and kinnikinnick (low manzanita) form the dominant ground cover.

Just beyond its reentry into pristine forest, the path encounters another trail leading left (north) toward Squaw Creek. Continue straight. The trail rises

Ancient river cobbles near Burger Pass in the Wallowa Mountains

steadily until it makes a single switchback at 2.4 miles into the hike (elevation 6800 feet), then rounds a curve at the top of the switchback grade and enters the Eagle Cap Wilderness.

Here the path crosses a long talus slope of granitic rocks, where rock pikas delight in tantalizing and frustrating dogs — squealing alarms, then ducking to safety beneath the boulders of the talus field. The trail offers a view of China Cap, a butte wearing a red topknot of basalt, to the north.

At 2.7 miles from the trailhead, the path encounters a wetland and then a small stream, both refreshing rests. Look for blue-eyed grass and shooting stars here, as well as an abundance of false hellebore. Beyond the stream, the trail ascends into an alpine environment at 7400 feet in elevation, leaving the grand fir behind. Whitebark pine appear, along with their companions, the Clark's nutcracker.

At 3.1 miles, the trail intersects Trail 1906, a trail along the ridge top that leads north toward China Cap and Meadow Mountain. Turn sharply right here (south) and continue toward Burger Butte instead. In another 0.5 mile of steady climbing, you reach Burger Pass (elevation 7830 feet) and glimpse the high Wallowa peaks which, from this perspective, seem to go on forever. There is also a collection of rounded cobbles strewn around the pass. These are the only witness to a 125-million-year gap in the geologic record between the 16-million-year-old basalts and the 140-million-year-old granitic rocks. They are the rounded cobbles deposited by an ancient stream of unknown age (possibly Cretaceous, about 100 million years old). Their source was in Idaho.

From the pass, Trail 1944 slants downslope to Burger Meadows, a sedge-filled wetland that was once a lake. Before you descend, look for elk grazing or relaxing in and around the meadows. The trail drops quickly, reaching the meadows in 0.9 mile, then contours north around the basin, dropping to meet Trail 1943 to Tombstone Lake and Diamond Lake 2.8 miles from Burger Pass. Turn south on this trail and cross Elk Creek. This 1.8-mile path to Tombstone Lake rises abruptly after crossing the creek, gaining 300 feet in a series of short switchbacks, crossing and flirting with a small stream that proves to be an outlet for Tombstone Lake. Here, the trees are mostly lodgepoles and subalpine fir, with whitebark pine increasing as you climb back toward timberline.

After a short flat stretch that touches an alpine meadow, the trail gallops upward another 300 feet, this time with longer and less regular switchbacks. About 0.2 mile past the top of this rise, look for a short spur trail that drops down to Diamond Lake. If you'd prefer not to lose any hard-won altitude here, continue on the main path another 0.6 mile along a flatter grade and casual switchbacks to Tombstone Lake (elevation 7421 feet). There are actually five lakes here in a pretty, glacially sculpted granitic basin, with a variety of fine and usually quiet campsites. Return as you came.

Hike 88

SUMMIT POINT TO CORNUCOPIA AND CRATER LAKE

Visit a coral reef and the mountain that harbored Oregon's richest gold deposit.

DISTANCE ■ 7.8 miles round trip

ELEVATION ■ 6800–8200 feet

DIFFICULTY ■ Moderate

TOPOGRAPHIC MAPS ■ Krag Peak, Cornucopia

GEOLOGIC MAP ■ 54

FEES/REGULATIONS ■ Northwest Forest Pass required for trailhead parking.

PRECAUTIONS ■ None

INFORMATION ■ Pine Ranger District, Wallowa-Whitman National Forest: (541) 742-7511

Directions: Take Oregon Highway 86 about 60 miles east from Baker City. Just past milepost 61 turn left (north) on USFS Road 77. Follow USFS Road 77 10.6 miles to McBride Campground and USFS Road 7715. Turn north on USFS

Limestone of the Summit Point Reef harbors corals, brachiopods, crinoid stems and other small fossils.

Road 7715, and at the first intersection in 0.25 mile, bear left. At the next intersection, at 1.6 miles, bear right. (Intersections are unsigned. Stay on the more traveled roads!) The trailhead parking area (elevation 6800 feet) is at mile 5.7 on this road.

About the Landscape: This relatively gentle hike takes you into the realm of mountain goats and crosses 200 million years of geologic time, a major fault, and the granitic intrusive that generated Oregon's richest gold deposit. Along the way there is a pretty alpine stream and what seems to be the most exceptionally clear, welcome, and pure spring in Oregon.

Trail Guide: The trail climbs a very rough 4WD road toward the lookout tower (one of the few staffed on this national forest, as of 2002), passing the gray limestone outcrops of the Triassic, 235-million-year-old Summit Point reef. You may find some poorly preserved fossils of crinoids, brachiopods, and corals here, though the fossils have been largely "cooked" by the intrusion of the adjacent Cornucopia stock. Near the top of this grade, the road to the lookout bears right, the trail continues to the north, crossing Columbia River basalts that are about 16 million years in age. For the next 1.9 miles the trail, lined with lupine, paintbrush, and dock, rises across basalt hills until it provides a view of Cornucopia across alpine meadows that in late July are a sea of fragrant blue lupine. This upland was severely overgrazed by sheep, removing most of the native grasses. Today, this area is still grazed by cattle, but the carpet of lupine indicates that it is beginning to recover from past severe abuse. Rocky Mountain goat kids now romp in these meadows in late July. (If you are hiking with a dog, keep Fido on a leash here in midsummer.)

The trail tracks past a shallow pond and turns toward the massive white mountain—Cornucopia stock. The white rock is granitic rock (a rare variety known as cordierite trondjehmite), which makes this mountain almost glow in morning light. The red streaks are basalt dikes—the conduits of flows similar to the basalts that you just walked across. The small lake and most of the high alpine meadows here conceal a jumbled fault zone known as the Eagle fault—an active system that has lifted the Cornucopia stock more than a mile, exposing the dikes and the granitic rocks that formed at considerable depth. These granitic rocks are really part of the Blue Mountain island arc sedimentary and volcanic rocks that melted and recrystallized during collision—and also, evidently, concentrated much gold. More than $20 million in gold was extracted from 36 miles of tunnels. The mine closed in 1938.

At 2.5 miles, the trail begins climbing Cornucopia at a steady pace, crossing several weathered basalt dikes and an impressive avalanche chute and leading past a refreshing spring. At 3.5 miles it grazes the rim of the mountain (elevation 8200 feet), and then continues north on Trail 1885 to Crater Lake—another glacial tarn in another 2.4 miles. Return as you came.

247

PINE LAKES
AND PINE CREEK

Visit two serene lakes far above Oregon's biggest gold mine.

DISTANCE ■ 15 miles round trip

ELEVATION ■ 4800–7300 feet

DIFFICULTY ■ Moderate to difficult

TOPOGRAPHIC MAPS ■ Cornucopia, Krag Peak

GEOLOGIC MAP ■ 1

FEES/REGULATIONS ■ Northwest Forest Pass required for trailhead parking.

PRECAUTIONS ■ Fording West Pine Creek can be a challenge early in the summer.

INFORMATION ■ Pine Ranger District, Wallowa-Whitman National Forest: (541) 742-7511

Directions: From Halfway, about 70 miles east of Baker City, follow the main street, Cornucopia Road, north 10.8 miles to a bridge across Pine Creek. Just before the bridge, turn right at a sign for Cornucopia Pack Station. Follow this road to a parking area and trailhead in 0.2 mile.

About the Landscape: The trail follows Pine Creek up a gentle, scenic valley, then travels a more arduous and rocky path to two small lakes in a beautiful alpine granitic basin. Many old mines can still be seen on the side of Cornucopia. This granitic body nurtured the largest gold-mine complex in Oregon, extracting $20 million of gold from 36 miles of tunnels. The mine closed in 1938, but placer mining continues along Pine Creek.

Trail Guide: From the trailhead, a broad path follows the West Fork of Pine Creek. The trail fords small creeks, and at 1 mile, bypasses a missing bridge and 100 yards farther, fords the main creek, which can be a daunting wade in the spring and early summer. The trail continues on the west side of the creek, providing excellent views of red-brown Columbia River basalt dikes in white granitic rocks—note the horizontal jointing in these dikes. Much of the

Pine Creek occupies a glacial valley just east of the main Cornucopia stock—a mountain of cordierite trondjemite.

hummocky, boulder-strewn bottomland along Pine Creek was placer mined and hydraulic mined (a process in which high-pressure hoses were used to wash sediment into sluice boxes where gold was removed) in the late 1800s and early 1900s.

At 2 miles, the trail crosses the West Fork of Pine Creek again, this time on a bridge. Here, it begins serious climbing, passing outcrops of layered Triassic (230-million-year-old) sandstones and shales that comprise Red Mountain. The heat of intrusion of the adjacent granitic rock hardened these rocks and baked them to a red color, oxidizing the iron in the sandstones. Some of the original layering and sedimentary features can still be found. Dikes of granitic rocks crosscut the sediments. The trail provides a good look at the contact between the granites and the sediments. The contact zone between granitic intrusions and the adjacent older rocks is where most mineral deposits are found, and Cornucopia is no exception.

Switchbacks take you higher. At 6.3 miles the trail enters Pine Lakes basin (elevation 7000 feet). It meanders through subalpine firs and lodgepole pines, with whitebark pines becoming more numerous. Whitebarks occupy the ridge top here, at elevations of about 8200 feet. You may glimpse white Rocky Mountain goats along the ridgeline or on higher outcrops.

Return as you came, or if possible, and you have a second vehicle and driver, you can return via Hike 88, continuing to the rim of Cornucopia on the trail and hiking 4 miles south to the Summit Point trailhead.

Hike

SUGARLOAF BUTTE

Explore some of the Wallowa Mountains' oldest and strangest granitic rocks and enjoy the view from a basalt-capped peak.

DISTANCE ■ 5.2 miles round trip

ELEVATION ■ 6615–7925 feet

DIFFICULTY ■ Moderate

TOPOGRAPHIC MAPS ■ Cornucopia, Deadman Point

GEOLOGIC MAP ■ 54

FEES/REGULATIONS ■ Northwest Forest Pass required for trailhead parking.

PRECAUTIONS ■ New trailhead, trail beginning, and trailhead entry road are not shown on topographic maps.

INFORMATION ■ Pine Ranger District, Wallowa-Whitman National Forest: (541) 742-7511

Directions: From Baker City, take Oregon Highway 86 56 miles to Halfway. Follow Main Street north, turn north on Fish Lake Road (USFS Road 66) and drive 24 miles to turnoff for trailheads for Clear Creek Reservoir and Dead-man Trail. (The turnoff is 0.1 mile past the Fish Lake Campground entrance.) Follow this road 0.3 mile to the trailhead.

About the Landscape: Follow streams through an old, recovering forest burn and across beautiful alpine meadows to an isolated lake and a basaltic butte with exceptional views.

Fire burned here in 1995, scorching some of the mostly lodgepole pine (and fire-adapted) forest. Sugarloaf Butte is a remnant of Columbia River basalts perched atop fault block and much older rocks; the area on and around the butte and reservoir is recovering from grazing, especially by sheep—but is now being grazed by cattle.

Trail Guide: From the trailhead, follow a path along the south side of a wet-land along cliffs, following switchbacks up a steep initial slope and detouring around downed trees as necessary. At the top of the grade, outcrops of dark gray, salt-and-pepper rocks greet you. These are gabbro—the oldest part of the Wallowa batholith—and some of these rocks are layered.

The trail leads to a junction. Turn right here, toward Sugarloaf Butte and Reservoir. In about 0.5 mile, the path dips into a small meadow, then follows a stream and enters a gaunt-looking, skeletal forest—the area burned in the 1995 Twin Lakes Fire.

For the next 0.5 mile the trail may be blocked in a few places by fallen trees—some can be simply stepped over, others require slight detours. Here, the fire was a "stand replacement" disturbance, and part of the fun of this hike is observing how the forest is recovering from seeming devastation. Plants growing here now include alder and ceanothis, both of which are nitrogen fixers that enrich soils. Flowers include fireweed, aster, larkspur, dogtooth violets, and pearly everlasting. Young ponderosa and lodgepole pine are grow-ing vigorously, a new generation replacing their parents and grandparents. This is great habitat for woodpeckers, including black-backed, three-toed, and downy, as well as flickers. This is a "disturbance" forest and ecosystem. In the geologic record, disturbance ecosystems are more often preserved than old growth or stable ecosystems.

After a 0.5-mile traverse, the trail emerges from the burn and enters a vast area of alpine meadow. A huge old-growth lodgepole pine—a fire survivor—guards the meadow entrance. Lupines, yarrow, and camas color the meadow pastel blue. Watch for occasional bull elephant's head and yellow monkey flower along the stream bank.

At a wooden marker halfway across the meadow, turn left (south) to find a dam and Sugarloaf Reservoir—a 30-acre lake. From the reservoir, you can trek cross-country toward Sugarloaf Butte, just to the west, or retrace your steps to the sign and follow trails to the junction with a USFS trail, a path that climbs

Dark granitic rocks along the trail to Sugarloaf represent the oldest part of the Wallowa batholith, about 145 million years in age.

Sugarloaf's eastern flank. Sugarloaf is a Columbia River basalt flow atop granitic rocks of the Wallowa batholith. You can find these older granitic rocks by taking a cross-country hike down Sugarloaf's south side.

The cross-country trip to the summit is easy from here and rewards you with views of Hells Canyon and the Seven Devils to the east, and the Wallowa Mountains (especially Cornucopia and Red Mountain) to the west and northwest. You can also check out the extent of the Twin Lakes fire and its mosaic pattern. To the north, the Imnaha River canyon yawns. Return as you came.

GEOLOGIC TIME CHART

ERA	PERIOD	EPOCH	MILLIONS OF YEARS BEFORE THE PRESENT	
Cenozoic	Quaternary	Holocene		
		Pleistocene	0.01	
	Tertiary	Pliocene	1.8	
		Miocene	5.0	
		Oligocene	24.0	
		Eocene	34.0	
		Paleocene	56.0	
Mesozoic	Cretaceous			65
	Jurassic		145	
	Triassic		208	
Paleozoic	Permian			248
	Pennsylvanian		290	
	Mississippian		323	
	Devonian		360	
	Silurian		410	
	Ordovician		440	
	Cambrian		505	
Precambrian				544

GLOSSARY

aa—Hawaiian term for lavas that cool with broken or fractured pieces on their surface

amphibole—a dark, iron- or magnesium-rich silicate mineral usually rectangular or elongate in outline

amphibolite—a dark metamorphic rock containing the mineral amphibole; develops under very high temperatures and pressures

andesite—a volcanic igneous rock intermediate between basalt and rhyolite, usually gray, named after the Andes volcanoes

argillite—a brittle, silica-rich, shalelike sedimentary rock, related to chert

basalt—a dark-colored, iron-rich volcanic igneous rock that contains pyroxene, olivine, and feldspar

batholith—a body of cooled plutonic rock greater than 100 square kilometers in area

bedding—the layers in which rock, especially sedimentary rock, is deposited

biotite—a dark, iron-rich silicate mineral, usually easily separated into paper-thin layers

biscuit mound (or biscuit scabland)—rough topography characterized by fine-grained silt mounds in a network of coarser stones or gravel

blueschist—a faintly blue-colored metamorphic rock that develops under conditions of very high pressure and low temperature

breccia—a rock composed of angular fragments of rock cemented or bonded together; usually created by explosions, rapid cooling, or movement along a fault

caldera—(1) a large basin-shaped depression in a volcanic summit, usually related to explosion; (2) a large, flat type of volcano that erupts explosive ash flows

chert—a sedimentary rock that develops as the small, silica-rich skeletons of single-celled marine animals called radiolarians accumulate on the deep ocean floor

cirque—a basin-shaped depression carved by ice at the head of a glacier

dacite—a light-colored volcanic igneous rock similar to andesite, with low magnesium, iron, and potassium contents; extrusive equivalent of granodiorite

dikes—narrow intrusions of magma that cut across bedding or layering in rock; feeder dikes serve as conduits of magma to surface eruptions

diorite—a gray-colored plutonic igneous rock intermediate between granite and gabbro, which looks like granite but contains less quartz; diorite usually contains the mineral amphibole or hornblende

dome—a bulbous accumulation, at a vent, of lava too viscous to flow

fault—physical break in the rock where one portion of the earth's crust has moved past another

feldspar—a white or gray silicate mineral composed of silica, aluminum, and some calcium, sodium, and/or potassium; most abundant component of igneous rocks

fold—bends or warped layering in rocks; the result of compression sometime in the rock's history

fumaroles—vents, often in the form of pipes or conduits through which hot gases trapped in an ash flow rise to the surface

gabbro—a dark-colored, iron-rich plutonic igneous rock, the intrusive equivalent of basalt

gneiss—a dark, hard, metamorphic rock that displays banding

graben—a valley or depression bounded and created by faulting

granite—a plutonic igneous rock that tends to be light in color, has a high content of quartz and potassium-rich feldspar, and often contains the dark mineral biotite

granitic, or granitoid, rock—a granite look-alike that may have a mineral composition different from granite

granodiorite—an intrusive igneous rock with less quartz and more feldspar than a "true" granite

greenstone—a catch-all term for gently metamorphosed basalt or other igneous rock that contains the minerals chlorite or epidote and has a greenish color

gutters—lava flow paths or channels

hornblende—a dark, hard, iron-rich mineral of the amphibole family; common in intermediate igneous rocks including diorite and andesite; often appears as shiny black rectangles

igneous rock—rock formed when lava or magma cools

ignimbrite—tuff or welded tuff that erupts in glowing clouds, moves at high speed, and solidifies into a hard, glassy but porous rock

intrusion—an emplacement of molten rock in already existing rock

island arc—a linear chain of volcanic islands that develops above a subduction zone

joints—cracks or separations along which there has been no movement; related to cooling or stress. Compare **fault**

lahars—volcanic mudflows, usually hot

lava—fluid, molten rock that flows on the surface; magma that has erupted

lava bomb—See **volcanic bomb**

maar—a crater left after volcanic explosions that produced only gas rather than a lava eruption

magma—fluid, molten rock beneath the earth's surface

mantle—the main bulk of the earth, 25 to 1800 miles deep, which lies between the core and the crust; composed of peridotite; rocks from the mantle may be faulted or carried to the surface when continents collide with island arcs or another continent

marble—heated, recrystallized limestone; a metamorphic rock

melange—a zone of mixed or different rocks held in a matrix of shale or serpentinite; usually associated with subduction zones

metamorphic rock—any rock changed from its original form by heat and/or pressure

moraine—unsorted gravels transported and deposited at the margin of a glacier

obsidian—a glassy form of rhyolite or dacite

olivine—an olive-green silicate mineral high in magnesium and iron that occurs in basalt and is abundant in peridotite

pahoehoe—Hawaiian term for a basalt lava flow with a smooth, ropy, and often glassy surface

peridotite—dense, magnesium-rich rock that composes the earth's mantle; on the surface, peridotite weathers to a bright reddish brown

pillow lava—molten lava, usually basalt, that chilled and solidified very quickly under water, resulting in globby forms and glassy exterior

pluton—a massive, dome-shaped intrusion of igneous rock

plutonic (or intrusive) rock—rocks formed if a lava never reaches the surface and cools slowly underground

pumice—porous, silica-rich volcanic glass produced in explosive eruptions; related to rhyolite and obsidian; may float

pyroxene—a dark, iron- and magnesium-rich silicate mineral common in basalt and gabbro; usually very small and fine-grained

quartz—silicon dioxide; one of the most abundant rock-forming minerals; colored forms include amethyst (purple) and rose quartz (pink)

rhyodacite—a fine-grained, light-colored volcanic rock; extrusive equivalent of granodiorite, containing slightly less silica and potassium than rhyolite

rhyolite—a quartz- and potassium-feldspar-rich, light-colored volcanic igneous rock; extrusive equivalent of granite; often banded; may contain biotite

sandstone—sedimentary rock composed of sand-sized particles

schist—a fragile metamorphic rock that develops thin layers of mica and other shiny minerals

scoria—oxidized, red-colored volcanic cinders

seafloor spreading—opening of the ocean floor at mid-ocean ridges; part of the plate tectonic process

seamounts—submarine volcanoes related to a stationary source of magma in the earth's mantle (a hotspot) rather than to a subduction zone

sedimentary rock—rocks deposited in layers by water or wind

serpentinite—metamorphosed peridotite, usually shiny green or black

shale—fine-grained sedimentary rock composed of silt and clay

shield volcano—a broad volcano with gentle slopes that erupts fluid basalt

sill—a flat-topped and flat-bottomed intrusion running parallel to bedding layers

slate—a low-grade metamorphic rock, usually formed from shale or mudstone

stratovolcano—a volcano composed of layers of ash and lava

striations—grooves worn by glacial ice or by rocks carried in ice

subduction—the process by which the seafloor is pushed and pulled down into the earth's mantle

subduction zone—the slanting zone where the seafloor plunges back down into the earth's mantle

terminal moraine—unsorted gravel that a glacier piles at its far or terminal end

terrane—a group of rock formations formed by similar or related processes over an extended time; often transported and added to a continent by plate tectonic processes

tonalite—a plutonic igneous rock with less quartz and more calcium-rich feldspar than a "true" granite; closely resembles granite in appearance

tsunami—tidal wave generated by an offshore earthquake

tuff—volcanic ash compressed into rock

vesicle—a cavity, usually small, formed by the entrapment of gas as a lava cools; found in volcanic igneous rocks

volcanic bomb—a blob of lava that was ejected while viscous and became rounded while in flight

volcanic (or extrusive) rock—rocks formed when lava erupts and solidifies

welded tuff—rock formed when very hot, nearly molten particles of ash stick or weld together

xenoliths—an inclusion of foreign rock in an igneous body; from the Greek *xeno*, "strange," and *lithos*, "rock"

RECOMMENDED READING

Allen, John Eliot. *The Magnificent Gateway*. Portland, Ore.: Timber Press, 1979.

Allen, John Eliot, Marjorie Burns, and Sam C. Sargent. *Cataclysms on the Columbia*. Portland, Ore.: Timber Press, 1986.

Benton, Michael. *When Life Nearly Died: The Greatest Mass Extinction of All Time*. Oxford, UK: Thames and Hudson, 2003.

Bishop, E. M. *In Search of Ancient Oregon*. Portland, Ore.: Timber Press, 2003.

_____. *Field Guide to Pacific Northwest Geology*. Portland, Ore.: Timber Press, 2004.

Compton, Robert. *Geology in the Field*. New York: John Wiley, 1985.

Dixon, Dougal, and Raymond Bernor. *The Practical Geologist*. New York: Simon and Schuster, 1992.

Gould, Stephen J., ed. *The Book of Life*. New York: W.W. Norton, 2001.

Harris, Stephen L. *Fire Mountains of the West*. Missoula, Mont.: Mountain Press, 1988.

Lahee, Frederick. *Field Geology*. New York: McGraw Hill, 1980.

McPhee, John. *Annals of the Former World*. New York: Farrar Straus Giroux, 1998.

_____. *Assembling California*. New York: Farrar Straus Giroux, 1991.

_____. *Basin and Range*. New York: Farrar Straus Giroux, 1986.

_____. *In Suspect Terrain*. New York: Farrar Straus Giroux, 1983.

_____. *Rising from the Plains*. New York: Farrar Straus Giroux, 1991.

Maley, Terry. *Field Geology Illustrated*. Boise, Idaho: Mineral Land Publications, 1994.

Orr, Elizabeth, and William Orr. *Geology of the Pacific Northwest*. New York: McGraw Hill, 2001.

_____. *Rivers of the West*. Salem, Ore.: Eagle Web Press, 1985.

Orr, Elizabeth, William Orr, and Ewart Baldwin. *Geology of Oregon*. Dubuque, Iowa: Kendall Hunt, 2001.

Potter, Miles. *Oregon's Golden Years*. Caldwell, Idaho: Caxton, 1976.

Reyes, Chris, ed. *The Table Rocks of Jackson County: Islands in the Sky*. Ashland, Ore.: Last Minute Publications, 1994.

Stanley, G. D. "Travels of an Ancient Reef." *Natural History* 87 (1986): 36–42.

Thorpe, Richard and Geoffrey Brown. *The Field Description of Igneous Rocks*. London: The Open University Press, 1985.

Tucker, Gerald. *The Story of Hells Canyon*. Joseph, Ore: Sheep Creek Publishing, 1993.

Tucker, Maurice. *The Field Description of Sedimentary Rocks*. London: The Open University Press, 1982.

Walker, Gabrielle. *Snowball Earth: The Story of the Great Global Catastrophe that Spawned Life*. New York: Crown Publishers, 2003.

Wallace, David Rains. *The Klamath Knot*. San Francisco: Sierra Club Books, 1983.

Williams, Ira A. *Geologic History of the Columbia River Gorge*. 1923. Reprint, Portland, Ore.: Oregon Historical Society, 1991.

Appendix A
MINERAL AND ROCK IDENTIFICATION

MINERALS AND ROCKS

Rocks are composed of minerals, rather like a fruitcake's mixture of cherries and raisins and bits of orange peel. The vast majority of rocks are composed of fewer than seven minerals. Six of these are silicate minerals that contain silicon dioxide. Of these top six silicate minerals, feldspar and quartz are the most abundant rock-forming minerals. They compose most granites and most sandstones. The other silicates (olivine, pyroxene, amphibole, and biotite) are dark minerals that bear iron and magnesium, and are most notable as the black specks in granite or other igneous rocks. The seventh common rock-forming mineral, calcite, is a carbonate, specifically calcium carbonate (the major ingredient in many antacid tablets). This is the only major mineral that is soft and easily soluble in faintly acid natural groundwater. It is resistant and stable in arid climates, but dissolves readily in more humid climates.

Rocks are subdivided into three genetic categories: igneous (cooled from lava), sedimentary (deposited by water or wind), and metamorphic (changed from one of the other two categories by heat and/or pressure).

IGNEOUS ROCKS

Most rocks in Oregon are igneous (a Greek word meaning "fire-formed"). Except for the Klamath Mountains, where most rocks are metamorphic, or on the coast, where most, except headlands and mountaintops, are sedimentary, your safest bet in Oregon is to claim you are standing on an igneous rock.

Igneous rocks are perhaps the earth's most fundamental. Igneous rocks are formed when a molten material (such as lava or magma) cools and solidifies. Most result from the melting of the earth's mantle. There are two broad categories of igneous rock:

Volcanic (or extrusive) rocks—the most abundant types of igneous rock in Oregon—erupt and flow along the surface as molten lava. They solidify quickly with little time for crystals to grow, are usually fine-grained, and may also display small holes, or vesicles, where gas bubbles collected as the lava flowed and chilled.

Common volcanic rocks include dark-colored basalt, gray andesite (named after the Andes volcanoes), and light-colored rhyolite and dacite. Basalt covers much of eastern Oregon and the Columbia River Gorge, supports coastal headlands, and provides a foundation for the High Cascades. The peaks of the

High Cascades are mostly andesite. Dacite, rhyolite, and obsidian (a quick-chilled, glassy version of rhyolite) are very viscous and cannot flow very far. These light-colored rocks usually compose domes—piles of viscous lava built atop the vent—high on volcanic peaks.

Some volcanic rocks are composed of ash rather than lava. Volcanic ash that is compressed into rock is known as tuff. A rock called welded tuff forms when ash that is still hot literally sticks or welds together. These rocks erupt in torrid clouds of ash called ignimbrites, and can form extensive layers.

Volcanic mudflows, or *lahars,* are considered both volcanic and sedimentary in nature. Modern lahars swept down Washington's Toutle River when Mount St. Helens erupted in 1980. These hot mudflows are unleashed when the heat of an eruption melts snow and glacial ice, sending a torrent of hot water, boulders, and ash with the consistency of hot concrete rushing down a volcano's slopes.

Plutonic (or intrusive) rocks are formed if lava never reaches the surface and cools slowly underground. Plutonic rocks are coarser-grained and often have a salt-and-pepper appearance. They include gabbro, a dark-colored equivalent of basalt; diorite, a lighter, often gray-colored rock which looks like granite; and granite, everybody's favorite, which tends to be light in color, although there are dark pink or red granites in the Colorado and Wyoming Rockies.

Most people use the term *granite* for any coarse-grained, light-colored igneous rock. But many rocks that look like granite are not really granite by geologists' definition. They do not have the right percentages of the minerals quartz and feldspar. In Oregon, most rocks that look like granite are technically granodiorite or tonalite, with less quartz than a "true" granite. The proper catch-all term for a granite look-alike is *granitic* or *granitoid* rock.

IGNEOUS ROCKS

COLOR Minerals	INTRUSIVE (Plutonic)	EXTRUSIVE (Volcanic)
Light-colored Quartz, feldspar, biotite	Granite Granodiorite	Rhyolite Dacite
Gray Feldspar, hornblende	Diorite	Andesite
Dark gray or green Feldspar, pyroxene	Gabbro	Basalt
Dark green with **red-brown outside** Pyroxene, olivine	Peridotite	No extrusive form in Oregon

Cooled bodies of plutonic rocks may represent the solidified magma chambers beneath long-extinct and eroded volcanoes, or may be a body of molten rock that cooled without erupting. They come in many different sizes and shapes. The largest bodies, by definition greater than 100 square kilometers in area, are known as batholiths. Oregon's most notable batholiths include the core of the Wallowas (Wallowa batholith), the northern end of

Cross-joints are common in granitic rocks.

the Elkhorns (Bald Mountain batholith), Mount Ashland (Ashland pluton), and the Grants Pass pluton west of Grants Pass. Smaller bodies of plutonic rock are known as stocks. The narrow conduits of magma en route to the surface that slice through rock are known as dikes. The red-brown stripes across the granitic rocks of the Wallowa Mountains are basalt dikes. On rare occasions dictated by the right tectonic circumstances, fragments of the earth's mantle arrive on mountaintops. In Oregon, mantle rocks, known as peridotite, are found in the Klamath Mountains (near Vulcan Peak) and in the Blue Mountains, on the north side of Canyon Mountain.

SEDIMENTARY ROCKS

The earth's history is archived in the layers of sedimentary rocks. These rocks are formed when silt, clay, sand, or other materials are deposited by water or wind; they most commonly display parallel layering (bedding, to geologists). Their fossils reveal primeval ecosystems, their textures evoke ancient seas. The most common Oregon sedimentary rocks are sandstones and shales. Coarse conglomerate, composed of sand, pebbles, and cobbles, is the trademark of an ancient river or beach. Very fine-grained

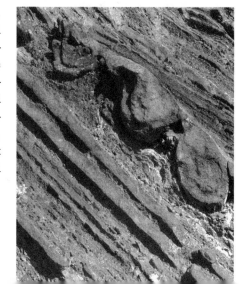

Sedimentary rocks near Illahe

sediments like shale and chert (a fine-grained, silica-rich sedimentary rock) indicate deep or very calm water. Limestone is a sedimentary rock associated with warm water and coral reefs.

Fossils are usually the only guide to the age of sedimentary rocks. In fine-grained rocks, microscopic fossils of one-celled plants or animals often provide clues to the age of the ancient seafloor. Fossils also help us understand how far dispersed the earth's plates have become: fossils of an Asiatic sea cap the Elkhorn Mountains; corals crown the summits of the Wallowas.

SEDIMENTARY ROCKS

PARTICLE SIZE	ROCK NAME
Pebbles and cobbles	Conglomerate
Sand	Sandstone
Silt and clay	Shale
Silica-rich ooze	Chert
Calcium-carbonate ooze or extremely fine-grained precipitation; coral reef	Limestone

METAMORPHIC ROCKS

Metamorphic rocks are merely igneous or sedimentary rocks that have been changed by heat and pressure. In Oregon, there are basically just four kinds of metamorphic rock: greenstone, marble, schist, and amphibolite. The textures and colors vary from rock to rock, but the names and mineralogy are the same. The metamorphic changes in heat and pressure vary from the barely discernible metamorphism of the sediments in the Wallowa or Aldrich Mountains to the extremely high-pressure metamorphism that changed seabed shales into *blueschist* near Mitchell and at Condrey Mountain in the Klamaths.

Greenstone—a catch-all term for gently metamorphosed basalt or other igneous rock—is the most abundant metamorphic rock in Oregon. It is green because iron-bearing minerals in the original rock alter to green minerals during metamorphism. Greenstones abound in Hells Canyon and along the Rogue River. A related rock, serpentinite, occurs in the Klamath Mountains.

Marble is heated and recrystallized limestone. Marbles can be hard, resistant rocks. Or they may be crumbly and difficult to climb, like some marbles in the Wallowa Mountains that have developed large calcite crystals and a texture like coarsely granulated sugar.

260

Schist is a fragile rock. This flaky, or friable, rock develops thin layers of mica and other shiny minerals. Schist is very rare in Oregon, found only in a few locations in the Blue and Klamath Mountains.

Amphibolite is a dark, banded rock that often exhibits small folds or flaky layers. It develops where very high temperature and pressure have affected rocks. It is even rarer than schist in Oregon.

FOLDS, FAULTS, AND STRUCTURAL GEOLOGY

The earth is neither a stable nor a gentle place. Continents collide. Seafloors spread. Mountains rise. Volcanoes erupt. All this activity stresses rocks. In people, stress produces wrinkles and gray hair. In rocks, it produces folds, faults, and cracks.

Although geologists classify different types of folds, the only thing the hiker need recognize is that folds—any type of fold at any scale—result from compression sometime in the rock's history. The broad, open folds in Columbia River basalt west of The Dalles, the crinkled chert at Rainbow Rock just north of Brookings, or the microscopic crenulations in the minerals of the Josephine peridotite at Vulcan Lake all mean the same thing: the rocks were subjected to stress, and folded or wrinkled as a result.

Faults are physical breaks in the rock where one portion of the earth's crust has moved past another. Like folds, they occur at all scales. Some faults develop where rock is pushed together and is too brittle to bend. Others develop where rocks are extended or pulled apart. All faults show offset—the displacement of one side relative to another. Motion along faults may be measured in millimeters, or in hundreds of miles. Joints are cracks or separations along which there has been no movement.

OREGON AND PLATE TECTONICS

The basic tenet of plate tectonics is that the earth's crust is composed of plates of low-density continental rocks (granites) and heavier oceanic crust (basalt) that move across the earth's surface. The motion is driven by convection currents in the earth's mantle—hot, dense material composed of the rock peridotite.

North America's westward motion was driven by the opening of the Atlantic Ocean—or *seafloor spreading*—that began 200 million years ago and continues today. The seafloor on which the continent rides is pushed and pulled back down into the mantle (rather like a huge conveyor belt). The process is called subduction, and the zone where the seafloor plunges back down into the mantle is called a subduction zone. Volcanoes usually develop above the subduction zone, and it is these volcanic islands that North America collided with to create Oregon's first land in the Klamaths and Blue Mountains.

The way cars are stacked in this wrecking yard resembles the way terranes are stacked in the Klamaths and Blue Mountains.

The islands and scraps of seafloor that were added to the continent are called terranes, or sometimes exotic terranes. A terrane can be defined informally as a group of rocks produced by unique geologic processes in one location and transported to a new location by plate tectonics. The terranes of the Blue Mountains are an example. Each terrane represents a different part of a complex island arc system—the volcanoes, the subduction zone, etc.—that collided with the adjacent continent. Sometimes, as in the Klamaths, the island arcs also collide with one another, producing a welter of terranes that are then added to the continent in one package. Western North America has long been a sort of terrane station, where the continent grows westward a little farther as each terrane arrives.

Other plate tectonic forces have contributed to Oregon's history as well. These include the clockwise rotation of the Klamath Mountains, Coast Range, and Cascades westward. During the last 20 million years, this linear band of tectonic blocks has swung westward like a pendulum with its pivot point just north of Longview, Washington. This rotational motion may be linked to the expansion of the Basin and Range in southeast Oregon, and to the faults of the Olympic-Wallowa Lineament fault in northeast Oregon.

There are undoubtedly other forces, as yet unrecognized, at work sculpting Oregon and our planet. After all, in 1965, plate tectonics was still the controversial hypothesis of a few graduate students, and tectonic rotation was not even dreamed of. As long as we continue to observe the earth, we will see new things and make fresh discoveries. Which is why, after all, we go hiking in the first place.

Appendix B
GEOLOGIC MAPS LIST

A geologic map is a great tool to help preview, review, or reconnoiter the geology you'll encounter on these hikes. These maps show the type and age of bedrock throughout the area mapped. They also show faults and other features of interest, and usually include a detailed description of the area's history and rock formations. Some, such as the map of the Bourne Quadrangle, provide a history of gold mines or other geologic endeavors.

The information about each hike includes a key to the geologic map that covers the area. Maps listed for each hike are keyed by number to a map list. (The number of the map is not related to the hike number.) The scale of the geologic map that covers each hike varies. For some, a detailed geologic map, based on the USGS 7.5' quadrangle is available. For others, mapping is only available on a 1:100,000 scale or on Oregon's state geologic map. Most maps currently in print (and a number of other books and pamphlets) are available from Oregon's Department of Geology and Mineral Industries, through their store: Nature of the Northwest, 800 Northeast Oregon Street, Suite 177, Portland, Oregon 97232. Phone: (503) 872-2750; TDD: (503) 872-2752; e-mail: *info@naturenw.org;* website: *www.naturenw.org.*

1. Geologic map of Oregon. G. Walker and N. McLeod. USGS, 1991. 1:500,000.
2. Preliminary geologic map of the Eagle Point and Sams Valley quadrangles, Jackson County, Oregon. T. J. Wiley and J. G. Smith. Oregon Dept. Geology and Mineral Industries, Open File Report. O-93-13. 1993.
3. Geologic map of the Kalmiopsis Wilderness, southwestern Oregon. N. J. Page et al. USGS, Map MF-1240-A. 1981. 1:62,500.
4. Mineral resource potential, Kalmiopsis Wilderness, southwestern Oregon. N. J. Page and M. S. Miller. USGS, Map MF-1240-E. 1981. 1:62,500.
5. Preliminary geologic map of the Medford 1x2 degree sheet. J. G. Smith et al. USGS, Open File Report. O-82-955. 1982. 1:250,000.
6. Lode gold characteristics of the Medford 1x2 degree quadrangle. N. J. Page et al. USGS, Map MF-1383-D. 1983. 1:250,000.
7. Geologic map of the Wild Rogue Wilderness, Coos, Curry, and Douglas Counties, Oregon. F. Gray et al. USGS, Map MF-1381-A. 1982. 1:48,000.
8. Geology of the south half of the Coos Bay 2 degree sheet. M. L. Blake Jr. and A. S. Jayco. USGS, Open File Map. 1989.
9. Geology of the Marys Peak and Alsea quadrangles, Oregon. E. Baldwin. USGS, Map OM-162. 1955. 1:62,500.
10. Geology and mineral resources of Coos County, Oregon. E. Baldwin et al. Oregon Dept. Geology and Mineral Industries, Bulletin 80. 1973. 1:62,500.

11. Geologic map of the Drake Crossing 7.5' quadrangle, Marion County, Oregon. Oregon Dept. Geology and Mineral Industries, GMS-50.

12. Geologic map of Elk Prairie 7.5' quadrangle, Marion and Clackamas Counties. Oregon Dept. Geology and Mineral Industries, GMS-51.

13. Geologic map of the Lake Oswego quadrangle, Clackamas, Multnomah, and Washington Counties, Oregon. M. H. Beeson et al. Oregon Dept. Geology and Mineral Industries, GMS-59. 1989. 1:24,000.

14. Geologic map of the Damascus quadrangle, Clackamas and Multnomah Counties, Oregon. I. P. Madin. Oregon Dept. Geology and Mineral Industries, GMS-60. 1994. 1:24,000.

15. Geologic map of the Portland quadrangle, Multnomah and Washington Counties, Oregon, and Clark County, Washington. M. H. Beeson et al. Oregon Dept. Geology and Mineral Industries, GMS-75. 1991. 1:24,000.

15a. Relative earthquake hazard map of the Linnton quadrangle, Multnomah and Washington Counties, Oregon and Washington. M.A. Mabey, Ian P. Madin, and others. Oregon Dept. Geology and Mineral Industries, GMS-104. 1995. 1:24,000.

16. Earthquake hazard map of the Portland quadrangle, Multnomah and Washington Counties, Oregon, and Clark County, Washington. M. A. Mabey et al. Oregon Dept. Geology and Mineral Industries, GMS-79. 1994. 1:24,000.

17. Earthquake hazard map of the Mount Tabor quadrangle, Clackamas, Multnomah, and Washington Counties, Oregon. Oregon Dept. Geology and Mineral Industries, GMS-89. 1995. 1:24,000.

18. Earthquake hazard map of the Beaverton quadrangle, Oregon. Oregon Dept. Geology and Mineral Industries, GMS-90. 1994. 1:24,000.

19. Earthquake hazard map of the Lake Oswego quadrangle, Clackamas, Multnomah, and Washington Counties, Oregon. Oregon Dept. Geology and Mineral Industries, GMS-91. 1994. 1:24,000.

20. Earthquake hazard map of the Gladstone quadrangle, Clackamas, Multnomah, and Washington Counties, Oregon. Oregon Dept. Geology and Mineral Industries, GMS-92. 1995. 1:24,000.

21. Geologic and neotectonic evaluation of north-central Oregon: The Dalles 1x2 degree quadrangle. James Bella. Oregon Dept. Geology and Mineral Industries, GMS-27. 1982. 1:250,000.

22. Geologic map of the Mount Hood Wilderness, Clackamas and Hood River Counties, Oregon. T. E. C. Keith et al. USGS, Map MF-1379A. 1982. 1:62,500.

23. Geothermal investigations in the vicinity of the Mount Hood Wilderness, Clackamas and Hood River Counties, Oregon. J. H. Robison et al. USGS, Map MF-1379 B. 1982.

24. Geology of the Mount Hood volcano. W. S. Wise. In: *Andesite Conference Guidebook*, H. Dole, ed. Oregon Dept. Geology and Mineral Industries, Bulletin 62. 1968.

25. Geologic map of Oregon. Oregon Dept. Geology and Mineral Industries. 1991. 1:500,000.

26. Geology of Mount Jefferson. Richard Conrey. Washington State University Ph.D., unpublished. 1990. 1:62,500.

27. Geologic map of the Three Sisters Wilderness, Deschutes, Lane, and Linn Counties, Oregon. E. M. Taylor et al. USGS, Map MF-1952. 1987. 1:63,360.

28. Geologic map of the Mount Bachelor Chain and surrounding area. W. E. Scott and C. A. Gardner. USGS, Map I-1967. 1992. 1:50,000.

29. Field geology of SW Broken Top quadrangle, Oregon. E. M. Taylor. Oregon Dept. Geology and Mineral Industries, Special Paper 2. 1978.

30. Roadside Geology of the Santiam Pass Area. E. M. Taylor. In: *Andesite Conference Guidebook*, H. Dole, ed. Oregon Dept. Geology and Mineral Industries, Bulletin 62. 1968.

31. Aeromagnetic and Gravity Surveys of the Crater Lake region, Oregon [Geology of Crater Lake]. H. Richard Blank. In: *Andesite Conference Guidebook*, H. Dole, ed. Oregon Dept. Geology and Mineral Industries, Bulletin 62. 1968.

32. Geologic map of the Eagle Butte and Gateway quadrangles, Jefferson and Wasco Counties, Oregon. G. A. Smith and G. A. Hayman. Oregon Dept. Geology and Mineral Industries, GMS-43. 1987. 1:24,000.

33. Geologic map of the Seekseequa Junction and a portion of the Metolius Bench quadrangles, Jefferson County, Oregon. G. A. Smith. Oregon Dept. Geology and Mineral Industries, GMS-44. 1987. 1:24,000.

34. Geologic map of the Madras East and Madras West quadrangles. G. A. Smith. Oregon Dept. Geology and Mineral Industries, GMS-45. 1987. 1:24,000.

35. Geologic map of the Smith Rock area, Jefferson, Deschutes, and Crook Counties, Oregon. P. T. Robinson and D. H. Stensland. USGS, Map I-1142. 1979. 1:48,000.

36. Geologic map of Newberry Volcano, Deschutes, Klamath, and Lake Counties, Oregon. USGS, Map MI-2455. 1995. 1:62,500 and 1:24,000.

37. Roadside Guide to the Geology of Newberry Volcano. R. A. Jensen. Cen. Ore. Geo. Pub. 1995.

38. Reconnaissance geologic map of the west half of the Bend and the east half of the Shelvin Park 7.5' quadrangles, Deschutes County, Oregon. USGS, MF-2189. 1992. 1:24,000.

39. Geologic map of the High Steens and Little Blitzen Gorge Wilderness Study Areas, Harney County, Oregon. Scott A. Minor et al. USGS, Misc. Field Studies Map MF-1876. 1987.

40. Geologic map of the Wildhorse Lake quadrangle, Harney County, Oregon. Scott A. Minor et al. USGS, Misc. Field Studies Map MF-1915. 1987.

41. Geologic map of the Alvord Hot Springs quadrangle, Harney County, Oregon. Scott A. Minor et al. USGS, Misc. Field Studies Map MF-1916. 1987.

42. Geologic map of the Krumbo Reservoir quadrangle, Harney County, Southeastern Oregon. J. A. Johnson. USGS, Misc. Field Studies Map MF-2267. 1994.

43. Mineral resources of the Pueblo Mountains Wilderness Study Area, Harney County, Oregon, and Humbolt County, Nevada. Roback et al. USGS, Bulletin 1740B. 1987.

44. Preliminary geologic map of the Three Fingers Rock quadrangle, Malheur County, Oregon. D. B. Vander et al. USGS, Open File Report. O-89-334. 1989. 1:24,000.

45. Geologic map of the Pelican Point quadrangle, Malheur County, Oregon. D. B. Vander Meulen et al. USGS, Misc. Field Studies Map MF-1904. 1987. 1:24,000.

46. Geologic map of the Rooster Comb quadrangle, Malheur County, Oregon. D. B. Vander Meulen et al. USGS, Misc. Field Studies Map MF-1902. 1987. 1:24,000.

47. Geology and mineral resources of the Grassy Mountain quadrangle, Malheur County, Oregon. M. L. Ferns and L. Ramp. Oregon Dept. Geology and Mineral Industries, GMS-57. 1989. 1:24,000.

48. Geologic map of the Owyhee Canyon Wilderness Study Area, Malheur County, Oregon. James G. Evans. USGS, Misc. Field Studies Map MF-1926. 1987. 1:62,500.

49. Geologic map of the Lower Owyhee Canyon Wilderness Study Area, Malheur County, Oregon. James G. Evans. USGS, Misc. Field Studies Map MF-2167. 1991. 1:48,000.

50. Geologic map of the Mahogany Mountain 30x60 minute quadrangle, Malheur County, Oregon, and Owyhee County, Idaho. Mark L. Ferns et al. Oregon Dept. Geology and Mineral Industries, GMS-78. 1993. 1:100,000.

51. Geologic map of the Vale 30x60 minute quadrangle, Malheur County, Oregon, and Owyhee County, Idaho. Mark L. Ferns et al. Oregon Dept. Geology and Mineral Industries, GMS-77. 1993. 1:100,000.

265

52. Geologic map of the Snake River Canyon, Oregon and Idaho. In: *A Preliminary Report on the geology of part of the Snake River Canyon, Oregon and Idaho.* T. L. Vallier. Oregon Dept. Geology and Mineral Industries, GMS-6. 1974.
53. Reconnaissance geology of the Wallowa Lake quadrangle. In: *Geology and Physiography of the Northern Wallowa Mountains, Oregon.* W. D. Smith and J. E. Allen. Oregon Dept. Geology and Mineral Industries, Bulletin 12. 1941. Approx. 1:100,000.
54. Reconnaissance geologic map of the Oregon part of the Grangeville quadrangle, Baker, Union, Umatilla, and Wallowa Counties, Oregon. G. Walker. USGS, MI-1116. 1979.
55. Geology and gold deposits of the Bourne quadrangle, Baker and Grant Counties, Oregon. H. C. Brooks et al. Oregon Dept. Geology and Mineral Industries, GMS-19. 1982. 1:24,000.
56. Geology and mineral resources map of the Elkhorn Peak quadrangle, Baker County, Oregon. M. L. Ferns. Oregon Dept. Geology and Mineral Industries, GMS-41. 1987. 1:24,000.
57. Geology and mineral resources map of the Mount Ireland quadrangle, Baker and Grant Counties, Oregon. M. L. Ferns et al. Oregon Dept. Geology and Mineral Industries, GMS-22. 1982.
58. Geology of the Canyon City quadrangle, northeastern Oregon. T. P. Thayer and C. E. Brown. USGS, Misc. Investigations Map MI-447. 1966.
59. Mineral resources of the Strawberry Mountain Wilderness and adjacent areas, Grant County, Oregon. T. P. Thayer et al. USGS, Bulletin 1498. 1981.
60. Reconnaissance geologic map of the east half of the Bend quadrangle, Crook, Wheeler, Jefferson, Wasco, and Deschutes Counties, Oregon. D. A. Swanson. USGS, Misc. Investigations Map MI-568. 1969. 1:250,000.
61. Reconnaissance geologic map of the John Day Formation in the southwestern part of the Blue Mountains and adjacent areas, north-central Oregon. P. T. Robinson. USGS, Misc. Investigations Map MI-872. 1975. 1:125,000.
62. John Day Basin Paleontology Field Trip Guide and Road Log. T. Fremd et al. Society of Vertebrate Paleontology. 1994. Variable scales.
63. Geologic map of the North Fork John Day Roadless Area, Grant County. James Evans. USGS, MF-1581-C.
64. Reconnaissance geologic map of the Lookout Mountain quadrangle, Crook and Wheeler Counties, Oregon. Swinney and others. USGS, I-543. 1968.

Appendix C
ADDRESSES

Alsea Ranger District (USFS), 18591 Alsea Highway, Alsea, OR 97324; (541) 487-5811

Applegate Ranger District (USFS), 6941 Upper Applegate Road, Jacksonville, OR 97530; (541) 899-3800

Ashland Ranger District (USFS), 645 Washington Street, Ashland, OR 97520; (541) 552-2900

Baker Ranger District (USFS), 3165 Tenth Street, Baker City, OR 97814; (541) 523-4476

Bend-Fort Rock Ranger District (USFS), 1230 NE Third, Bend, OR 97701; (541) 383-4000

Beverly Beach State Park, 198 NE 123rd Street, Newport, OR 97365; (800) 551-6949

Burns District, Bureau of Land Management, HC-74, 12533 Highway 20 West, Hines, OR 97738; (541) 573-4400

Cape Arago State Park, c/o Oregon State Parks Regional Office, 365 North Fourth Street, Suite A, Coos Bay, OR 97420; (800) 551-6949

Cape Blanco State Park, c/o Humbug Mountain State Park, P.O. Box 1345, Port Orford, OR 97465; (800) 551-6949

Cape Lookout State Park, c/o Oregon State Parks Regional Office, 416 Pacific Street, Tillamook, OR 97141; (800) 551-6949

Chetco Ranger District (USFS), 555 Fifth Street, Brookings, OR 97415; (541) 412-6000

Columbia River Gorge National Scenic Area, 902 Wasco Avenue, Suite 200, Hood River, OR 97031; (541) 386-2333

Cove Palisades State Park, 44300 Jordan Road, Culver, OR 97734; (800) 551-6949

Crater Lake National Park, P.O. Box 128, Crater Lake, OR 97604; (541) 594-2211

Detroit Ranger District (USFS), HC 73, Box 320, Mill City, OR 97360; (503) 854-3366

Diamond Lake Ranger District (USFS), 2020 Toketee Ranger Station Road, Idlewild Park, OR 97447; (541) 498-2531

Eagle Cap Ranger District (USFS), 88401 Highway 82, Enterprise, OR 97828; (541) 426-4978

Fort Rock State Natural Area, c/o Oregon State Parks Regional Office, P.O. Box 5309, Bend, OR 97708; (800) 551-6949

Gold Beach Ranger District, 1225 South Ellensburg Street, Box 7, Gold Beach, OR 97444; (541) 247-3600

Guy W. Talbot State Park, c/o Oregon State Parks Regional Office, 3554 SE 82nd Avenue, Portland, OR 97266; (800) 551-6949

Hells Canyon National Recreation Area, 88401 Highway 82, Enterprise, OR 97828; (541) 426-4978

Hood River Ranger District (USFS), 6780 Highway 35 South, Parkdale, OR 97041; (541) 352-6002

Humbug Mountain State Park, P.O. Box 1345, Port Orford, OR 97465; (541)332-6774

Jackson County Parks and Recreation, 400 Antelope Road, White City, OR 97503; (541) 774-8183

John Day Fossil Beds National Monument, 32651 Highway 19, Kimberly, OR 97848; (541) 987-2333

LaGrande Ranger District (USFS), 3502 Highway 30, LaGrande, OR 97850; (541) 963-7186

Lane County Parks Division, 3040 North Delta Highway, Eugene, OR 97401; (541) 341-6900

La Pine State Recreation Area, c/o Oregon State Parks Regional Office, P.O. Box 5309, Bend, OR 97708; (541) 388-6211

Lava Lands Visitor Center, 58201 South Hwy 97, Bend, OR 97707; (541) 593-2421

Lookout Mountain Ranger District, Ochoco National Forest; (541) 416-6500

Malheur National Forest, 431 Patterson Bridge Road, PO Box 909, John Day, OR 97845; (541) 575-3000

McKenzie Ranger District (USFS), 57600 McKenzie Highway, McKenzie Bridge, OR 97413; (541) 822-3381

Medford District (BLM), 3040 Biddle Road, Medford, OR, 97504; (541) 618-2200

Mount Hood National Forest, Visitor Information Center, 65000 East Highway 26, Welches, OR 97067; (503) 622-7674

The Nature Conservancy, 1234 NW 25th Street, Portland, OR 97828; (503) 228-9561

Nature of Oregon Information Center, 800 NE Oregon Street, Portland, OR 97232; (503) 731-4444

Newberry National Volcanic Monument, Deschutes National Forest, 1230 NE Third, Bend, OR 97701; (541) 388-4000

North Fork John Day River Ranger District (USFS), PO Box 158, Ukiah, OR 97880; (541) 427-3231

Ochoco National Forest, Supervisor's Office, P.O. Box 490, 3160 NE Third Street, Prineville, OR 97754; (541) 416-6500

Oregon Caves National Monument, Cave Junction, OR 97523; (541) 592-3400

Oregon Department of Fish and Wildlife, Sauvie Island Wildlife Area, 18330 NW Sauvie Island Road, Portland, OR 97231; (503) 621-3488

Oregon Department of Geology and Mineral Industries, 800 NE Oregon Street, Suite 941, Portland, OR 97232; (503) 731-4100

Oregon Dunes National Recreation Area, Siuslaw National Forest, 855 Highway Avenue, Reedsport, OR 97467; (541) 271-3611

Oregon Museum of Science and Industry, 1945 SE Water Avenue, Portland, OR 97214; (503) 797-4545

Oregon State Parks and Recreation Department, 1115 Commercial Street, SE, Salem, OR 97301; (800) 551-6949

Pine Ranger District (USFS), General Delivery, Halfway, Oregon 97834; (541) 742-7511

Portland Bureau of Environmental Services, 1120 SW 5th Ave., Portland, OR 97204; (503) 823-7740

Portland Parks and Recreation Department, Hoyt Arboretum, 4000 SW Fairview Boulevard, Portland, OR 97221; (503) 823-3655

Prairie City Ranger District (USFS), 327 Front Street, Prairie City, OR 97869; (541) 820-3800

Prospect Ranger Station (USFS), 47201 Highway 62, Prospect, OR 97536; (541) 560-3400

Rogue River-Siskiyou National Forest Headquarters, 333 West Eight Street, Medford, OR 97501; (541) 858-2200

Saddle Mountain State Park, c/o Oregon State Parks Regional Office, 416 Pacific Street, Tillamook, OR 97141; (800) 551-6949

Salem District (BLM), 1717 Fabry Road SE, Salem, OR 97306; (503) 375-5646

Shore Acres State Park, c/o Oregon State Parks Regional Office, 365 North Fourth Street, Suite A, Coos Bay, OR 97420; (800) 551-6949

Silver Falls State Park, c/o Oregon State Parks and Recreation Division, 525 Trade Street SE, Salem, OR 97310; (800) 551-6949

Sisters Ranger District (USFS), P.O. Box 249, Highway 20, Sisters, OR, 97759; (541) 549-7700

Siuslaw National Forest, Supervisors Office, 4077 Research Way, Corvallis, OR 97333; (541) 750-7000

Smith Rock State Park, c/o Oregon State Parks Regional Office, P.O. Box 5309, Bend, OR 97708; (800) 551-6949

Sunset Bay State Park, c/o Oregon State Parks Regional Office, 365 North Fourth Street, Suite A, Coos Bay, OR 97420; (800) 551-6949

Sweet Home Ranger District (USFS), 3225 U.S. Highway 20, Sweet Home, OR 97386; (541) 367-5168

Tahkenitch Lake State Park, c/o Oregon State Parks Regional Office, 365 North Fourth Street, Suite A, Coos Bay, OR 97420; (800) 551-6949

Umpqua National Forest Headquarters, 2900 NW Stewart Parkway, Roseburg, OR 97470; (541) 672-6601

US Forest Service, Region Six Headquarters, Pacific Northwest Regional Office, 319 Pine Street, Portland, OR 97208; (503) 221-2877

USGS, Branch of Distribution/Information Center, P.O. Box 25286, Federal Center, Denver, CO 80225; (888) ASK-USGS

Vale District (BLM), 100 Oregon Street, Vale, OR 97918; (541) 473-3144

Wallowa–Whitman National Forest, Supervisors Office, P.O. Box 907, 1550 Dewey Avenue, Baker City, OR 97814; (541) 523-6391

Zigzag Ranger District (USFS), 70220 East Highway 26, Zigzag, OR 97049; (541) 622-3191

INDEX

aa (basaltic) 137, 148, 149
Aldrich Mountains 14, 67
Alvord desert 67, 193
ammonites 31
amphibolite 46, 54, 56
andesite 35, 131, 153
Angels Rest 106-107
Anthony Lake 229, 230
anthophyllite 39
argillite 89, 101, 232
Astoria Formation 65, 76, 77

Bald Mountain batholith
    229-232
Banks-Vernonia Trail 68-70
basalt 11, 16-18, 70-72, 77-78,
    96, 99, 104, 105, 131
Basin and Range 22, 67, 199
batholith 215
Big Obsidian Flow 177, 180,
    182-183
biscuit mounds 36, 113
Blue Basin 216-217
Blue Mountain island arc
    12-14, 208-210, 229
Blue Mountains 14-15, 21, 29
Boring volcanic field 87-92,
    103, 107
brachiopods 209, 246
breccia 67, 71
Broken Top 120, 142-14
Buckhorn Overlook 233

caldera 191, 207
Canyon Mountain 209, 221-223
Cape Arago 84
Cape Blanco 62-63, 66
Cape Kiwanda 75-76
Cape Lookout 17, 66, 72-74
Cascade Mountains 115-165
Cayuse Cone 120, 140, 145
chert 232
Chetco Lake 44, 55-57
Chetco Peak, 44, 48, 49, 55-57
Coast Range 22, 65-85
Collier Cone 120, 145-148
Columbia River (ancestral)
    65-66, 70-71, 102-103, 110
Columbia River basalt 66, 77,
    87-88, 104-106, 210, 218
Columbia River Gorge 18,
    22, 27, 70, 79, 100, 102-113

concretions 79, 84, 85
conglomerate 58, 60, 61, 62
Coon Hollow 234-235
Cornucopia (intrusion,
    mountain) 22-23, 210
Cove Palisades 169-171
Crater Lake (Mount
    Mazama) 153-157
Crater Rock (Mount Hood)
    118, 125, 127
crinoids 68, 246

dacite 10, 119, 124, 127, 128
Deschutes Basin 22, 167-176
Devils Punchbowl 78-79
Diamond Craters 189-191
dikes 77, 79, 122, 197, 244, 248
dome (volcanic) 118, 125,
    127, 141, 142, 177-178,
    183-184
dunes 76, 82-83
dunite 53
Eagle Creek 110-111
Echo Lake 45-48
Egan Cone 120-121
Elkhorn Crest 230
entelodont 218
Erratic Rock State Natural
    Site 88, 100-101
Eureka Mine 235, 237
exotic terranes 11, 14, 30-32
    65, 208-210, 227

faults 11, 18, 19-20, 67
feldspar 38
flow-banding 182
folding 11, 67
foliation 39
Foree Basin 218
Fort Rock 178, 187-189
fossils 15-16, 62, 65, 68-69,
    76, 110, 195, 209, 218-219,
    221, 234, 246
Frenchman Springs basalt
    flows 70-71, 105-106
fumaroles 118, 156, 157

gabbro 46, 54-55, 58, 80, 81,
    222, 232, 236
gastropods 76
Gin Lin Mine 41-42
Gold Beach terrane 31, 62

gold, gold deposits 15, 41-42,
    49, 116, 210, 214, 226,
    232, 247
gomphothere 36
graben 191
Grande Ronde basalt 104,
    105, 109
granitic intrusions 13, 15,
    37-39, 51, 210
Grayback pluton 52, 215
greenstones 33-34, 48-49, 59,
    61, 209, 226, 227, 232

harzburgite 53
Hells Canyon 8, 14, 27, 209,
    235, 237
High Cascade graben 116
High Cascades 18-19, 22,
    116
High Lava Plains 22, 177-191
Hoffer Lakes 12
hornblende 40, 41
Hug Point 77-78
Humbug Mountain 59-61
Hurricane Creek 241-243

igneous rocks, 12-13
ignimbrite 170, 190
Imnaha basalt 16, 104, 238
Imnaha River 236-237
island arc system, 32

Jack London Trail 33
Jefferson Park 133
John Day Fossil Beds 15,
    116, 132, 216-221
joints 168
Jordan Craters 205-207
Josephine ophiolite 44, 49, 56

Kalmiopsis Wilderness 15,
    44, 53-54, 56-57
Klamath microcontinent 56,
    59-60, 62
Klamath Mountains, 14-15,
    21-22, 29-32, 45-47, 65, 67

Larch Mountain 108-109
Latourell Falls 105-106
lava bombs 91
Lava Butte 185-186
Lava Cast 184-185

LeConte Crater (cone) 120, 140, 142
Leslie Gulch, 18, 201, 204-205
limestone 13, 51, 209
Little Belknap Crater 148-150
London Peak 33-34
Lookout Mountain 213-215
Lost Creek Nature Trail 129-131

maar 190
marble 31, 50, 52, 242
Marys Peak 65, 80-81
Maxwell Lake 239
McKenzie Pass 11, 148-149
McKenzie River 136-137
metamorphic rocks, 11
Metolius River 137-139
Missoula Floods 18, 88, 100-101, 112-113
Mount Ashland 37-39
Mount Hood, 10, 19, 20, 21, 117-118, 124, 128
Mount Jefferson 118-119, 134
Mount Scott (Crater Lake) 122, 153-154
Mount St. Helens 113, 124
Mount Tabor 88, 90-91
Mount Thielsen 121, 151-153
mudstone 13, 68-69
Multnomah Falls 108-109

Natural Bridge (Rogue River) 160-162
Nee Mee Poo Trail 238
Newberry Volcano 10, 124
normal faults 67
North Fork, John Day River 209, 226-228

obsidian 10, 141, 180, 182-183
Old Maid eruption 117-118, 129-131
Olympic-Wallowa lineament 11, 19, 67
Oregon Caves National Monument 50-52
oreodont 219
Otter (Otter Crest) 78-79
Owyhees, 18, 22, 201-207

pahoehoe 11, 165, 190, 206
Painted Hills 27, 132, 219-221
palagonite 121
peridotite 30, 39, 45-46, 53, 54-55, 56-57, 223, 224

pillow basalts, pillow lavas 65, 80-81, 108, 179, 228
Pilot Rock 16, 17, 39-41
placer mining 41-42
Pomona basalt flow 70, 113
Powell Butte 92-93
Priest Rapids basalt 13, 105-106
Pueblo Mountains 197-198
pumice 135, 140

Ramona Falls 125-126
Red Buttes Wilderness 45-48
reverse fault 67
rhyodacite 122, 141
rhyolite 124, 174, 177, 198, 201, 202-203, 221
ring dikes 79
Rock Mesa 120, 140, 141-142
Rogue River (ancestral) 35
Rogue River (modern) 48-49, 58
Rooster Rock 132-133
Rowena Crest 112

Saddle Mountain (coast) 17, 70-72, 74
Sand Mountain 136-137
sandstone 13, 36, 68, 71, 79, 81
Sandy Glacier volcano 117, 125-126
Sauvie Island 93-95
scoria 91, 135, 190
Seal Rocks 66
sedimentary rocks 13, 36, 71, 84-85
serpentinite 48
shale 13, 36, 81
sheeted dikes 58, 59
shield volcano 109, 120, 124, 149, 158
Shore Acres 83-85
sill 80-81
slate 49, 235
slickensides 50, 67
Smith Rock 171-175
Snow Camp terrane, 30-31, 58-59
South Sister 19, 120, 139-141
Spencers Butte 87, 96-97
stalactites 51, 52
stalagmites 51
Steens Mountain 194-197
Steins Pillar, 211
stratovolcanoes 116, 124, 125, 143

Strawberry Lake 224-225
Strawberry Volcanics 224-225
subduction zone earth-quake, 20, 66
subduction zone 16, 20, 32, 40
Summit Lake 43-45, 246
Sunset Bay 83-85

Table Rock (Molalla) 131-132
Table Rocks (Medford) 34-36, 63
Tahkenitch Dunes 82-83
Takelma Gorge 162-163
terraces (coastal) 63
The Pinnacles 155
The Watchman 154
Three Forks 202
Three Sisters 120
Tidbits Mountain 132, 150
Timberline Trail 127
Todd Lake 142-143
Toketee Falls 157-158
Tombstone Lake 245
Troutdale Formation 91, 103
tuff 116, 170-171, 172, 173, 178, 180, 187, 188-189, 207, 217
turbidites 81
Twin Pillars 211-213

Upper Table Rock 34-35

Valen Lake fault 55, 67
volcanic bombs 136, 146, 184, 190
Vulcan Lake, 44, 48, 49, 53-55

Wallowa batholith 215, 241
Wallowa Mountains, 8, 14, 15, 19, 51, 208-210
Wallowa terrane 236-237
Wanapum basalts 70, 104
Western Cascades 16, 22, 87, 102, 115-116, 131, 150-151
White River 129, 175-176
Willamette Valley 18, 19, 20, 22, 68, 87-101
Wineglass tuff 123

xenoliths 38-39

Yapoah Cone 120, 145-147, 149
Yellowstone (caldera) 207
Yellowstone (hotspot) 12, 104, 192-193

ABOUT THE AUTHOR

Ellen Morris Bishop, a specialist in igneous petrology and the exotic terranes of eastern Oregon, received her Ph.D. in geology from Oregon State University in 1982. She has worked as a science journalist, is an accomplished large-format landscape photographer, and has written and photographed two other books about the Pacific Northwest's geology: *In Search of Ancient Oregon* and *Field Guide to Pacific Northwest Geology*. Her landscape and documentary photographs have been commissioned by The Nature Conservancy, Oregon Natural Desert Association, and other conservation organizations. As a complement to her interest in geology, Bishop has also written *Best Hikes in Oregon with Dogs* (The Mountaineers Books, 2004). She lives in Oregon, with her husband, David, two dogs (Meesha and Dundee), and a precocious cat named Alley.

THE MOUNTAINEERS, founded in 1906, is a nonprofit outdoor activity and conservation club, whose mission is "to explore, study, preserve, and enjoy the natural beauty of the outdoors . . . ." The club sponsors many classes and year-round outdoor activities in the Pacific Northwest, and supports environmental causes through educational activities, sponsoring legislation and presenting educational programs. The Mountaineers Books supports the club's mission by publishing travel and natural history guides, instructional texts, and works on conservation and history.

Send or call for our catalog of more than 500 outdoor titles:

The Mountaineers Books
1001 SW Klickitat Way, Suite 201
Seattle, WA 98134
800-553-4453
mbooks@mountaineersbooks.org
www.mountaineersbooks.org

The Mountaineers Books is proud to be a corporate sponsor of Leave No Trace, whose mission is to promote and inspire responsible outdoor recreation through education, research, and partnerships. The Leave No Trace program is focused specifically on human-powered (nonmotorized) recreation. Leave No Trace strives to educate visitors about the nature of their recreational impacts, as well as offer techniques to prevent and minimize such impacts. Leave No Trace is best understood as an educational and ethical program, not as a set of rules and regulations. For more information, visit *www.LNT.org*, or call 800-332-4100.

MORE TITLES IN THE HIKING GEOLOGY SERIES
FROM THE MOUNTAINEERS BOOKS

Hiking the Grand Canyon's Geology, Lon Abbot & Teri Cook

Hiking the Southwest's Geology: Four Corners Region, Ralph Lee Hopkins

Hiking Arizona's Geology, Ivo Lucchitta

Hiking Colorado's Geology, Ralph Lee Hopkins & Lindy Birkel Hopkins

Hiking Washington's Geology, Scott Babcock & Bob Carson

OTHER TITLES YOU MIGHT ENJOY FROM
THE MOUNTAINEERS BOOKS

Best Hikes with Dogs:
Oregon, Ellen Bishop

100 Classic Hikes in Oregon,
Douglas Lorain

Best Old-Growth Forest Hikes: Washington
& Oregon Cascades, John & Diane Cissel

Exploring Oregon's Wild Areas:
A Guide for Hikers, Backpackers,
Climbers, Cross-Country Skiers,
& Paddlers, William Sullivan

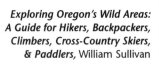

Oregon State Parks: A Complete
Recreation Guide, Jan Bannan

Available at fine bookstores and outdoor stores, by phone at 800-553-4453
or on the Web at www.mountaineersbooks.org

THE MOUNTAINEERS BOOKS